D1670192

History

for the IB Diploma

PAPER 3

Imperial Russia, Revolution and the Establishment of the Soviet Union (1855-1924)

SECOND EDITION

Sally Waller

Series editor: Allan Todd

CAMBRIDGE
UNIVERSITY PRESS

University Printing House, Cambridge CB2 8BS, United Kingdom

One Liberty Plaza, 20th Floor, New York, NY 10006, USA

477 Williamstown Road, Port Melbourne, VIC 3207, Australia

314–321, 3rd Floor, Plot 3, Splendor Forum, Jasola District Centre, New Delhi – 110025, India

79 Anson Road, #06–04/06, Singapore 079906

Cambridge University Press is part of the University of Cambridge.

It furthers the University's mission by disseminating knowledge in the pursuit of education, learning and research at the highest international levels of excellence.

Information on this title: education.cambridge.org

© Cambridge University Press 2016

First published 2012
Second edition 2016
20 19 18 17 16 15 14 13 12 11 10 9 8

Printed in Italy by Rotolito S.p.A.

A catalogue record for this publication is available from the British Library

ISBN 9781316503669

Cambridge University Press has no responsibility for the persistence or accuracy of URLs for external or third-party internet websites referred to in this publication, and does not guarantee that any content on such websites is, or will remain, accurate or appropriate.

Contents

Introduction

1

Imperial Russia and the Soviet Union (1855–1924)

This book is designed to prepare students for *Imperial Russia, Revolution and the Establishment of the Soviet Union (1855–1924)*. This is Topic 12 in HL Option 4, History of Europe for Paper 3 of the IB History Diploma examination. This option examines the conflicting parts played by modernisation and conservatism in Tsarist Russia and explores reasons for the eventual collapse of the Tsarist autocracy in 1917. It explores continuity and change through the revolutions of 1917, the Civil War and the rule of Lenin. There is a particular focus throughout on the interaction of the social, economic and political factors responsible for change.

Figure 1.1: This 1853 illustration shows Nicholas I, father of Alexander II, being driven through St Petersburg; at this time, the Tsar was all-powerful.

Figure 1.2: The 1924 funeral procession of Vladimir Lenin, attended by four million people. By 1924, Russia had undergone huge changes and was a communist state.

Themes

To help you prepare for your IB History exams, this book will explain the specified content for *Imperial Russia, Revolution and the Establishment of the Soviet Union (1855–1924)* as set out in the IB *History Guide* and explore major themes with regard to change and continuity, causation and consequence, significance and perspectives. These cover:

- the emancipation of the serfs and the other military, legal, educational and local government reforms of Alexander II (1855–81)
- the nature of Alexander II's rule and the extent of tsarist reaction in his later years
- the nature of tsardom and policies under Alexander III (1881–94), including the drive towards economic modernisation
- the growth of opposition movements in the last quarter of the 19th century

- the policies of Nicholas II (1895–1917) and the various factors, including the Russo-Japanese War, that led to the revolution of 1905
- the work of Stolypin and the experiment with the *dumas* (elected town councils)
- the impact of the First World War (1914–18) on Russia
- the causes and impact of the February/March revolution in 1917 and the issues faced by the Dual Power and the Provisional Government
- the parts played by Lenin and Trotsky in the build-up to – and the carrying out of – the October/November 1917 revolution
- the type of state created by Lenin (1917–24), including the impact of the Russian Civil War, economic policies such as War Communism and the New Economic Policy (NEP), terror and coercion, and the Soviet state's foreign relations.

Terminology and definitions

Since the title of this topic is *Imperial Russia, Revolution and the Establishment of the Soviet Union (1855–1924)*, it might be helpful at the outset to have some idea of the changing nature of the Russian state. The book begins with Russia as an Empire under a hereditary ruler known as a Tsar, which means Emperor. This Empire collapsed in 1917 when 'revolution' – a complete overthrow of the old political, economic and social system – took place. The Russian Revolution brought to power a Bolshevik government, named after the group which led it. The Bolsheviks were Communists, following the ideology of Karl Marx and in Chapter 4 you will read more about the Marxist stage theory of history and how the Bolsheviks, led by Vladimir Lenin adapted communism to suit the circumstances they found themselves in. Imperial Russia became the USSR (the Union of Soviet Socialist Republics), sometimes known as the Soviet Union, in 1922.

In the course of this book, you will find references to groups and parties on the right- and left-wings of politics. The political spectrum below will help you to appreciate the various groupings that form those 'wings'.

Figure 1.3: The political spectrum: Left/Centre/Right.

In this book, you will meet a number of key terms that are particularly pertinent to the study of Russian history between 1855 and 1924. The most important of these are provided here for reference:

- **Autocracy:** complete power in the hands of one man
- **Communism:** an economic and social system in which everyone works together for the common good
- *Duma:* an elected council at municipal or state level
- *Kulak:* a wealthy peasant
- *Mir:* a village commune where peasants worked
- **Soviet:** an elected council, usually of workers, soldiers, sailors and sometimes peasants controlling an area
- *Zemstva:* elected local government assemblies.

Key Concepts

Each chapter will help you to focus on the main issues, and to compare and contrast the main developments that took place during the various periods of Russian history between 1855 and 1924.

In addition, at various points in the chapters, there will be questions and activities which will help you focus on the six Key Concepts – these are:

- change
- continuity
- causation
- consequence
- significance
- perspectives.

KEY CONCEPTS ACTIVITY

Change and continuity: The state you will be studying is variously described as imperial Russia, tsarist Russia, the Russian autocracy, the Dual Power, the Soviet state and the USSR during the years 1855 to 1924. Try to find definitions for these terms and draw a timeline showing Russia's political progression through the different regimes from 1853 to 1924.

Theory of Knowledge

In addition to the broad key themes, the chapters contain Theory of Knowledge links, to get you thinking about aspects that relate to history, which is a Group 3 subject in the IB Diploma. The topic, *Imperial Russia, Revolution and the Establishment of the Soviet Union (1855–1924)* has several clear links to ideas about knowledge and history. As you study the material in this book, try to think about the nature of power, what is meant by 'the state', what forces move history forward and what forces hold it back. You should also reflect on the importance of different ideologies, particularly the impact of Marxism in Russia.

The Soviet state became a strongly ideological communist regime after 1917. International travel was restricted, and a strict system of censorship was imposed. Writers and historians were given limited access to state archives and were not permitted to write about controversial subjects, particularly anything that implied criticism of the government. Instead, they often found themselves having to produce propaganda on behalf of the Russian state. This has made it difficult for historians, even in the more open post-communist era, to establish the truth about life in Soviet times.

Theory of Knowledge

History and propaganda

Winston Churchill (1874–1965) once said: *'History will be kind to me, for I intend to write it.'* It is sometimes said that history is the record of the victors. Is this a fair comment? What is the difference between history and propaganda?

Western historians have not been immune to political developments either. For example, during the Cold War the West was highly critical of communist ideology. This fact needs to be kept in mind when reading Western commentators who wrote during the Cold War period, in order to understand the forces that influenced their thinking. All interpretations of this period are affected by the political prejudices of their authors and by the time and place in which they were written. You should bear this in mind as you read and, in particular, when looking at the sections which examine historical debate.

When considering all historical interpretations, you should be making links to the IB Theory of Knowledge course. For example, when trying to explain aspects of particular policies, political leaders' motives and their success or failure, historians must decide which evidence to select and use to make their case, and which evidence to leave out.

But to what extent do the historians' personal political views influence them when selecting what they consider to be the most relevant sources, and when they make judgements about the value and limitations of specific sources or sets of sources? Is there such a thing as objective historical truth? Or is there just a range of subjective historical opinions and interpretations about the past, which vary according to the political interests of individual historians?

You are strongly advised to read a range of publications giving different interpretations of the theory and practice (and the various economic, political and social policies covered by this book) in order to gain a clear understanding of the relevant historiographies (see Further reading).

IB History and Paper 3 questions

Paper 3

In IB Diploma History, Paper 3 is taken only by Higher Level students. For this paper, IB History specifies that three sections of an Option (in this case, History of Europe) should be selected for in-depth study. The examination paper will include two questions from each of the eighteen sections – and you have to answer three questions in total.

Unlike Paper 2, where there are sometimes regional restrictions, in Paper 3 you would be advised either to choose a question from the content of each of the three sections you have been prepared for, or to choose two questions from one content area and a third question from another. The questions are in-depth analytical essays. It is therefore important to study all the bullet points set out in the *IB History Guide*, if you wish to give yourself the widest possible choice of questions.

Exam skills

Throughout the main chapters of this book, there are activities and questions to help you develop the understanding and the exam skills necessary for success in Paper 3. Your exam answers should demonstrate:

- factual knowledge and understanding
- awareness and understanding of historical interpretations
- structured, analytical and *balanced* argument.

Before attempting the specific exam practice questions that come at the end of each main chapter, you might find it useful to refer first to Chapter 8, the exam practice chapter. This suggestion is based on the idea that, if you know where you are supposed to be going (in this instance, gaining a good grade), and what is required, you stand a better chance of reaching your destination!

Questions and mark schemes

To ensure that you develop the necessary knowledge, skills and understanding, each chapter contains comprehension questions and examination tips. For success in Paper 3, you need to produce essays that combine a number of features. In many ways, these require the same skills as the essays in Paper 2.

However, for the Higher Level Paper 3, examiners will be looking for greater evidence of **sustained** analysis and argument – linked closely to the demands of the question. They will also be seeking more depth and precision with regard to supporting knowledge. Finally, they will be expecting a clear and well-organised answer so it is vital to make a rough plan before you start to answer a question. Your plan will show straight away whether you know enough about the topic to answer the question. It will also provide a good structure for your answer.

It is particularly important to start by focusing **closely** on the wording of the question so that you can identify its demands. If you simply assume that a question is 'generally about this period/leader', you will probably produce an answer that is essentially a narrative or story, with only vague links to the question. Even if your knowledge is detailed and accurate, it will only be broadly relevant. If you do this, you will get half-marks at most.

Another important requirement is to present a **well-structured** and **analytical argument** that is clearly linked to **all the demands of the question**. Each part of your argument/analysis/explanation needs to be supported by carefully selected, precise and relevant own knowledge.

In addition, showing awareness and understanding of relevant historical debates and interpretations will help you to access the highest bands and marks. This does not mean simply repeating, in your own words, what different historians have said. Instead, try to **evaluate** particular interpretations **critically**. For example, are there any weaknesses in some arguments put forward by some historians? What strengths does a particular interpretation have?

Examiner's tips

To help you develop these skills, all chapters contain several sample questions, with examiner's tips about what to do (and what *not* to do) in order to achieve high marks. These chapters will focus on a specific skill, as follows:

- Skill 1 (Chapter 2) – understanding the wording of a question
- Skill 2 (Chapter 3) – planning an essay

- Skill 3 (Chapter 4) – writing an introductory paragraph
- Skill 4 (Chapter 5) – avoiding irrelevance
- Skill 5 (Chapter 6) – avoiding a narrative-based answer
- Skill 6 (Chapter 7) – using your own knowledge analytically and combining it with awareness of historical debate
- Skill 7 (Chapter 7) – writing a conclusion to your essay.

Some of these tips will contain parts of a student's answer to a particular question, with examiner's comments, to give you an understanding of what examiners are looking for.

This guidance is developed further in Chapter 8, the exam practice chapter, where examiner's tips and comments will help you focus on the important aspects of questions and their answers. These examples will also help you to avoid simple mistakes and oversights that, every year, result in some otherwise good students failing to gain the highest marks.

For additional help, a simplified Paper 3 mark scheme is provided in Chapter 8. This should make it easier to understand what examiners are looking for in your answers. The actual Paper 3 IB History mark scheme can be found in the syllabus and on the IB website.

This book will provide you with historical knowledge and the necessary understanding to help you answer all the specific content bullet points set out in the IB *History Guide*. Also, by the time you have worked through the various exercises, you should have the skills you need to construct relevant, clear, well-argued and well-supported essays.

Background to the period

Russia in 1855

Figure 1.4: The Russian Empire in about 1855.

Note: The Julian calendar in use in Russia until February 1918 was 13 days behind the Gregorian calendar used in the West. This book uses the old Julian calendar for dates up to February 1918, and the Western Gregorian calendar for dates after 1918. The account of the two revolutions of 1917 therefore uses the 'old' dates in February and October, rather than the Western equivalents in March and November. However, sample questions on the revolutions use the terms 'February/ March revolution' and the 'October/November revolution', as in the IB examination papers.

In 1855, the Russian Empire was a land of extreme contrasts, encompassing frozen northern plains, eastern forests and the fertile 'bread basket' (wheat fields) of Ukraine. The sparsely populated Asiatic lands east of the Urals contrasted with the heartland of European Russia, where 75% of the people lived. There were also racial differences, with less than half the population being 'Russian' by birth. Instead, there were many varied ethnic groups, bringing together diverse cultures, languages and religions. These groups included Lutheran Finns, Baltic Germans, Estonians and some Latvians, Roman Catholic Lithuanians, Poles, Orthodox and other Belorussians and Ukrainians, Muslim peoples along the empire's southern border, Orthodox Greeks and Georgians, and members of the Armenian Apostolic Church.

There was also a far deeper contrast, although it was less obvious at the time. This was the huge difference between Russia's reputation as a giant among nations (covering one-sixth of the world's surface area, with 69 million people and an army of 1.5 million) and the reality of its economic and military weakness.

Between 1825 and 1855, the Russian Empire was ruled by Tsar **Nicholas I**, a member of the imperial Romanov dynasty. Like his predecessors, Nicholas believed that he had been divinely appointed (chosen by God to be ruler). The tsar's title, 'Emperor and Autocrat of all Russia', was associated with ruthless authoritarianism and the tsar's *ukases* (decrees) were law.

> ### Nicholas I (1796–1855):
>
> Nicholas was the youngest son of Tsar Paul I of Russia. When Nicholas was only five years old, his father was killed in a palace revolution. Nicholas's eldest brother, Alexander, then became Tsar Alexander I. When Alexander died unexpectedly in 1825, the second eldest, Constantine, was declared ineligible to rule the empire because he had married a Pole. That left Nicholas, but he faced a military revolt (by a group called the Decembrists) before he was accepted as tsar. He lived in fear of conspiracies for the rest of his life. Nicholas ruled from 1825 to 1855 and his great passion was the Russian army. He also had an overwhelming sense of duty, driven by his religious convictions.

Controlling this vast empire was a constant challenge, and Russia's economic under-development – compared with the industrialised Western European powers – posed a threat to its future. In 1855 Russia was totally reliant on serfdom, a system whereby the majority of people were serfs or poor peasants 'owned' by wealthy landowners and forced to work for them. These serfs were also liable to be conscripted into (forced to join) the so-called 'mighty' Russian army. The army may have been large, but the serfs could only be made to serve through fierce discipline and often had little idea what they were fighting for. Even Russia's military reputation was therefore based on a myth.

In 1833, Nicholas's minister of education, Sergei Uvarov, proposed that 'Autocracy, Orthodoxy and Nationality' should be the guiding principles of the tsarist regime. These principles demanded that Russians should show unswerving loyalty to the unlimited authority of the tsar, to the traditions of the Russian Orthodox Church, and to the Russian nation. To enforce such principles, Nicholas I re-established the secret police (or Third Section) in 1826. Minorities were repressed, censorship was enforced, there was no freedom to travel abroad and any hint of rebellion was crushed.

In the 1850s, the structure of government had not changed since the early 1800s. All the central government departments were accountable to the tsar, who was advised by a personal chancellery (replaced in 1861 by a Committee of Ministers). There was also an imperial Council of State, whose members were appointed by the tsar to advise on legal and financial matters. In addition, there was a Council of Ministers, which discussed draft legislation. There was also the Senate, which was the final court of appeal on major legal matters.

However, the vast empire was poorly administered and there was an ever-widening gap between state income and expenditure. Russia's huge army and rather smaller navy absorbed around 45% of the government's annual spending. Russia's agriculture was stagnating and its transport systems were left undeveloped. Furthermore, Russia was no longer able to dominate the European markets with its traditional exports of grain and raw materials.

This lack of progress was partly due to the regime's commitment to a serf-based economy as the only means of supporting the upper classes, the government and the military forces. Most European countries were already making great progress towards full industrialisation. In these countries, there was massive private investment in railways, mills, factories, coal pits and quarries, but Russia was held back by its social structure. Its serf-based economy no longer served the needs of the state.

In the 1850s, Russia still had a feudal social hierarchy that divided the élite (the privileged minority of nobles) from the tax-paying peasants

– the 90% of the population who not only served the state with their labour in the fields but also provided its revenue and the manpower for its army.

Most Russian peasants managed to scrape a living from the land in the summer but often suffered starvation during the winter. They had neither the income nor the incentive to fuel industrial demand. In addition, there was no bourgeoisie (middle class), whose drive to better themselves and make a profit had forced industrial change in Western European countries.

The serfs (peasants) could be selected to do military service for a period of 25 years. This condemned the chosen individuals to spend most of their adult lives in a military colony – a village compound run by the army, where whole families lived under military direction and the men spent their days training as soldiers.

The forced conscription system produced a reluctant army and regular periods of unrest in the countryside. In 1825, there were at least 20 outbreaks of serf violence each year; and in 1848 there were 64 such incidents.

The official emphasis on Russian nationalism led intellectuals to adopt one of two positions. Some thinkers, known as 'Westernisers', believed that Russia could only remedy its situation by copying developments in Western Europe. The 'Slavophiles', on the other hand, believed the Russian Empire possessed superior traditional values and should follow its own path. For the Slavophiles, the Russian peasant commune (community) provided an alternative to Western capitalism. Yet most of this talk merely provided heated discussion for the nobles' leisure hours and was never put into practice.

Nicholas I considered change and appointed several commissions to investigate serfdom. However, it was not until the Crimean War exposed Russian weaknesses that the then Tsar, Alexander II finally took action.

ACTIVITY

Find out more about the 'Westernisers' and 'Slavophiles' and their differing views of Russia's future. Which group had the more convincing arguments, and why?

The Crimean War

The ruler of the Turkish Empire in 1853 was the Ottoman Sultan and his empire extended from Turkey into the Balkans and the Middle East. The sultan's power over his non-Turkish peoples in Europe was increasingly challenged from the 1820s onwards. Tsar Nicholas I seized this opportunity to extend Russia's power in the Balkans and the Middle East. However, this Russian expansion caused conflict with the British and French, who had their own trading interests in the region.

Figure 1.5: Russian troops fighting French and British soldiers in the Crimean War; the Russians were poorly equipped, with old-fashioned muskets.

Russian troops arrived in Moldavia and Wallachia in June 1853 and the Turks declared war a few months later – on 4 October 1853. When the Russians refused to withdraw, and sank a squadron of the Turkish Black Sea fleet (which was at anchor in Sinope Bay), the British and French decided to teach Russia a lesson.

In September 1854, a joint British–French expeditionary force of over 60 000 men landed on the Crimean coast and mounted a combined land and sea attack on Sebastopol. It was a bitter conflict and there was some incompetent fighting on both sides, made worse by the spread of cholera though the troops. Nevertheless, Sebastopol eventually fell to the British–French forces on 9 September 1855.

Nicholas had died on 18 February 1855. It was therefore his son, Alexander II, who immediately agreed to an armistice (ceasefire) that led to the Treaty of Paris on 30 March 1856. This treaty was not particularly harsh in practical terms. However, one of its clauses insisted on the neutrality of the Black Sea, thereby preventing Russia from maintaining a fleet there in the future. This loss of naval power was a severe blow to Russian national pride.

The war effort showed how far Russia lagged behind its enemies in technological terms. Russia suffered from inadequate transport and communications, and it took the Russians longer to get equipment to the front line than it took France and Britain to send equipment from the channel ports. Russian equipment was also outdated, with inferior muskets (and only one musket to every two soldiers). The Russian navy still used sails and wooden-bottomed ships, while Western ships had metal cladding and were powered by steam. Furthermore, Russia's inshore fleet still contained galley boats, rowed by conscripted serfs.

KEY CONCEPTS ACTIVITY

Causation: Find a map of the Crimea in 1853–55. Indicate the main areas of conflict and, around the edge, list the reasons why Russia lost the Crimean War. You can use those given here and research others for yourself. In particular, try to find out about the state of Russian weaponry, the Russian transport system and the Russian navy. When you have created your diagram, use a colour code to indicate which reasons were political, economic, social, military or just bad luck. Use your diagram as the basis for a class discussion on why Russia lost the Crimean War.

Summary

By the time you have worked through this book, you should be able to:

- explain why – and with what results – Alexander II undertook a series of reforms
- understand the extent to which the tsarist government changed between 1855 and 1917, and the forces promoting that change as well as those holding it back
- explain how and why Russia undertook a drive towards economic modernisation and agricultural improvement, and describe the results of that drive by 1917
- identify the reasons for – and the impact of – opposition to tsardom until 1917
- assess the extent of change brought about by the revolution of 1905, and explain why change was limited
- understand the impact of the First World War on the Russian state
- analyse the reasons for the two Russian revolutions of 1917, and assess their outcomes
- explain why the Soviet state evolved as it did under Lenin, and assess the legacy that Lenin left behind.

2

Alexander II, reform and the emancipation of the serfs, 1855-61

TIMELINE

1855 **Feb:** Alexander II becomes tsar

1856 **Mar:** Treaty of Paris ends Crimean War

1857 **Jan:** Secret committee considers serf emancipation

1858–59 Alexander II tours Russia giving pro-emancipation speeches; landlords prepare inventories of peasant holdings

1860 **Oct:** Emancipation order drawn up

1861 **Feb:** Emancipation Edict proclaimed

1861 **Mar:** Emancipation of serfs made law

KEY QUESTIONS

- Why is Alexander II associated with the 'modernisation' of Russia?
- Why did modernisation demand the emancipation of the serfs?
- How was emancipation carried out and how did this change Russia?

The consequences of the Crimean War were profound. Russia had lost its status as a great naval power and the humiliation ran deep. The weakness and backwardness of Russia's social and economic structure had been exposed and the folly of reliance on serfs revealed. Alexander II would try to address these issues, beginning with Russia's greatest 19th-century reform – the emancipation of the serfs. However, in allowing the tsarist autocracy to relax a little, he unwittingly encouraged opposition from those for whom 'a little' would never be enough.

Overview

- Alexander II's accession to the throne coincided with Russia's disastrous defeat in the Crimean War.
- The military and administrative inadequacies demonstrated by that war persuaded Alexander that Russia had to make reforms.
- The most pressing of Russia's problems was the issue of the serfs, whose bondage was obstructing both economic progress and military efficiency.

• The serfs were emancipated in 1861 but the terms of the Emancipation Edict left a number of problems unresolved.

2.1 Why is Alexander II associated with the 'modernisation' of Russia?

The new Tsar: Alexander II (1818–81)

Like the empire he inherited, **Alexander II** was a man of contrasts and contradictions. He was gentle, sensitive and charming to those who were close to him, but he was also very sure of his own autocratic powers. He was a mixture of timidity and forcefulness, an enlightened thinker and a strong conservative. He was capable of compassion and yet he could also be ruthless and stubborn.

Alexander II (1818–1881):

Alexander was the eldest son of Tsar Nicholas I and Alexandra Feodorovna. Before her marriage and baptism into the Orthodox Church, Alexandra had been the Protestant Princess Charlotte of Prussia. On the one hand, Alexander had grown up respecting but also fearing his overpowering autocratic father. On the other hand, he had been encouraged to think more liberally by his tutor, the poet Vasily Zhukovsky, who was chosen for him by his mother. He was a rather lazy young man of average intelligence; but he felt the heavy weight of responsibility when he succeeded to the throne aged 36, following his father's death.

Historians have found it hard to categorise Alexander II. He has traditionally enjoyed a reputation as 'the Liberator', a term that was used by the writer **Fyodor Dostoevsky** in his novel *The Brothers Karamazov*.

Figure 2.1: Alexander II's coronation in Moscow in 1856.

Fyodor Dostoevsky (1821–81):

Dostoevsky was a journalist, novelist and short-story writer who liked to examine individual motivation. In 1847 he joined the Petrashevsky Circle, a group of intellectuals who discussed reform and change. However, he was arrested in 1849 and sent to prison camp for four years, followed by a period in the army. This experience had a marked effect on his later writing, which explored extremes of human experience. Dostoyevsky spent much of the 1860s in Western Europe, where he wrote his most famous novels such as *Crime and Punishment*, *The Idiot*, *The Possessed* and *The Brothers Karamazov*.

Although Alexander II brought much–needed change to the Russian Empire, he left the essentials of tsarist autocracy untouched and his reforming bursts were interrupted by periods of reaction. According to historian Edward Crankshaw, 'There was no hard centre to the reign. There was no discernible pattern. In the end everything turned sour.'

Crankshaw perhaps made an over-harsh judgement on a tsar about whom the historian John Westwood wrote, 'with the possible exception of Khrushchev [Soviet leader 1953–64], no other Russian ruler did so much to reduce the suffering of the Russian people'.

Despite his reforming legislation, Alexander still left an empire that was politically, economically and socially backward compared with the rest of Europe. At the end of his reign in 1881, around 80% of Russians still could not read or write and peasants regularly died of starvation. None of Alexander's reforms could be judged unqualified successes, and most were left incomplete. Another negative factor was the growth of revolutionary opposition and violence during his reign. This increasing violence ended in the assassination of Alexander II himself in 1881.

The tsar's training

As the eldest son of Tsar Nicholas I, Alexander was well prepared for the throne. In line with his father's interests, he was made to endure a rigorous military training. Yet, rather strangely, Nicholas also allowed him to be educated by an enlightened, liberal-minded private tutor (chosen by his Prussian wife), the poet Vasily Zhukovsky. Zhukovsky and the reforming bureaucrat Mikhail Speransky have together been credited with developing some of Alexander's more humanitarian and reforming impulses. For example, when Alexander was just 11 years old, Zhukovsky composed a homily (lesson) on 'the Perfect Ruler' for his young pupil. It read: '[The Tsar should] respect the law and let his example make others respect it; a law disregarded by the Tsar will not be kept by the people... A sovereign's real strength lies in the well-being of his subjects and not in the numbers of his soldiers...' In view of such sentiments, it is surprising that Nicholas I allowed Zhukovsky to tutor his son.

Alexander was also given the opportunity to travel around the Russian Empire, taking a seven-month tour when he was 19 years old. Nicholas's motives in allowing this remain unclear, but this journey gave Alexander an opportunity to see his future inheritance at first hand. Uniquely for a tsar, he developed an ability to understand and sympathise with the people. For example, he wrote to his father from Siberia, pleading with him to do something about the awful living conditions of prisoners there.

Alexander defied his father's wishes by marrying Marie Alexandrovna, the daughter of the Grand-Duke of Hesse-Darmstadt, in April 1841. However, he was forgiven and brought into government, acting as his father's deputy during Nicholas's absences from the capital. Alexander served ten years on the Council of State, took part in a committee on railways and acted as chairman of an enquiry into serfdom. The insights he gained through this work, together with the bleak evidence emerging from the Crimean War of the serious deficiencies in the empire's administration and army, convinced him that reform could no longer be delayed. Not surprisingly, liberals welcomed his reign with a sense of expectation. Here, they hoped, was indeed a 'modernising tsar'.

Theory of Knowledge

History and truth

This paragraph includes a number of comments that could be considered opinions: 'Alexander defied his father's wishes', 'he was forgiven', 'the insights he gained... convinced him'; 'not surprisingly, liberals welcomed his reign'; 'they hoped'.

How would you test whether these statements represent definite truth, possible truth, untruth or deliberate deception? In pairs, choose another paragraph from this chapter. Each of you should note the 'opinions' it contains. Check whether you have both identified the same words and phrases. Are opinions important in history?

Early changes

Although Alexander retained most of his father's 17 ministers, the unpopular Alexander Bibikov (minister for internal affairs) and Count Peter Kleinmichel (director of roads and public buildings) were immediately dismissed, signifying a change of attitude. Other early proclamations allowed the Catholic Church in Poland greater freedom and permitted less censorship in Russian universities. Alexander's coronation, in September 1856, was accompanied by the release of political prisoners, including those involved in the 'Decembrist' plot to assassinate his father in December 1825. In addition, the government cancelled tax arrears (taxes owed) and recruitment to the armed services for the next three years, and eased the restrictions on travel outside Russia.

Imperial Russia and the Soviet Union (1855–1924)

Nevertheless, it should not be assumed that Alexander was a liberal. He was supported in taking a more enlightened approach by his liberal-minded brother, Grand-Duke Constantine, and by his aunt, the Grand-Duchess Elena Pavlovna. However, the Grand-Duchess noted that 'he is jealous of his power' and he had no intention of weakening his own autocracy. Alexander surrounded himself with enlightened, Westernising bureaucrats like the Milyutin brothers, Nikolai and Dmitri, who became, respectively, Minister for Internal Affairs from 1859 to 1861 and Minister of War from 1861 to 1881 (see 3.1, Military reforms, 1874). But he was equally happy to appoint conservatives such as Prince Alexei Orlov (see 2.1, Steps to emancipation) to important positions. Alexander liked to think of himself as a 'mediator', maintaining a balance between tradition and progress as a way of ensuring orderly change.

In a move that has acquired greater significance in retrospect, Alexander summoned representatives of the nobility to Moscow on 30 March 1856. There, he gave them an address that included the words: 'It is better to abolish serfdom from above than to wait until the serfs begin to liberate themselves from below. I ask you gentlemen to think of ways of doing this. Pass on my words to the nobles for consideration.' The idea was not a new one, but it was the first time that any tsar had taken the step of publicly committing himself to reform.

Alexander certainly had no intention of rushing through immediate changes to a system that provided the basis of Russia's economic and social structure. After he had spoken his now-famous words, very little actually happened. Most landowners probably hoped that if they did nothing, the issue of reform would simply go away. But in the aftermath of the Crimean War, with the constant threat of peasant rebellion, the need for action had grown ever more urgent.

There has been some debate as to whether Alexander proceeded with the emancipation of the serfs because he felt he had to, or because he was genuinely committed to reform. For example, Crankshaw has written, 'The Emancipation had to be, he knew, but he did not like it.' Meanwhile, Alan Wood has said, 'It was fear, not philanthropy, which forced him on a path that was essential for the economic and political survival of the empire.' But according to J. Stephen Graham, 'Since he was a child, Alexander believed that ownership of serfs was contrary to the teachings of the Bible and spoke of this idea to his father.'

Whatever his motivation, once committed to the idea, Alexander pursued it with determination. He made it clear to landowners and opponents that it was not emancipation itself that he invited them to consider, nor the fact that the measure would be accompanied by the granting of land to the serfs (such decisions were not open to question), but only the details of how these changes were to be achieved. It took until 1861 for these aspects to be worked out.

KEY CONCEPTS ACTIVITY

Change and continuity: Make a two-column chart. Head one side 'Evidence of modernising ideas' and the other 'Evidence of conservative ideas'. Complete the chart using the knowledge of Alexander II that you have gained so far. You should add to your chart as you work through this chapter and the next.

2.2 Why did modernisation demand the emancipation of the serfs?

The serfs

There were around 53 million serfs in the Russian Empire, making up 90% of the population. Of these, roughly half were *pomeshchik* (privately owned serfs). Most of the others were state serfs, whose conditions had been marginally improved by laws passed in 1838. The majority in both groups worked the land. There were differences between those who paid their masters with labour (*barschina* – traditionally three days a week, although this could vary) and those who paid rent (*obruk*) and were therefore often able to practise a trade in addition to farming. However, there was no great incentive to make large profits through trade, since landlords could raise the rent if a serf was seen to be doing well. There were also about 1.4 million household serfs who had no land and had to perform domestic duties for their masters. Most serfs lived in rural communes, where the elder (head of the household), in consultation with the landowner or his bailiff, controlled their lives.

Some historians have argued that Russian peasants were actually better off than free peasants and agricultural labourers elsewhere in Europe, including England, because of the support they received from their communes and because landlords took some responsibility for their serfs. For example, it was not in a landowner's interest to neglect his serfs totally, since they could become unproductive or he might lose them altogether. Consequently, good Russian landlords had a rather paternalistic attitude towards their workers.

Figure 2.2: This 19th-century cartoon shows Russian landlords using serfs instead of money when playing cards; serfs could actually be used to pay off gambling debts, transferred as gifts in marriage dowries or exiled to Siberia at the whim of their owner.

Many landlords tried to argue that the serfs were actually better off living under the protection of a master, but the reality was rather different. Most peasants were at the mercy, not of the landlords but of their stewards, who wanted to make a profit for themselves and who treated the serfs like animals. The commune was also as much a form of control as support, and the serfs remained their master's property. For instance, they could be separated from their families and sold like cattle. They were subject to corporal punishment and liable to be conscripted into the army, and they could not marry without their lord's permission. There was sexual abuse and exploitation. Short of executing them, the landowner could treat his serfs as he wished.

Serfs also suffered dreadful living conditions. In an empire the size of Russia's, it would be wrong to make too many generalisations but a report on the condition of the serfs (compiled for Nicholas I in 1841) confirms that whole communities lived on the edge of starvation. Some 'escaped' by getting drunk on cheap, home-distilled alcohol. It was reported that 'A peasant – always facing compulsion, desperate in his worries, on the edge of destitution – relies on cunning and deceit to see him through life's difficulties. Without any education, they grow up like savages.'

Early attempts to reduce serfdom

With the abolition (in 1762) of the requirement that nobles serve the state in the civil service, the original justification for serfdom – which was to free the nobles for state duty – had disappeared. However, despite some attempts to regulate the position of the serfs in the first half of the 19th century, the institution lingered on. This was because the task of reform was so huge and the opposition to change was so deeply entrenched. Serfdom was abolished (although it took further laws to ensure that peasants gained access to land) in the Baltic states of Estonia, Livonia and Courland in 1816–19. Meanwhile, in 1847–48 serfdom was regulated in Ukraine – with systematic records made of peasants' land allotments and landlords' obligations.

Nicholas I described serfdom as 'an evil palpable to all' and convened ten secret committees to look into the practice. There were two minor decrees in 1842 and 1847. The first permitted landlords to abandon the master/serf relationship in favour of fixed contracts creating 'obligated serfs'. The second (in 1847) allowed peasants to purchase their freedom to help repay owners' debts when an estate had to be sold at auction. Apart from these decrees, little had been achieved.

DISCUSSION POINT

Is it possible to know how Russian serfs felt about their lives at this time? Could our assumptions about the feelings of the serfs actually be completely wrong?

Arguments in favour of emancipation

The economic argument

A crucial argument put forward in favour of emancipation was that it was needed for the Russian Empire's industrial development. Tied serfs could not move to cities to work in factories, where – the emancipationists argued – free labour would be more efficient than forced labour. Furthermore, serfdom kept standards of living low, reducing internal demand for goods, without which there was little incentive to industrialise. In any case, the capital needed for industrial investment was not being generated. On the contrary, the serf-owning nobles were falling ever more heavily into debt, as old-fashioned agricultural practices failed to produce a grain surplus for export. This was particularly true since the empire's population had doubled in the first half of the 19th century and internal consumption had increased accordingly. By 1859, 66% of serfs had been mortgaged as security against landowners' loans from the state bank. This situation was also contributing to government debt. Agricultural stagnation left peasants unable to pay taxes and they owed a total of 54 million roubles in tax arrears by 1855.

The military argument

The historian Alfred Rieber has argued that serfdom had to be abolished in preparation for reforming the Russian army along Western lines. The Crimean War had shown that Russia's forces were in desperate need of reorganisation. The empire could no longer afford a large peacetime army, and maintaining an army of 25-year conscripts was both costly and inefficient. Reformers such as Dmitri Milyutin (see 3.1, Military reforms, 1874) argued that conscripts should spend less time on active service. Instead, he favoured a short period in the armed forces, for military training, followed by a longer time in 'reserves'.

However, this proposed system was thought to be unworkable while serfdom continued. It was claimed that demobilised soldiers could not be sent back to their communes as trained soldiers after a few years because of the danger that they would lead peasant uprisings. Serfdom therefore had to be dismantled, for the sake of internal and external security. There was a second argument too. It was customary to free serfs after their military service, assuming they survived it. If this were to be continued, with relatively short periods of service, serfdom would end in two to three generations in any case. It would therefore be best to tackle the issue straight away, rather than allow serfdom to crumble 'from below' and without regulation.

The moral and intellectual arguments

Intellectuals argued the need for change in Russian society on moral grounds. They believed that bondage was morally wrong and that serfdom was incompatible with the humanitarian standards expected of a civilised country. Westernisers, in particular, wanted to bring about the changes that had enabled the West to achieve social and industrial progress. They argued that serfdom degraded not only the serfs, by slavery, but also the 'slave-owners' in the nobility. They claimed that serfdom weakened the moral character of the upper classes, making them lazy and unable or unwilling to contribute to the well-being of the state.

Among the thinkers putting forward such ideas were the socialist Alexander Herzen and the author Ivan Turgenev (see 3.1, Cultural and educational reforms). Turgenev wrote *A Sportsman's Sketches*, a collection of short stories, which showed that serfs were normal human beings who were just as capable of feeling human emotion as any of their so-called 'betters' in society, and therefore deserved more respect. One particular group of reformers called themselves *Nihilists*, from the Latin word *nihil* ('nothing'). They believed that the need to make a dramatic change to the structure of Russian society outweighed all other considerations in the search for a better future. To them, nothing else mattered.

The practical arguments

There were other immediate practical issues that encouraged reform, including a growing feeling of discontent among the peasants themselves. The constant pressure to produce more grain, coupled with conscription, had provoked more than 300 separate peasant uprisings in the decade before the Crimean War. At the beginning of his reign, Alexander II did not give the customary proclamation of freedom for those who had fought in the war. This led to further unrest. Alexander held back from making this proclamation, in anticipation of more radical reform. But the longer it took to make any real changes, the higher the level of tension in the country became. Even in Russia's police state, it was increasingly difficult for the authorities to keep control.

Figure 2.3: A group of Russian intellectuals photographed in 1856, including Ivan Turgenev (bottom row, second from the left).

SOURCE 2.1

In 1856, the novelist Leo Tolstoy (then still a young landowner aged 28) wrote a letter to Count Bludov, a reform-minded Minister, urging abolition and warning of mounting danger in Russia.

> Time is short. If the serfs are not free in six months, we are in for a holocaust. Everything is ripe for it. Only one criminal hand is needed to fan the flames of rebellion and we shall all be consumed in the blaze.

Troyat, H. (trans. N. Amphoux). 1967. **Tolstoy.** *New York, USA. Doubleday. p. 140.*

QUESTION

With reference to the origin and purpose, assess the value and limitations of this source for historians studying the reasons behind the decision to emancipate the serfs.

Leo Tolstoy (1828–1910):

Tolstoy came from an aristocratic family. He served in the army and travelled around Europe, where he began writing short stories. On returning to Russia, he managed the family's estate, set up a school for peasant children, and wrote novels in the 1860s and 1870s, including War and Peace and Anna Karenina. He had an acute social conscience and was concerned about the forces that shape lives, particularly catastrophe and coincidence. Eventually Tolstoy had a spiritual crisis of his own and he spent his later years living a simple life, devoted to social reform.

ACTIVITY

Create a spider diagram to show the various factors that led Alexander II to emancipate the serfs. Use a colour code to group the different types of reasons in your diagram.

2.3 How was emancipation carried out and how did this change Russia?

Steps to emancipation

In 1857, Alexander set up a secret committee of leading officials under the chairmanship of 71-year-old **Prince Alexei Orlov**, the president of the Council of State. In line with Alexander's desire to remain in ultimate command, this group was mainly composed of conservative representatives. Crankshaw has suggested that Alexander was deliberately trying to make the 'old guard' face up to new realities so that 'Orlov and his friends would be forced on to the defensive and made to retreat by inches'. However, as Alexei Levshin (assistant minister of internal affairs from 1856 to 1859) observed, 'the composition of the committee was extremely unfortunate and thus it was not surprising that for the first half year it only gazed at the beast that was shown it and walked around it, not knowing which side to approach it.'

In August, when this committee seemed to be making little progress, Alexander brought in his brother Constantine, a vocal pro-abolitionist. By 1858, Alexander gave up all attempts at secrecy and instead began a personal tour of the country, during which he delivered many speeches in favour of emancipation. Alexander invited provincial committees to draw up records of peasant holdings, terms and dues and provide their own contributions to the 'peasant question'.

> ### Prince Alexei Orlov (1786–1861):
>
> Prince Orlov fought in the Napoleonic Wars but opposed the radical ideas of many officers. He helped suppress the Decembrist revolt in 1825, for which he was made a count. Orlov accompanied Nicholas I on foreign tours and served on a secret committee (1839–42) that considered the peasantry. In 1844, he was appointed chief of the Third Section (head of the secret police). Orlov helped negotiate the Treaty of Paris in 1856 and Alexander II consequently made him a prince. He was named president of both the Council of State and the Council of Ministers, and in 1858 he became chairman of the committee on serf emancipation. He opposed emancipation and died shortly after its proclamation.

The 'Nasimov rescript' of November 1857 (so-called after some correspondence with Nasimov, the governor-general of Vilna) made it clear that the government had already decided on certain principles. These included a commitment to giving freed serfs their own land. Nevertheless, Alexander also made it clear that the landowners' concerns would be most important. He still wanted the final emancipation measure to seem like a gesture from the entire nobility, and he liked to talk of 'national renewal'. However, in the press it was Alexander himself who was hailed as the 'supreme benefactor'.

SOURCE 2.2

By 1860, Alexander was growing impatient and he made the following declaration.

> The matter of the liberation of the serfs, which has been submitted for the consideration of the State Council, I consider to be a vital question for Russia, upon which will depend the development of her strength and power. I am sure that all of you, gentlemen, are just as convinced as I am of the benefits and necessity of this measure. I have another conviction, which is that this matter cannot be postponed; therefore I demand that the State Council finish with it in the first half of February so that it can be announced before the start of work in the fields; I repeat – and this is my absolute will – that this matter should be finished right away.

From: www.corvalliscommunitypages.com

QUESTION

With reference to Source 2.2, why did Alexander issue this declaration in 1860?

There was heated debate among the provincial committees. Some of them sent in two reports: one representing the majority view and the other the concerns of the minority. Inaccurate data on peasants' holdings and obligations was sometimes deliberately submitted.

To curb this tendency, Alexander tightened censorship again, ordered editors to confine themselves to the official line, and established a new Commission of 38 (with 38 men) under Nikolai Milyutin (see 3.1, Military reforms, 1874). Milyutin's proposals were finally submitted to the Council of State in October 1860.

The Emancipation Edict

The Emancipation Edict was read out in churches all over Russia on 19 February 1861. However, its actual wording, composed by the reactionary Metropolitan (leading provincial bishop) Filaret, was so legalistic and obscure that it was difficult for the serfs to understand exactly what it said. Furthermore, it was not until 5 March that the decree actually came into force. By this time, the tsarist government had ensured that extra police and soldiers (as well as a great many whips and canes) had been sent to the provinces.

For many people, the edict was almost an anti-climax. First, it only applied to the privately owned serfs. (A similar but slightly more generous measure came into force for the state serfs in 1866, whereby they were allowed to redeem more land, at a lower price.) Second, emancipation was not to be fully granted immediately but would come through a gradual three-stage process.

Finally, as anticipated, Alexander was able to reassure the landowners in a speech to the Council of State on 28 February 1861, saying: 'I hope, gentlemen, that when you have examined the projects put before you, you will be convinced that everything that it was possible to do to protect the interests of the landowners – has been done.'

Figure 2.4: This card, commemorating the emancipation of the serfs, features the following extract from the edict: 'Cross yourself, Orthodox people, and ask for God's blessing for your freed labour, the guarantee of your domestic well-being and benefit for society.'

SOURCE 2.3

Alexander Nikitenko (1804–77) was born a serf but managed to get an education and received his freedom in 1861. He reported his reaction to the edict in his diary.

> March 5 [1861], Sunday. A great day: the manifesto on freedom for the peasants. They brought it to me around noon. With an inexpressible feeling of joy, I read through this precious act, the likes of which has surely not been seen throughout the thousand-year history of the Russian people. I read it aloud to my wife and children and one of our friends in the study before the portrait of Alexander II at whom we all gazed with deep reverence and gratitude. I tried to explain to my ten-year-old son as simply as I could the meaning of the manifesto, and I instructed him to enshrine forever in his heart the fifth of March and the name of Alexander II, the Liberator.

From: http://academic.shu.edu

QUESTION

Do you think Source 2.3 is typical of the way peasants reacted to the Emancipation Edict throughout Russia? Explain your views.

The Emancipation edict was carried out in three stages as follows:

Stage 1 – freedom

Serfs received their personal freedom, which gave them the right to marry, own property, run businesses, travel and have legal protection. But they had to continue to fulfil their labour service for another two years. Meanwhile, lands would be surveyed and valued, and the administrative details would be drawn up for the next stage.

Stage 2 – temporary obligation

During the second stage, the peasants continued to pay rent and were under the landlord's control until they were ready to redeem their land. Regulatory charters were drawn up for each estate by the landowners. These charters recorded the amount of land to be given to the freed serfs and any remaining obligations to landowners. The charters were subject to peasant approval under the supervision of 'peace mediators'. Every non-domestic serf was granted his own cottage and the land immediately around it (*usad'ba*), plus a further allotment of farmland. Although the state laid down maximum and minimum sizes of allotments in different regions, the amount of land allocated had to be negotiated between peasants and landowners, and it could vary considerably from one area to another. This temporary obligation period ended whenever the landowner chose.

Stage 3 – redemption operation

In the third stage, peasants began to pay for their land allotments with redemption payments. The amount due was divided up into 49 annual payments, with a 6% interest charge added on. Reconstituted village communes or new township organisations of 2000–3000 people (known as *volosts*) were responsible for collecting the peasants' payments.

Peasants lived in farmsteads called *obshchina*, although they preferred to refer to them as *mir*, meaning 'world'. (The farmsteads were effectively the peasants' world.) Several *mirs* were united to form a *volost*, which was run by an assembly of delegates elected from the *mirs*. Taxes, including the redemption dues, were collected annually by the *mirs* and handed over to the *volost*, to be given to the government as a lump sum. The size of the redemption payments varied according to the size and quality of the land, but was roughly equal to the amount the peasants had formerly been paying in feudal dues.

The administrative and judicial authority of the landowners was also handed over to the *mirs* and *volosts*, which became responsible for ensuring that the terms of the Emancipation Edict were carried out.

The freed serfs had to remain in their *mir* until their redemption payments were complete. Communal open fields were held by the *mir* for the community's use. The *mir* also controlled when the fields were planted, when crops were harvested and ploughing began, and redistributed land allotments if the village population changed.

Landowners received the price of the land in long-term bonds issued by the government. Some chose to sell additional land above their allocated share, to peasants. The landowner also retained ownership of meadows, pasture and woodland, as well as his own land, which was subsequently worked by hired labour.

ACTIVITY

Draw a flow diagram to illustrate the stages by which the serfs achieved emancipation. Below each stage comment on the significance of the change.

KEY CONCEPTS QUESTION

Significance: Using your diagram to help, answer the question: How significant was the decision to emancipate the Russian serfs?

Theory of Knowledge

History, language and understanding

Did the Emancipation Edict make serfs free? Why is this a difficult question to answer? Can language be a barrier to historical understanding?

Results of the edict

Many historians have praised Alexander's courage in carrying out this emancipation measure. Terence Emmons, a Western historian, called this reform 'the greatest single piece of state-directed engineering in modern European History before the 20th century'. However, more recent historians have been less complimentary. Professor John Grenville described the Emancipation Edict as nothing more than 'a cruel joke' and Westwood wrote that 'Alexander did little for the serfs'. Although Crankshaw did not go quite so far, he still commented, 'Nobody was satisfied'.

As with almost any change, there were some 'winners'. Some peasants did very well out of the land allocations. Indeed, the hard-working or lucky ones were able to supplement their allocations by purchasing additional land and even buying out other ex-serfs who chose to leave the countryside and move to the towns. Some of these enterprising peasants then found that they were able to produce a surplus for sale and export. Forming a small sub-class of relatively wealthy peasants, they became known as *kulaks* or, less commonly, *miroedy*. Both were derogatory terms (*kulak* meaning 'a fist', referring to the way such peasants fought their way to the top; and *miroedy* meaning 'commune-eater'). Some peasants, who sold their land allocation and so forfeited their *mir* rights, also did quite well by moving to nearby towns and obtaining regular employment and reasonable wages.

As for the landowners, those who used the compensation payments to write off their debts and invest in business increased their wealth. Meanwhile, those who continued to live as country gentry benefited by using their influence to ensure that they received the best land and the peasants paid prices that were well above the land's market value.

In some less fertile areas (where peasants had given landlords part of their earnings from non-agricultural occupations), land was valued up to 90% higher than it should have been, supposedly to take these other earnings into account. But even in the more fertile south, prices were often inflated by up to 20%. The more unscrupulous landlords charged such high prices that the peasants were forced to continue working for their old masters. Alternatively, some of the peasants had to pay the landowners with crops, or continue to pay them rent, in exchange for land to farm. As a result, around 15% of peasants were still 'temporarily obligated' until 1881 – when redemption was finally made compulsory.

The edict also appeared to fulfil some of Alexander's wider aims. For example, Russian industry expanded in the wake of emancipation, and cities, communications and banks also grew. In Ukraine and the East, the emancipation (combined with improvements in transport) led to increased grain production. Grain exports therefore went up steeply – from 31% of exports between 1861 and 1865 to 47% between 1891 and 1895. This shows that the measure did have some positive effect.

However, there were plenty of 'losers' too – these were people who gained little from emancipation. Peasants who received poor or over-priced land allocations, and were faced with high redemption payments, struggled to survive. Sometimes whole peasant communities fell into arrears with their redemption dues and had to pay an additional penalty. This could extend the period of repayment and drag the peasants down further into debt. The loss of the former benefits of the common land, pastureland and the woods (where firewood was traditionally gathered), as well as the removal of the landlords' protection, was enough to put many peasant families well below subsistence level.

The average peasant holding of around 3.6 hectares (9 acres) was too small to farm at a profit. Peasants generally lost around 20% of their former land. Even more land disappeared in fertile areas like Ukraine, where most peasants lost nearer 30% of their land. Furthermore, land could still be taken away and reallocated by the *mir* to ensure that all male children born within the commune had allotments. By 1878, only 50% of peasants could produce a surplus to sell.

Of the remainder, many had fallen into debt and were forced to sell out to the landowners or *kulaks*. Emancipation merely turned these people into migrant labourers. The edict had the same result for the ex-domestic serfs, who were also without land and dependent on wages. For these people, life became even more difficult.

Figure 2.5: Even after emancipation, many people in the countryside continued to suffer; here, peasants who have fallen into debt and been forced to sell their land, say goodbye to their family and friends before going in search of work elsewhere.

For those peasants who remained in the countryside, the *mir* exerted a controlling force that was almost as oppressive as that of the former landowners. The commune had judicial powers and it could banish members to Siberia or refuse to accept back those who were prosecuted in courts. Peasants could still be flogged on the orders of the *mir*, and travel was only possible with an internal passport issued by the *mir*. The *mir* also regulated personal relationships as much as the old feudal system. For example, it enforced customs whereby a father-in-law was entitled to have sex with his daughter–in–law during his son's absence, and newly married couples had sexual relations in front of the whole community.

Some landowners also faced problems after the edict, including disputes over land holdings and payments which led to continuing peasant unrest. In the four months after emancipation, there were 647 incidents of rioting and the army had to be called upon in places to restore order. The most notorious incident occurred in Bezdna in April 1861. Here, a military commander opened fire on peasants who were protecting the cottage of a man called Anton Petrov. This man was a literate peasant who had led peasants in the area to believe that a messenger was on his way from the tsar to increase their freedoms. Nearly 500 peasants were killed and Petrov was executed, in what became known as the Bezdna Massacre.

Since around 50% of landowners had already mortgaged at least some of their land to banks before the Emancipation Edict, the landowners ended up using much of their compensation money to pay off their existing debts. By 1905, the nobles had sold about 30% of the land held in 1861, and 50% of the remaining land was mortgaged. This left the nobility worse off than before, and increased their resentment of the tsarist government.

ACTIVITY

Just as events and developments have long-term and short-term causes, they also have long-term and short-term consequences. Using the information in this chapter, make a chart listing the short- and long-term consequences of the Emancipation Edict. The outline is given below.

	Consequences for the peasants	Consequences for the landowners	Other general consequences
Short-term			
Long-term			

The standard view of Soviet historians, and many Western ones until the 1970s, was that the reforms left the peasantry with very heavy burdens. These included 'land hunger' (the problem of not having enough land), which was made worse by the growing population. Furthermore, the peasants faced annual redemption payments, the poll tax and indirect taxes on food and goods. It has been suggested that emancipation was 'too little too late'. Despite initial hopes, discontent increased and the drain of the redemption payments reduced the peasants' purchasing power. The measure consequently failed to stimulate industry.

In his book *The Shadow of the Winter Palace* (quoted below), Edward Crankshaw poses an alternative argument: that emancipation was 'too much, too soon'. He emphasises the scale of the change and the sense of disorientation it provoked – not just for the freed serfs but also for the poorly compensated landowners.

SOURCE 2.4

It is arguable that with the tide of feeling against serfdom as a national disgrace slowly rising, Alexander would have been wiser to rely on the growth of humanitarianism and the pressures of economic development to do his work for him…

Emancipation could not have been carried out as it was, peacefully, in any society other than an autocracy. It could not have been carried out in any society which set a high value on the rights of the individual or was seized with a conviction of the sacredness of private property.

Crankshaw, E. 1976. **The Shadow of the Winter Palace: Russia's Drift to Revolution, 1825–1917.** *New York, USA. Viking Penguin. pp. 199 and 207.*

KEY CONCEPTS ACTIVITY

Perspectives: You are given two opposing historical interpretations of emancipation to consider: 'too little, too late' and 'too much, too soon'. One group in the class should take the first interpretation ('too little, too late') and the other group the second ('too much, too soon'). Each group should prepare a convincing speech to deliver in favour of their view. The teacher can decide which is the more persuasive speech, based on the arguments and evidence put forward.

Paper 3 exam practice

Question

'Considering the **difficulties he inherited**, Alexander II of Russia should be **praised**, not **criticised**, for his **bold** decision to emancipate the serfs in 1861.' To what extent do you agree with this statement?
[15 marks]

Skill

Understanding the wording of a question

Examiner's tips

Although it seems almost too obvious to state, the first step in producing a high-scoring essay is to look **closely** at the wording of the question. You need to remember that an essay is an argument, and it is important to identify exactly what you are being asked to argue about. Every year, students throw away marks by not paying sufficient attention to the actual words (and dates!) of the question.

It is therefore important to start by identifying what argument the question requires you to address.

Here, you are essentially being asked to evaluate the strengths and limitations of the decree that emancipated the serfs. The argument centres around whether the measure was praiseworthy or not.

You are also being asked to place your argument in the context of Alexander's inherited difficulties. This should actually help you to focus your answer.

The **key words** in the quotation given in the question are as follows:

- difficulties he inherited
- praised/criticised
- bold (decision).

The **key or 'command' words** in the question are:

- **to what extent...?** All these key words are carefully chosen in order to give you clear instructions about what you need to cover in your essay. If you ignore them, you will not score high marks, no matter how precise and accurate your knowledge of the subject matter.

For this question, you will need to consider:

- **inherited difficulties:** Russia's geographical, political and economic weaknesses; the tradition of autocracy and the social hierarchy versus growing moral and intellectual pressures; the failure of earlier regimes to reduce or remove serfdom
- **specific difficulties revealed by the Crimean War:** the inadequacies of the Russian army; administrative and communications problems; peasant discontent; differences between Russia and the West
- **bold:** given the failure of his ancestors, the need to maintain the support of the nobles, and the dangers of change, Alexander's move was bold; it was carried out in the face of considerable criticism
- **praise:** bold move that ended serfdom; permitted development of a money-based economy; allowed hard-working peasants (*kulaks*) and enterprising landlords to flourish; stimulated railways, banking, industry, cities; led to further reforms
- **criticism:** peasants still tied to *mir* (redemption payments); some lost a lot of land and were hard pressed by high land valuations; nobles continued to go bankrupt; unrest in countryside, with continuing social division; positive economic impact less than anticipated
- **to what extent...?:** requires you to develop an argument in which you express your own view as to whether Alexander II deserves more praise than criticism, or vice versa. This will form your thesis (view) and you should support this throughout your answer. However, your essay will need to be structured to show that you understand both sides of the argument and can bring relevant evidence to bear on a variety of possible interpretations, while still showing that 'your' view is the most convincing.

Common mistakes

Under exam pressure, it is easy to get side-tracked and to start writing narrative or description in response to a question that has been explicitly designed to invite argument (analysis). For example, a common error here would be to pick on the words 'emancipation of the serfs' and to write in detail about the provisions of the measure. However, you should really be concentrating on Alexander's 'daring' in introducing the measure at all. You should also be evaluating its successes and limitations, for which he might be praised or criticised.

By looking carefully at the key words in the quotation and question **before** you begin to plan, you will see that you need to concentrate on the 'boldness' of the measure and its outcomes. This will help you avoid wasting time on irrelevant description, which will detract from your argument.

Another mistake would be to see this simply as a question in which you must write all you know about Alexander II. Once again, you would fail to answer the question.

For more on how to avoid irrelevant and narrative answers, see Chapter 5 and 6 respectively.

Activity

In this chapter, the focus is on understanding the question and producing a brief essay plan. Look again at the question, the tips and the simplified mark scheme in Chapter 8. Now, using the information from this chapter and any other sources of information available to you, draw up an essay plan (perhaps in the form of a two-column chart), which has all the necessary headings for a well-focused and clearly structured response to the question.

Paper 3 practice questions

1   Examine the nature of tsardom in Russia in the mid 19th century.

2   To what extent do you agree that political considerations were more important than economic considerations in the decision to emancipate the serfs in 1861?

3   'The lives of the Russian peasants were worse after 1861 than they had been before the emancipation measure.' To what extent do you agree with this statement?

4   Evaluate the reasons for, and results of, Alexander II's decision to carry out the emancipation of the serfs in 1861.

Alexander II's subsequent reforms and their impact 1861–81

TIMELINE

1863 Reform of education; University Statute passed

1863–64 Second Polish rebellion – suppressed in May 1864

1864 **Jan:** Polish autonomy abolished

1864 *Zemstva* law passed; reform of judiciary; Secondary Education Statute passed

1865 Greater freedom of publication and press permitted; Elementary Education Statute passed

1866 Attempted assassination of Alexander II

1870 Reform of municipal government creates town *dumas*

1874–75 Military reforms

1875–78 Balkan crisis from August 1875; Eastern crisis brings war with Turkey

1876 Land and Liberty founded

1877 Trial of the 50

1878 **Jan:** Vera Zasulich shoots military governor of St Petersburg but is not convicted; government steps up its exile of people suspected of supporting terrorism

1880 People's Will set up

1881 **Mar:** Assassination of Alexander II by People's Will

KEY QUESTIONS

- How, and with what success, did the regime address the need for further modernisation in the empire?
- Was there a conservative reaction in the later years of Alexander II's rule?

The Emancipation Edict was followed by further reforms that changed the status and rights of both the peasantry and the landowners. These reforms were partly a natural consequence of the Emancipation Edict but they were also the result of mounting pressure to bring Russia into the modern world. This modernising urge was shown by the attitudes and activities of the reformist brothers Nikolai and Dmitri Milyutin, who wished to complete the job that emancipation had begun. Sadly for Alexander II, his reforms would never be considered sufficient. The growing opposition movement was not appeased, and Alexander II was assassinated in 1881.

Overview

- The emancipation of the serfs meant that further change was needed, and gave more influence to reformers such as the Milyutin brothers. For instance, Dmitri Milyutin was behind a series of military reforms in 1874–75. These reforms removed abuses and created a smaller, more efficient, more professional and less expensive army.
- Educational reforms (1863–64) extended opportunities and reduced Church control at all levels.
- The legal reforms of 1864 established a fairer and less corrupt court system, with trials by jury and the opportunity for outsiders to attend trials and for journalists to report on court proceedings.
- Censorship was reduced from 1865 onwards.
- Between 1864 and 1870, local government was reformed and two types of elected councils were established – provincial *zemstva* and town *dumas*.
- Industrial development was promoted by Mikhail von Reutern, and agriculture flourished.
- There was limited reform in the Church and in the treatment of ethnic minorities.
- After an attempt on his life in 1866, Alexander became more reactionary, notably in education and in the government's use of the police and the legal system.
- Alexander's reign saw the emergence of an opposition. This came mainly from intellectuals, as the intelligentsia became increasingly active; the Populist intellectuals attempted to rouse the peasants, but their failure led to more extreme 'terrorist' opposition.
- Tsar Alexander II was assassinated in March 1881, on the very day when he took the first step towards creating a form of elected national assembly.

3.1 How, and with what success, did the regime address the need for further modernisation in the empire?

Military reforms, 1874

General **Dmitri Milyutin** was the older brother of **Nikolai Milyutin**. Dmitri was Minister of Defence from 1862 and it fell to him to address the Russian Empire's military needs. Between 1833 and 1855, around one million conscripted peasant soldiers had died owing to a combination of ill-health, lack of warm clothing, outdated equipment and low morale. Dmitri Milyutin wanted to close the gap between Russia's inadequate army and the highly efficient, successful Prussian armed forces, which had been modernised by Albrecht von Roon under Otto von Bismarck, the Chancellor.

Figure 3.1: Russian troops in Warsaw, Poland, in 1864.

Dmitri Milyutin (1816–1912):

Dmitri Milyutin came from a well-connected but not very wealthy noble family. He trained as a soldier but had to give up active service after being wounded. Instead, he involved himself in military scholarship and analysed the reasons for the Russian defeat in the Crimea. Alexander II made Dmitri Milyutin minister of war from 1861 to 1881, and Milyutin implemented some important army reforms. He was made a count and in 1898 became Russia's last Field Marshal.

Nikolai Milyutin (1818–1872):

Nikolai (younger brother of Dmitri Milyutin) joined the ministry of internal affairs in 1835. He favoured reform in the Slavophile tradition. Nikolai Milyutin rose to a position of influence within a few years and by 1859 he had become an assistant minister. He helped to draw up the emancipation *ukase*. He was also involved in the development of the *zemstva* but he resigned in 1866, shortly before these provincial councils were actually established.

In 1863, General Dmitri Milyutin started trying to raise morale and end some of the cruellest forms of punishment in the Russian army. Flogging and 'running the gauntlet' (running through a tunnel of soldiers armed with wooden clubs or whips) were both abolished, and changes were made to military court procedure. A new code of conduct for soldiers and sailors was introduced, and courts could no longer punish people by making them serve in the army.

The length of military service had already been reduced from 25 to 16 years. In 1868, Dmitri Milyutin reduced it further – to ten years, with five years in the reserves. He created the office of 'chief of staff' and improved organisation by establishing 15 military districts. To improve training and discipline, he set up military cadet schools (with specialist schools for military, infantry and cavalry) and colleges (which accepted non-nobles) to train officers. The last of the military colonies – where conscripts had been forced to live, isolated from the rest of society and subject to unremitting discipline – were abandoned. Furthermore, the army medical services were modernised. Milyutin also lobbied for the provision of modern rifles and iron-clad, steam-driven battleships, as well as strategic railways to improve the transport of troops and supplies.

Milyutin's reforming impulses were given another boost by Prussia's success in the 1870–71 Franco-Prussian War. This enabled him to overcome opposition from the landowners and bureaucrats to bring about radical change in the army. His reforms helped to create a fairer system and produce a smaller, more efficient and less expensive army.

The Conscription Act of 1 January 1874 included the following measures:

- nobles' exemption from military service was ended
- all male subjects became eligible for military service at the age of 20
- those not ruled out on health grounds, or as 'only' sons or sole breadwinners, were chosen by drawing lots within each military district; each military district was given a quota for recruitment
- a quarter of men aged 20 would serve each year
- the full term of service was 15 years but active service was reduced to six years plus nine years in reserve
- men with formal education had shorter terms of active service, so university graduates only served six months, those with partial secondary education served three years, those with full secondary education two years, and men with primary education served four years; this was a concession to the nobility but also encouraged peasants to send their sons to school
- those with no education were taught to read.

There was some strong opposition from nobles, merchants and even aristocratic soldiers, such as Prince Baryatinsky, who objected to being placed on the same level as peasants. Nevertheless, the reforms were approved and took effect from 1875.

Results

These changes helped to create a new spirit of professionalism within the smaller, better-trained army, in which promotion depended less on social status than on actual merit. They also had the desired effect of considerably reducing government spending on the army from its high level (45% of total expenditure) in 1846. Although the 1877–78 campaign against Turkey took longer than expected, it brought a Russian victory. The reforms therefore helped to restore Russia's international reputation. It was also reassuring for the government to know that there was a core of well-trained soldiers in every province. In theory, these troops could be used to help maintain civil order at home, as well as being mobilised to fight for Russia abroad.

Other benefits included the improved literacy that resulted from the army education campaigns, and the boost to education created by reducing the length of military service. However, there were still substantial numbers of illiterate peasant recruits, and their illiteracy reduced the effectiveness of some of the army training. Other issues also remained. For example, better-off individuals might manage to avoid military service by finding others to serve as substitutes in their place. The officer class also remained largely aristocratic and retained its old-fashioned values. For instance, officers still preferred bayonets to rifles because they believed that long-range weapons would encourage cowardice.

Despite some notable achievements, Russia did not keep pace with the West in terms of producing rifles, machine guns, artillery, ships, naval equipment or ammunition. Nor was the victory of 1877–78 repeated. The war against Japan in 1904–05 ended in defeat, and the Russian effort against Germany in the First World War proved disastrous.

KEY CONCEPTS ACTIVITY

Significance and consequence: In pairs or small groups, choose one of the areas of reform mentioned in this chapter (e.g. military; legal etc.). Write down what you consider to be the strengths and limitations of your area of reform for satisfying discontent and ensuring political stability in Russia. Share your ideas with the class and decide whether these reforms, taken together, were likely to help or impede the tsarist autocracy.

Legal reforms

Before the Emancipation Edict, the administration of justice was inefficient, slow, socially discriminatory and appallingly corrupt. So-called trials took place in secret, without the accused, witnesses or any legal representatives present. The cases were frequently judged by men without legal training, purely on the basis of written evidence that had often been altered by the police. Even before the trial took place, the accused could be held in prison, sometimes for years, unaware of the charges against them. If the accused person was a peasant, they were assumed to be guilty until proven innocent.

In 1862, work began on a new legal code. In November 1864, Alexander issued a statute 'to establish in Russia, courts of justice that are swift, fair, merciful and equal to all our subjects; to raise the authority of the judiciary and to give it the independence that benefits it.' This system was based on a mixture of English and French practice, which introduced the adversarial system into Russian courts for the first time. The accused would be granted a defence lawyer, who would argue the details of the case with the prosecutor in front of a jury. Juries were to be chosen from lists of wealthy people (using a property qualification), drawn up by the *zemstva*, the new local government councils.

Both sides could call witnesses, the jury would deliver the verdict and the judge would decide on the sentence for those who were found guilty. These judges were specifically instructed to consider each case on its merits and not to follow precedents (previous similar cases). The rights of the defendant would be taken into account, courts would be open to the public, and the press would be permitted to report on trials. Furthermore, judges would be given proper training and their pay would be increased to make them less open to corruption. Once appointed, they would hold their positions for life.

These legal reforms gave Russia one of the most progressive legal systems in Europe. A court hierarchy was established, from the town magistrates' courts at the lowest level to the higher crown courts and above them the Senate, which acted as the final court of appeal. The legal system became much fairer and better organised. Most importantly, the fundamental principle that the judiciary was separate from the legislative powers and executive authority of the state (known as 'the separation of powers') was established.

However, there were some limitations. Juries could not handle cases involving treason. Furthermore, since the government lacked the income to extend the court system to the villages, traditional peasant justice continued to operate through peasant *volost* courts, with minimal interference from provincial officials. These not only followed quite different procedures; they also gave their own punishments, including corporal punishment.

Results

Alexander's legal reforms introduced the theory of equality before the law (although the continuation of the *volost* courts diluted that principle). The reforms also helped bring more impartial justice. In addition, they gave rise to a new legal profession, whose work became a focus for popular interest, as Russians flocked to the courts to see justice in action for the first time. Some trials caught the popular imagination. One of these was the trial of Vera Zasulich, who was accused of attempting to murder the governor of St Petersburg in 1878 (see 3.2, The 'crisis' of the 1870s). This case attracted crowds and produced some heated press reports. By providing a forum for the voicing of critical opinion, the courts served the regime by making it more aware of popular feeling. However, the courts also weakened the government, as they allowed critics of the regime to speak out.

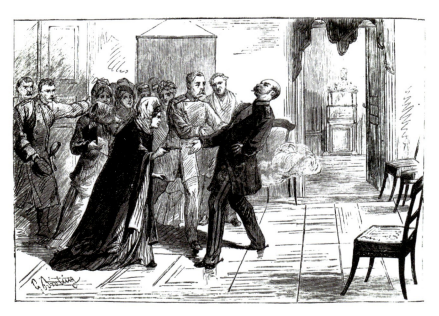

Figure 3.2: The revolutionary Vera Zasulich shot and wounded the governor of St Petersburg in 1878, but she was acquitted by a sympathetic jury.

This new legal system was slow to spread, partly because of the shortage of trained lawyers. Although the first courts were established in Moscow and St Petersburg in 1866, they were never fully introduced throughout the Russian Empire. There were none, for example, in Poland. In addition, the police still had extensive powers. The Third Section could stop, search and arrest people as it wished, punishing the politically or socially undesirable without bringing them to trial. What is more, cases were increasingly (and even more so after Alexander II's death) withdrawn from the crown courts and assigned to special tribunals. It seems strange that Alexander II never anticipated the problem of reconciling a fairer and more impartial judicial system with autocracy. However, once the dangers of open jury trials were revealed, the government tried to reverse some of its earlier reforms.

Cultural and educational reforms

Other major cultural and educational reforms took place. Before 1855, under Nicholas I, all books and newspapers had to be submitted to the government censor. Strict controls had been put in place and any writers who were critical of the regime had been sent to Siberian prison camps. This was the fate of Fyodor Dostoevsky (see 2.1, The new Tsar: Alexander II (1818–81)).

In 1863, under Alexander II, censorship was made the responsibility of the ministry of the interior. In 1865, a new set of rules was issued for writers and editors. Daily newspapers no longer had to be submitted for censorship prior to publication, and books and periodicals of over 160 pages and all academic works no longer needed prior approval. However, the government tried to protect itself against the effects of subversive or damaging literature by warning that the ministry could still order the withdrawal of publications and prosecute the publishers. This threat proved less effective in practice than in theory, since the authorities were often unable to respond to dangerous articles without breaching state security. Furthermore, if a newspaper was fined or closed down, readers automatically assumed that the government had something to hide.

For the first time, Russian newspapers were able to discuss both international and domestic politics. Information and ideas circulated more freely, and bold editors with strong financial backing could push the boundaries and build up a curious and committed readership. For example, the poet Nikolai Nekrasov edited a popular journal that offered radical and critical articles. Authors returned from Siberia and culture flourished with the writings of men such as Leo Tolstoy and **Ivan Turgenev**.

Ivan Turgenev (1818–83):

Turgenev was influenced by Western ideas of progress while studying at the University of Berlin, Germany. In his subsequent novels and plays, he analysed the problems of Russian society, showing an awareness of the acute need for a change in attitudes. His short-story collection, **A Sportsman's Sketches** (1852), is said to have awakened its upper-class readers to the value of emancipation. Although Turgenev lived abroad while Nicholas I was on the throne, he returned in 1861 after the Emancipation Edict and published **Fathers and Sons**, his most profound work, in 1862.

Nikolai Pirogov (a surgeon), Konstantin Ushinsky (an official at the ministry of education) and Alexander Golovnin (minister for education from 1861 to 1866) organised a campaign to bring more widespread, more effective and less class–ridden education to Russia. They favoured an education system that would create 'whole men', rather than rote-learners. They also stressed the importance of the humanities, as well as science.

In 1863, Golovnin introduced the University Statute. This measure gave universities greater autonomy (independence). It also enabled faculties to control their own admissions and staffing, including allowing women to attend courses (though not to take degrees). Universities were permitted to establish their own research programmes and teaching syllabuses, and to discipline their own students.

Higher-education reform was fundamental to Russia's modernisation, which required experts in both administration and economics. But it also raised a problem for the government, since reform would allow more critical and independent thinkers to emerge through the universities. The educational reforms led to a huge increase in the number of students going to university. In particular, when universities took up the option of offering scholarships and reducing fees, the reforms enabled many people from non–noble backgrounds to obtain the benefits of university education.

Theory of Knowledge

Independent thought

Is it necessary to attend university to become an independent thinker? Is it actually possible for anyone to be a truly independent thinker?

The Secondary Education Statute of 1864 and the Elementary Education Statute of 1865 addressed primary and secondary education. These measures made it easier to open schools, as long as certain basic moral and religious principles were upheld. Schools were still inspected regularly, and changes to their curriculum could be ordered. But they became much freer and were opened to children of all classes and religions. In addition, village schools were no longer controlled by the Church and its Holy Synod (ruling body).

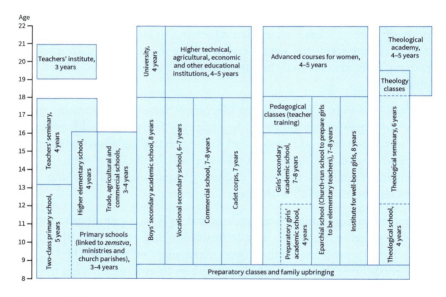

Figure 3.3: The Russian educational structure as established by Alexander II's reforms.

Alexander's educational reforms led to a rapid growth in the number of schools. In 1856 only 400000 children attended primary schools, but by 1878 over a million children were benefiting from primary education. Such expansion was largely made possible by the funding provided by the *zemstva*. By 1914, these councils were running almost half the primary schools in the Russian Empire.

The military reforms also played their part in improving overall literacy levels, although it is important not to exaggerate success in this sphere.

Local government reforms

As the nobles had lost their legal and judicial control over the serfs, a reform of local government was needed. In 1860, Alexander appointed a commission to look into this. The commission was initially chaired by the liberal reformer Nikolai Milyutin and later by Pyotr Valuev (as Minister for Internal Affairs). Following the commission's report, several changes were put into effect in 1864.

Most local government in the European part of Russia would be organised into provincial (*guberniya*) and district (*uezd*) elected councils, known as *zemstva*. Their members would be chosen by three separate electoral colleges: one for the local landowners, another for town dwellers and a third for the peasant members of the rural communes. These elected councillors would meet annually to decide matters of policy.

In addition, the measure provided for the establishment of permanent paid civil servants to administer policy, and for qualified professional employees (such as doctors, school teachers, lawyers, agricultural experts, veterinarians and technical experts) to carry out day–to–day work on behalf of the *zemstva*. The duties of the *zemstva* included: staffing local schools; providing medical care; undertaking light engineering projects such as building roads and bridges; providing a fire service; maintaining prisons, mental asylums and orphanages; promoting local industry; administering poor relief (monetary support and other help for the poor); and advising on industrial projects and agricultural problems.

In 1870, similar elected councils were set up in towns and cities to provide municipal self-government. These were known as *dumas*. Like the *zemstva*, *dumas* could raise taxes and levy labour to support their activities.

Results

At a local level, the *zemstva* and *dumas* proved very effective. John Westwood observed that their local knowledge 'enabled them to do a good job' because there was a natural incentive for local professionals to 'look after their own affairs'. They promoted public health and welfare, considerably improving hygiene, literacy, mortality rates and the environment. However, despite their willpower and enthusiasm, they were only able to make limited progress on alcoholism, poverty, epidemics and famines.

Like the new court system, the *zemstva* and *dumas* were not universal and were only established in a piecemeal fashion. There were none in Siberia, and as late as 1914 they existed in only 43 of the Russian Empire's 70 provinces. They also had limited capacity to implement more radical change. Although they had some powers to raise local taxes, they were mostly dependent on the central government for funding. Meanwhile, many aspects of local government (such as powers to levy state and local taxes, appoint officials and maintain law and order) remained with the provincial governors. These governors were appointed by the tsar or the police and were directly responsible to the ministry of internal affairs.

The system for voting councillors on to the *zemstva* and *dumas* has also been criticised. As the system was based on property qualifications, it produced councillors who were overwhelmingly from the landowning nobility or very wealthy urban classes (although there was also some peasant representation). In total, 41% of the people who voted members on to *uezd* assemblies were nobles, and in some areas the nobles used the system to their own advantage.

However, the *zemstva* and *dumas* also offered a valuable opportunity for the intelligentsia to serve in a professional capacity, helping such men develop a greater understanding of the lives and needs of the peasants. These councils provided a chance for intellectuals to participate in government and created a new pool of critical thinkers, as members developed a greater understanding of local issues and appreciated the need for centrally led reform. The councils also enabled peasants to hear the ideas of reformers. According to Alan Wood, 'It was this gradual intellectual osmosis, as much as the propaganda and agitation of professional revolutionaries, that encouraged the process of social and political fermentation which built up into such an explosive head in the revolutionary events of 1905.' Westwood referred to the *zemstva* as 'seedbeds of liberalism'.

Part of the frustration stemmed from the tsar's refusal, in the 1860s, to consider extending the *zemstva* system to create an elected national assembly. His belief in autocracy was too strong to countenance such a move. The country could so easily have taken a step towards democracy by building on the *zemstva* experiment, but the tsar's refusal meant that the autocracy was condemned to a slow death, worn down by continual political opposition. Nevertheless, Alexander II had a great deal of support. The creation of a national representative body was opposed by the landowners, who thought it would remove what remained of their authority. It was also opposed by reforming bureaucrats, who believed that such an assembly would be dominated by landowners who would limit the bureaucrats' power and reforming endeavours. The 'enlightened' Nikolai Milyutin therefore cautioned against it.

SOURCE 3.1

Count Pyotr Valuyev, minister of the interior from 1861 to 1868, warned Alexander II of the dangers of an elected national assembly.

To give the **zemstva** a voice in matters common to the whole Empire would be to break up the unitary executive power of the empire and distribute it among forty or fifty bodies. This would expose the social order and the entire imperial structure to perils which must be evident to all.

Quoted in Crankshaw, E. 1976. **The Shadow of the Winter Palace: Russia's Drift to Revolution, 1825–1917.** *New York, USA. Viking Penguin. p. 213.*

QUESTION

What does Pyotr Valuyev believe the consequences of an elected national assembly would be? What do you think he means by 'perils'? Do you think his fears were justified?

Other reforms: financial and economic developments

Economic growth was essential for Russia's future. Without a strong economic base, it would be impossible to achieve the imperial and military success needed to restore Russia's international status and prestige. Although the Emancipation Edict had provided the groundwork for the development of a money-based economy, government intervention was still needed to channel investment along the right paths. It was not enough to leave such matters to chance, particularly since Russia lacked the entrepreneurial middle class that had driven industrial revolutions elsewhere in Europe.

The appointment of **Mikhail von Reutern** as minister of finance in 1862 signalled this move towards greater state involvement in industry. Reutern has been described as 'a financial wizard'. He managed to reform the Treasury, establishing budgeting and auditing procedures for all government departments. He also abolished the previous practice of tax-farming (whereby private companies bought the right to collect taxes) and established a new system of collecting taxes; and he produced Russia's first comprehensive budget in 1862.

> ### Mikhail von Reutern (1820–90):
>
> Reutern was a Baltic landowner who began his career in the Naval Office, where he reduced the number of state-owned enterprises and instead made contracts with private firms. He served on railway and bank committees and helped found Russia's first state bank in 1860. He became minister of finance (1862–78) and produced the first published budget in 1862. He reformed the tax system to include more indirect taxation, promoted private railway construction and encouraged private investment in companies. In 1881, Alexander III appointed him chairman of the Council of Ministers. He retired following illness in 1886.

Reutern extended credit facilities and helped set up the state bank in 1860. He also promoted municipal banks in 1862 and a savings bank in 1869. These changes helped to put the national currency on a firmer footing and gave more opportunities to those who wanted to borrow in order to develop businesses. In addition, he promoted trade by reducing import and export duties after 1863.

He was particularly interested in expanding the railway network. Russia's first railway was completed in 1837 and a line between St Petersburg and Moscow was opened in 1851, in the reign of Nicholas I. Reutern built on this foundation, seeking investment in Russian railways from overseas investors. He also proposed that the government would guarantee to provide finance if it was needed for particular projects.

Figure 3.4: Newly built railways spread to distant parts of the Russian Empire; in this 1868 illustration, some Russian peasants look shocked on seeing a train for the first time.

Such policies proved very successful, and produced a sevenfold increase in the amount of railway track between 1862 and 1878, from 3532 km (2190 miles) to 22 498 km (13 950 miles). By 1880, 94% of railway lines had been built and were being run by private companies. These improved transport networks helped produce a 6% annual average growth rate in Russia during Reutern's term of office. The historian Clive Trebilcock has referred to this as Reutern creating 'the first state-managed exercise in industrial advance'.

The use of foreign technical expertise and capital also helped modernise and expand older industries, such as iron, coal and textiles, as well as some newer industries such as oil. The government guaranteed an annual dividend for foreign investors, and drew up legislation to regulate joint-stock companies (which were owned by shareholders). One notable success was the establishment of the Naphtha Extraction Company by the Nobel brothers in 1879, which opened up new potential for coal and oil extraction in Russia.

During Alexander II's reign, agriculture also enjoyed a boom, less through any direct intervention than because of other reforms, such as serf emancipation and Reutern's financial changes. Reduced tariffs (taxes on imports and exports) boosted trade, while the availability of credit benefited enterprising landowners as much as new industrialists.

Church reforms

In 1858, a priest called Ivan Belliustin wrote a report 'on the poverty and lack of skill of the rural clergy'. This highlighted some fundamental problems. Belliustin spoke of rural priests who were too poor to carry out their duties and too ignorant (or even illiterate) to perform essential rites. It also criticised bishops, whose only interests were political. The report alarmed the government, which relied on the Orthodox Church as an essential ally in maintaining control. The loyalty of believers was seen as vital in upholding the autocracy. Consequently, in 1862 Pyotr Valuev (the minister for internal affairs) set up a commission to examine the practices and organisation of the Orthodox Church.

The commission reported back in 1868 and changes were made to allow more capable priests to rise through the Church hierarchy. However, by this time some of Alexander's earlier reforming impulses had weakened. Little was therefore done about clerical poverty or the inability of many rural priests to perform their duties.

DISCUSSION POINT

Why was it easier for Alexander II to carry out reforms in some areas than in others? Share your ideas with a partner and then hold a class discussion.

Reformer or not? Alexander's treatment of the Jews, Finns and Poles

The Jews

Alexander II was far more tolerant of the Jews than any tsar before him. The tradition of Russian anti-Semitism dated back to the Middle Ages, when Jews were viewed as 'Christ-killers'. At that time, Jews were banned from entering the heartland of old Muscovy Russia (from Kiev to Moscow). However, the number of Jews under Russian administration grew as Russia expanded, and new ethnic and economic hostilities were added to the religious ones. In 1791, Catherine the Great established 'the Pale of Settlement' (see Figure 4.3), as a separate area, in which Jews were forced to live. Subsequent laws limited the professions they could engage in and the property they could own.

Despite the entrenched anti-Semitism that existed in Russia, Alexander II allowed Jews to attend universities and permitted the appointment of the first Jewish professor. He was prepared to encourage Jewish participation in the expanding commerce and industry of the empire. He therefore allowed Jews with academic degrees to live in Russian towns beyond their allocated areas in 'the Pale', though they were still barred from owning land (except through trade) and from living in central and eastern Russia. The Jews who took part in the Polish rebellion of 1863 (see below) were harshly dealt with. However, these Jews were just as likely to be persecuted by anti-Semitic Poles (who believed the Jews had betrayed Polish secrets to the Russians) as by the Russians.

The Finns

Alexander II believed in winning over his Finnish subjects by responding to their desire for greater independence, rather than trying to control them by force. Consequently, in 1863 he recalled the Finnish Diet of the Four Estates (a representative assembly), which had not met since 1809. He also allowed Finnish to become the sole official language in Finland from 1863, and several Finnish journals were founded. He created a separate currency for the area, and under the military reforms of 1874 Finnish soldiers could not be made to serve outside Finland.

The Poles

The 1815 Congress of Vienna had divided Poland between Prussia and Russia. In theory, Poland retained its own constitution (but had the Russian tsar as its king). However, in practice the Russians frequently tried to impose their own culture and destroyed the flourishing University of Vilnius. A major uprising broke out in Warsaw in 1830. As a result, an independent Polish government had been created.

The Russians had crushed the uprising in September 1831, annulled the Polish constitution, destroyed the Polish army, closed Warsaw University, and built a Russian military base in Warsaw. They had confiscated property and exiled 10 000 Polish rebels. Nevertheless, a Polish independence movement had been kept alive, led by Prince Adam Czartoryski. Many Poles had therefore pinned their hopes on the accession of Tsar Alexander II, in the belief that he would make concessions.

Alexander II began his reign compassionately with regard to Poland. He relaxed restrictions on the practice of Catholicism and the use of the Polish language, and appointed committees to consider Polish grievances in 1861. He gave the Poles more local autonomy and greater freedom of expression, permitting displays of Polish national identity. He even allowed Polish nobles to form their own nationalist organisation – the Agricultural Society of Poland.

However, there were limits as to how far Alexander was prepared to go. His early concessions were not followed up with any others, and Polish demands for a separate constitution provoked the response 'Point de rêveries, Messieurs' ('No daydreaming, Gentlemen'). This triggered nationalist demonstrations in 1861, in which several hundred Poles were killed, wounded or arrested. Two further years of unrest – and an ill-advised attempt to press Polish nationalists into the Imperial Russian army in January 1863 – led to the formation of a Polish Central National Committee. This committee declared the country to be in a state of rebellion against Russian rule.

Figure 3.5: Wounded Polish rebels receive medical attention after the 1863 uprising.

The rebel Poles only held out for 16 months, after which they were crushed by Russian armed forces. Russian victory was also helped by divisions within Polish society. These divisions were partly the result of the deliberate Russian policy to win over the Polish peasants by giving them more land (and giving their communes wider powers) than their Russian counterparts. The rebel leaders were executed and 80 000 Poles were sent to Siberia – the largest political contingent in tsarist history. By 1866, the Kingdom of Poland had been destroyed. It lost its status and simply became the Vistula region of the Russian Empire, named after the River Vistula. The power of the Polish nobility had been broken.

3.2 Was there a conservative reaction in the later years of Alexander II's rule?

The spread of opposition

The reforms implemented by Alexander II were controversial. Not all his ministers agreed with what he was doing, and there were times when he was uncertain himself. More worryingly for the regime, outsiders (mostly intellectuals and students but even merchants, small businessmen and prosperous peasants) were also critical. But in most cases their criticisms were not that the reforms went too far, but that they did not go far enough.

Discussion of Russia's future was stimulated by the excitement and disappointment brought about by Alexander's attitude to reform and the changed atmosphere within the country. The relaxation of censorship allowed ideas to spread more freely. At the same time, the growth of education and the greater autonomy of the universities produced a larger and more critical student body. The legal reforms also created a new group of skilled, professional debaters, who were ready to question and challenge the autocracy. Meanwhile, the establishment of the *zemstva* and *dumas* provided a new setting for debate in the provinces.

A new intelligentsia therefore emerged. Although they were small in number, these intellectuals proved influential in pressing for further reform and, in particular, greater individual liberty. Furthermore, their actions were not merely confined to books and debate. Some of them became involved in more active opposition and therefore posed a real threat to the tsar and his regime.

The uncertainty surrounding the Emancipation Edict led to demonstrations by students from the universities of St Petersburg, Moscow and Kazanin during 1861–62. In St Petersburg, flyers, pamphlets and proclamations found their way onto the city streets. There were also fires in St Petersburg and several provincial towns.

Land and Liberty, Russia's first truly revolutionary political society, was founded in 1861, the year of the Emancipation Edict. Although the organisation had no coherent programme, its members strongly believed that there was an alternative to autocracy. They looked to the peasants, led by the intelligentsia, to change Russia, creating an agrarian–socialist society of peasant communes.

Such thinking was encouraged by the work of socialist thinkers. The socialists believed in greater equality of wealth and they were deeply influenced by the works of Karl Marx (see 4.3, The 1880s). Marx had written his *Communist Manifesto* in 1847 (with Friedrich Engels), encouraging the working-class 'proletariat' to rise up against its masters. It was published in 1848. Mikhail Bakunin provided the first translation of the *Communist Manifesto* into Russian in 1869. But although Marxist thinking was intellectually attractive, even Bakunin thought it was largely irrelevant to Russia in the 1870s, since Russian society was mainly rural. Bakunin's own writings concentrated on replacing the private ownership of land with collective ownership, although he also held the revolutionary view that 'the state' should be destroyed.

A fellow socialist, Alexander Herzen, who wrote for the journal *The Bell* (published in London between 1857 and 1867 and secretly distributed in Russia), also believed that a new peasant-based social structure was needed in Russia. In 1869, he urged his followers to 'go to the people'. Meanwhile, Nikolai Chernyshevsky, editor of the radical journal *The Contemporary* and author of the novel *What is to be Done?*, expressed similar thoughts.

Figure 3.6: The 15 November 1861 issue of *The Bell*, an influential dissident journal.

While some students expressed interest in socialist theories, others were more extreme in their criticisms, as seen in Source 3.2 below.

SOURCE 3.2

In 1862, a manifesto entitled 'Young Russia' was produced by a group of students influenced by the Nihilist movement. They resented the restraints imposed by both the autocracy and Orthodox Church. The Young Russia manifesto included the following statement.

> Society is at present divided into two groups that are hostile to one another because their interests are diametrically opposed. The party that is oppressed by all and is humiliated by all is the party of the Common people. Over it stands a small group of contented and happy men. They are the landowners, the merchants, the government officials; in short all who possess property, either inherited or acquired. At their heart stands the Tsar. They cannot exist without him or he without them. If either falls the other will be destroyed. There is only one way out of this oppressive and terrible situation which is destroying contemporary man, and that is revolution – bloody and merciless revolution – a revolution that must radically change all the foundations of contemporary society without exception and destroy the supporters of the present regime.

Quoted in G Vernadsky et al. (eds.) 1972. **A Sourcebook for Russian History from Earliest Times to 1917**, *New Haven, USA. Yale University Press; and Christian, D. 1997.* **Imperial and Soviet Russia**. *Basingstoke, UK. Palgrave Macmillan. p. 93.*

QUESTION

With reference to the origin and purpose, assess the value and limitations of this source for historians studying the reasons for the growth of opposition in Russia during the reign of Alexander II.

A call for violent action was repeated in Bakunin's writings and also in Sergei Nechaev's *Catechism of a Revolutionary*. Nechaev's book was smuggled into Russia from Switzerland, where it was published in 1869. It called on the opponents of autocracy to pursue revolution, to the exclusion of 'family, friends, love, gratitude and honour'.

ACTIVITY

ACTIVITY

Try to find out more about *Nihilism*. If you have time, read Turgenev's *Fathers and Sons*, which features a *Nihilist*. This novel will give you an insight into 19th-century Russian society and provide a different perspective of later 19th century Russia.

The turning point, 1866

Before 1866, the criticisms and actions of the intelligentsia were broadly controlled by the tsarist secret police. For example, Chernyshevsky was arrested in 1862. He was convicted of inciting revolution and sentenced in 1864 to exile and hard labour in Siberia. His departure, coinciding with the suppression of the Polish revolt and the waning of peasant unrest, marked a lull in activity over the next two years.

In April 1866, Dmitri Karakozov, a member of a revolutionary student cell known as the Organisation, tried to assassinate the tsar as he was stepping out of his summer garden. This attempt on his life shook Alexander II, particularly as it came just a year after his eldest son and heir, Nicholas Alexandrovich, had died and his wife had fallen ill with tuberculosis. His immediate thought was that his would-be assassin was a Pole. When he heard he was a Russian (and, worse, a student of noble blood), it threw him into still greater despair.

The assassination attempt undermined Alexander's confidence in his reforming mission, and made him more willing to listen to the conservatives and churchmen who had been urging him to greater caution. His new mistress, Caterina Dolgoruki (whom he eventually married in 1880), also distanced him from his pro-reform brother and aunt. According to the historian Richard Pipes, 'The Emperor faced the solid opposition of the rank and file of the bureaucracy as well as that of his son and heir-apparent, the future Alexander III'.

Karakozov was publicly hanged, other Organisation leaders were sent to Siberia, and there was a crackdown on subversives, agitators, *Nihilists* and other 'enemies of the state'. This is sometimes seen as the turning point in Alexander's rule, from reform to reaction. However, it was probably less of a turning point than has traditionally been believed.

The year 1866 saw Alexander replace the liberal minister for education, Golovnin, with the staunch conservative and Orthodox believer,

Dmitri Tolstoy. He also appointed Pyotr Shuvalev as head of the Third Section, and replaced Pyotr Valuev with Alexander Timashev as minister of internal affairs. Konstantin Pahlen was promoted to minister of justice, and police powers were increased. Meanwhile, the power of the *zemstva* was restricted by limiting the amount of money they could raise in taxation.

> **Dmitri Tolstoy (1823–1889):**
>
> Count Dmitri Tolstoy had served in the ministry of the navy before becoming over-procurator (head) of the Holy Synod in 1865–80. He also became a member of the Council of State in 1866 and held the position of minister for education between 1866 and 1880, when he promoted Classics as the basis of education. From 1882 to 1889, he served as minister for internal affairs and chief of the gendarmerie under Alexander III.

A conservative reaction?

Education

Dmitri Tolstoy took immediate action to halt the tide of reform in education, which was blamed for the growth of student radicalism. He reduced the power of the *zemstva* over education and restored the position of the Church in the village schools. The high schools were ordered to follow a traditional Classical curriculum and abandon the natural sciences. Maths, Latin, Greek and Divinity replaced the teaching of subjects that encouraged critical thinking (such as History).

From 1871, only students from traditional high schools could go on to universities; those from modern technical schools were only able to move to higher technical institutions. Here, too, controls were tightened. New censorship laws were passed in 1873, forbidding students to discuss certain topics. There was also a strict ban on forming extra-curricular student organisations. While Tolstoy allowed Moscow University to organise lectures for women, he also used his right to veto university appointments. This led many students to seek greater freedom by studying abroad.

Theory of Knowledge

Thinking point

How far are social and cultural values moulded by education? Is it possible to control and influence society through interference in educational establishments?

Public education continued to expand throughout Alexander's reign, and new teacher-training colleges were set up to cope with the increased demand for teachers. Yet, education still came to be seen as another way of reinforcing obedience to traditional moral principles, rather than something that offered new opportunities for individual learning and advancement.

The police and the law courts

Shuvalev worked to strengthen the police and root out subversion. The Third Section became particularly active during these years. Even those who fled abroad were likely to be tracked down by its agents and brought back to Russia to face trial. Shuvalev worked in association with Pahlen, who used the judicial system to expose and condemn anyone accused of subversive political activity.

A number of open show trials were held. But this strategy backfired when the juries (created as a result of Alexander's legal reforms) acquitted many of those who had been 'brought to justice'. In the famous 'Trial of 193', 153 of the 193 accused were acquitted and others were given only light sentences by a sympathetic jury.

In addition, the speeches of the defence lawyers were reported in the press, again in accordance with Alexander's reforms. This provided useful publicity for opponents of tsardom. Frustrated, the government ruled in 1878 that future political crimes would be heard in military courts. There, the cases could be heard and the sentences could be passed in secret.

KEY CONCEPTS QUESTION

Change and consequence: To what extent did the conservative reaction after 1866 undermine all the reforming work of Alexander II's earlier years?

ACTIVITY

Try holding your own trial of an opponent of tsardom, with a prosecution lawyer, defence lawyer, witnesses and jury. The accused should think about which group in society they belong to, and which opposition movement (if any) they support – and why. The accused should write a brief for their lawyer, explaining why they have opposed the autocracy.

The 'crisis' of the 1870s

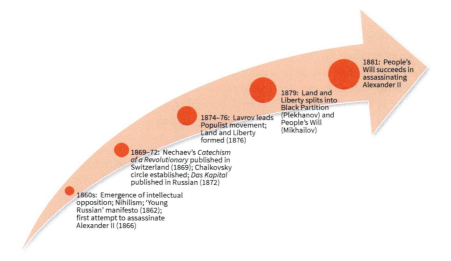

Figure 3.7: A diagram showing the growth of opposition to tsardom from the 1860s to 1881.

In 1871, Nechaev returned illegally from Switzerland to St Petersburg. There, he formed a circle of young revolutionary thinkers – the Chaikovsky circle. Although Nechaev himself was soon forced to flee again, the group produced pamphlets and smuggled books into Russia. These publications spread the idea that true reform could only occur if the peasants were persuaded to support socialist change and rebel against their lack of land and their heavy tax burden.

From this circle, Pyotr Lavrov emerged in 1874 to lead a group of around 2000 young men and women (mostly students). These individuals were quite literally prepared to 'go to the people' in order to spread their socialist views. Known as Populists or *narodniks* (from *narod*, meaning 'to the people'), they left their homes, universities and jobs to go into the countryside. There, they took posts in villages or poor areas of towns as doctors, teachers or even labourers, to share the life of the peasants.

However, the movement lacked any advance planning or clear leadership and ended in failure. Some of the Populists were struck down by diseases that were common in rural areas. Others were rapidly disillusioned by the response they received from the peasants, who were very suspicious of their activities. Local people sometimes thought the Populists were really secret police and spies. Indeed, some of them were even handed over to the police by the *volosts*. After a second disastrous attempt to encourage a peasant rising in 1876, around half of those involved were arrested and imprisoned. Many then appeared in public show trials in St Petersburg in 1877.

The sentences they received were comparatively lenient, but the branding of the Populists as revolutionaries and subversives actually encouraged the most extreme members to live up to their name and go further. Hence, a second Land and Liberty organisation was set up in 1876. This was a much more disciplined body, with a select membership of about 200, inspired by Bakunin and committed to more extreme action. Its members, including **Georgi Plekhanov**, were trained in spying and sabotage. They sought work in peasant communes and used their positions to stir up resistance to tsarist officials and state demands.

Georgi Plekhanov (1856–1918):

Plekhanov was initially attracted to the Populist movement and he became a leader of Land and Liberty and the Black Partition. On being sent into exile in 1880, he studied Marxism in Geneva and came to see it as the solution to Russia's troubles. He co-founded Emancipation of Labour with Lev Deutsch and Vera Zasulich in 1883. This organisation merged with other socialist groups to form the Russian Social Democratic Labour Party (RSDLP) in 1898. In 1903, when the party split, Plekhanov became a Menshevik (see 4.3, The 1890s and early 1900s) and he lived in exile until 1917. Although hailed as the 'Father of Russian Marxism', he never agreed with Lenin's leadership and spent his final year in Finland.

3

Imperial Russia and the Soviet Union (1855–1924)

In 1877–78, Russia became involved in another war – this time against the Turks. Russia was supposedly fighting on behalf of the breakaway Christian principalities in the Balkans that were seeking independence from their Muslim masters.

Although Russia eventually won this war, it proved to be a longer and more debilitating struggle than expected after Milyutin's military reforms. An industrial recession was beginning, following a wider economic depression in Europe. Russia's problems were made worse by a famine following a bad harvest in 1879.

All these factors bred a state of extreme tension in Russia in the late 1870s. The Land and Liberty movement assassinated General Mezemstev, the head of the Third Section, in St Petersburg in 1878. In the same year, Vera Zasulich shot and wounded General Trepov, the governor of St Petersburg. However, she was found 'not guilty' by a sympathetic jury. Although the tsar ordered her re-arrest, she was smuggled out of the country and went to Germany.

Internal disputes over methods caused Land and Liberty to break up in 1879. The organisation divided into two groups: Plekhanov's *Cherny Peredel* ('Black Partition'), which continued to operate among the peasantry, working peacefully to spread socialist propaganda; and Timofei Mikhailkov's *Narodnaya Volya* ('the People's Will'), which advocated violence and was committed to the removal of the tsar.

There were several further attempts on the tsar's life. In April 1879, Alexander Soloviev, a 33-year-old former student, fired five times at the tsar as he was out walking, but missed. Soloviev was sentenced to death and hanged. In December 1879, the People's Will organised an explosion on the railway from Livadia to Moscow, but missed the tsar's train. In February 1880, another member of the People's Will, Stephan Khalturin, set off a charge under the dining room of the Winter Palace. This killed 11 people and wounded 30. However, the tsar arrived late for dinner and was unharmed.

In view of such developments, it was perhaps not surprising that Alexander II should implement a final 'reactionary' measure in 1879. He declared a state of emergency and divided the country into military-style governor-generalships, with instructions that the military courts should be used to prosecute and exile political offenders. Nevertheless, even at this stage Alexander had not abandoned all thoughts of reform.

Count Loris-Melikov, a hero of the Turkish war and formerly a strict but effective governor-general, was appointed the head of the Supreme Administrative Commission to examine ways of combating the revolutionary agitation. Loris-Melikov was aware that the terrorists were actually only a small minority. If they could be separated from the well-meaning liberals and reformers, he believed they could be rapidly dealt with. To this end, he presented Alexander with a series of administrative and economic proposals. In August 1880, Alexander appointed him as minister of internal affairs, with exceptional powers to carry through his ideas.

Loris-Melikov's proposed measures included releasing political prisoners, relaxing censorship, removing the salt tax (which put a heavy burden on the peasants who relied on this everyday item), lifting restrictions on the activities of the *zemstva*, and transferring the powers of the Third Section to the regular police (where its 'secret police' activities continued but under a new name – the *Okhrana*). He also drew up a modest set of legislative proposals in 1880, which would have allowed representatives of the rural *zemstva* and urban *dumas* to scrutinise and advise on legislative bills before they went to the Council of State for ratification. These proposals were ready by the middle of February 1881 but nothing came of them.

On 13 March 1881, another assassination plan devised by the People's Will finally succeeded. Tsar Alexander II was killed on the very day that he signed a *ukase* (decree) to create several commissions to prepare Loris-Melikov's proposed reforms. He was due to present this decree to his Council of State that afternoon. However, a hand grenade was thrown at the tsar's coach as he was returning to the Winter Palace from a military ceremony. It missed its target and instead killed a soldier and a passing tradesman's boy.

Foolishly, the tsar got out of his carriage to see what had happened, thereby providing a target for another assassin, who threw a bomb at the tsar's feet, mortally wounding him. In this way, according to the historian Harry Hearder, 'his reign which had started in high hope ended in futile tragedy'.

Figure 3.8: This contemporary wood engraving shows the explosion that ended Alexander II's life in March 1881.

Problems of interpretation

The conventional view of Alexander II is that of the 'Tsar Liberator'. A contemporary, Boris Chicherin, wrote, 'Alexander set out to remodel completely the enormous state which had been entrusted to his care'. Subsequent historians have tended to accept this view, at least in part. Certainly, despite the many limitations of his reforms, there is little doubt that the changes he instituted helped to propel Russia into the modern world and stimulated economic growth and social movement.

Yet certain criticisms still stand, and these are linked to the intention behind the reforms. While Alexander may have genuinely intended to act in the best interests of his people (in line with the promises made by a tsar at his coronation), it has been suggested that his main motivation for reform was to preserve the autocracy. He therefore carried through reforms in accordance with his duty to improve a system that had failed Russia in the Crimea. The historian Alfred Rieber has gone still further, suggesting that the emancipation and reform process was motivated solely by military considerations. Rieber believes that the reforms were linked to the desire to strengthen and protect the autocratic state by developing a strong, efficient army. Furthermore, Alexander was content to concentrate his energy on foreign policy and Russian expansion in the Far East, leaving domestic issues to others.

Alexander II's refusal to countenance any form of National Assembly or change the fundamental basis of tsardom also suggests that he valued autocracy very highly. The tsar and most of his officials assumed that Russian autocracy was the best way of ruling and that Russia would remain an agrarian country, with nobles and peasants as the most important groups in society. They did not see the reforms as steps towards creating a new force of entrepreneurs and wage-earners. Instead, they tried to protect traditional nobility and peasantry as the basis of tsarist power.

Another interpretation is that Alexander's character was flawed and that his approach to reform was inconsistent. He had a limited understanding of the likely impact of his reforms, and began his reign with an exaggerated confidence in the regime's ability to control their results. When the effects were not as he expected, he was ready to retract. David Saunders has written, for example, 'the laws which freed the serfs emerged from a process that the tsar barely understood and over which he had only partial control'.

Hugh Seton-Watson has described Alexander as being at the crossroads between autocracy and modern liberal constitutional development. He judged the tsar a failure for seeking an unrealistic compromise between the two, and refusing to abandon autocracy. According to Crankshaw, 'During all his 25 years as tsar, he was to display an alternation between enthusiasm and apathy, stubbornness and defeatism, vision and myopia.'

In carrying through a number of reforms, Alexander unwittingly encouraged the transformation of Russia's old class structure and threatened the classes on which the power of the autocracy rested. In the short-term, the changes caused disillusionment among the liberal intelligentsia and provoked an increasingly radical response from growing groups of socialist thinkers. In the long-term, the government would pay a heavy price for Alexander's lack of vision.

In 1881, organised opposition (which had been made possible by his own reforms) was already becoming difficult to control, and the 'Tsar Liberator' met his end through an assassin's bomb. As Werner Mosse has written, 'Alexander proved himself a disappointing liberal and an inefficient autocrat'.

It is interesting to note the striking parallel between this era of the 'Great reforms' and *perestroika* in the late 1980s, as identified by David Christian: 'In both periods a new generation of young, reforming politicians launched sweeping changes from above, after a prolonged era of political oppression and economic stagnation. In one case the reformed system survived for another 60 years; in the other it collapsed.'

KEY CONCEPTS ACTIVITY

Change and continuity: Was Alexander II's reign more a time of change or a time of continuity? Draw up a balance sheet and discuss your conclusions with a partner.

Paper 3 exam practice

Question

To what extent does Alexander II deserve the title 'Tsar Liberator'?
[15 marks]

Skill

Planning an essay

Examiner's tips

As discussed in Chapter 2, the first stage of planning an answer to a question is to think carefully about its wording so that you know what is required and what you need to focus on. Once you have done this, you can move on to the other important considerations.

Decide your **main argument/theme/approach before** you start to write. This will help you identify the key points you want to make. For example, this question clearly invites you to make a judgement about Alexander II, weighing up positive and negative interpretations of the tsar and his reign. You will need to show your understanding of 'Tsar Liberator'. You will also need to decide on an approach that helps you produce an argument that is clear, coherent and logical. Your argument should show whether this title is a good description of Alexander II – or whether you would prefer to support an alternative.

Plan **the structure of your argument** – i.e. the introduction, the main body of the essay (in which you present precise evidence to support your arguments), and your concluding paragraph.

For this question, whatever overall view you have of Alexander II, you should try to make a **balanced** argument. The question is primarily about differing interpretations of Alexander II, so you will need to cover a **range** of interpretations: Alexander as a traditional autocrat, as a reformer only to protect autocracy, as an inefficient reformer, as an inconsistent leader, as a figurehead who left reform to others, as a genuine reformer, and so on. However, it is also about the 'liberating' nature of the reforms. For example, were they genuinely liberating?

3 Imperial Russia and the Soviet Union (1855–1924)

Were they only half measures? Were they too restricted? Take care with questions at Higher Level. There is often more than one focus.

The amount of time you devote to the varying interpretations will very much depend on the view you choose to adopt. But you will obviously want to develop your ideas fully, while allowing time to consider (even if only to dismiss) the alternatives.

Whatever the question, try to **link** the points you make in your paragraphs, so that there is a clear thread that follows through to your conclusion. This will help to ensure that your essay is not just a series of unconnected paragraphs.

You may well find that drawing a spider diagram or mind map helps you with your essay planning. For this question, your spider diagram might look like this.

When writing your essay, include **linking phrases** to ensure that each smaller 'bubble' (factor) paragraph is linked to the 'main bubble' (the question). For example:

While Alexander was in many ways a traditional autocrat, he nevertheless accepted the need for some reform, even if his motives can be questioned…

However, Alexander was not only driven by autocratic tendencies. He was also inconsistent in his attitude to reform…

Furthermore, the tsar's lack of genuine concern for reform can be seen in the way that he allowed others to draw up the details...

In addition, not all the reforms were genuinely liberating...

There are clearly many factors to consider. Drawing up a five-minute plan of this type, with brief details (such as dates and main supporting evidence) under each heading, will help you cover what you want to say in the time available. Your plan should enable you to keep your essay balanced, so that you do not spend too long on any one aspect. It should also ensure that you remain focused on the question and do not wander off into description.

Common mistakes

It is very easy to look at questions and see just one clear argument emerging from them. In this case, was Alexander a 'Tsar Liberator' or not? Saying 'yes he was' in these ways... but 'no he wasn't' in those ways... would provide an answer to the question, but it would be over-simplistic and would ignore the varied interpretations suggested.

Furthermore, many Higher-level IB questions have a subtext that invites consideration of less obvious arguments. Here, an important secondary argument concerns the degree to which Alexander's reforms were 'liberating'. The tsar's intentions might also be considered in deciding whether or not the term 'Tsar Liberator' is well deserved. Did Alexander have genuinely liberating intentions, and how far was he restricted by his responsibilities and inheritance as tsar?

Trying to weave several arguments together is never going to be easy, but it is the mark of a high-achieving student. Always reflect on the full demands of a question **before** you begin and consider how you will link your various arguments. Remember, just as builders need scaffolding before they can construct a solid house, essay writers need a plan before they can develop a convincing answer.

Remember to refer to the simplified Paper 3 mark scheme in Chapter 8.

Activity

In this chapter, the skills focus is on planning answers. Using this chapter and any other sources of information, produce essay plans – using spider diagrams, charts or mind maps – with all the necessary headings (and brief details) for well-focused and clearly structured responses to at least two of the following Paper 3 practice questions.

Paper 3 practice questions

1 'Alexander II was a failure in all that he set out to do.' To what extent do you agree with this statement?

2 Evaluate the extent to which Russia was modernised in the reign of Alexander II.

3 Discuss the success of Alexander II's efforts to reform Russian institutions.

4 To what extent were Alexander II's policies in Russia revolutionary?

5 'Alexander II's reforms created more problems than they solved.' To what extent do you agree with this statement?

Alexander III (1881–1894) and Nicholas II (1894–1917): Modernisation, repression and the growth of opposition to 1904

4

TIMELINE

1881 **1 Mar:** Assassination of Alexander II brings Alexander III to power

Apr: Manifesto of Unshakable Autocracy

Aug: Statute on Measures for the Preservation of Political Order and Social Tranquility; Jewish pogrom; Russification programme begins

1882 **Mar:** Statute on Police Surveillance

1883 **Apr:** Peasant land bank set up

1884 Educational decrees passed

1885 **Jun:** Nobles' bank established

1886 **Jan:** Poll tax abolished

1887 **Mar:** Attempted assassination of Alexander III

1889 Land captains introduced

1891–92 Great famine

1894 **14 May:** Nicholas II is crowned

Oct: Alexander III dies

1898 Establishment of Russian Social and Democratic Party

1903 SDP splits between Bolsheviks (under Lenin) and Mensheviks (under Martov)

KEY QUESTIONS

- What was the nature of tsardom under Alexander III and Nicholas II?
- In what respects was Russia underdeveloped and what attempts were made at modernisation?
- Why and how did opposition movements grow?

Between 1881 and 1904, tsardom returned to the path of political repression and reaction. Alexander III began his reign with the public hanging of his father's assassins. When Nicholas II came to the throne in 1894, he somewhat feebly tried to preserve his father's policies. Both these tsars were strong believers in 'Autocracy, Orthodoxy and Nationality'. They lived in the past, either ignoring or brutally attempting to crush those who called for political change and economic modernisation. Three factors made it increasingly difficult for these last two tsars to rule as their ancestors had done. These issues were the emergence of a liberal, professional middle class; changes in the position of the peasants; and – most importantly – the development of a large and vocal urban industrial workforce. Yet their governments offered no alternative to autocracy. Popular demands therefore erupted into Russia's first 20th-century revolution in 1905.

Overview

- When Alexander III came to the throne, he was determined to re-assert the tsar's autocracy, after what he saw as the dangerous innovations of Alexander II's reign.
- Loris-Melikov's cautious plans for constitutional reform were abandoned, and the powers of the nobility were re-established with the institution of land captains.
- Changes were made in judicial and educational policy, and there was greater censorship, repression and control.
- Ethnic minorities were subjected to a policy of Russification and anti-Semitism escalated.
- The Russian Orthodox Church was strongly supported and restored to a position of supreme power.
- Nicholas II continued his father's policies, though he was a less forceful character than Alexander III and found leadership difficult.
- The Russian economy expanded, under Vyshnegradsky and Witte, but this brought increasing social problems and discontent.
- Repressive measures and economic change encouraged the growth of opposition, divided between moderate liberal and more extreme socialist and Marxist groups.

Figure 4.1: The coronation of Tsar Alexander III in 1881.

4.1 What was the nature of tsardom under Alexander III and Nicholas II?

What kind of ruler was Alexander III?

Alexander III was 36 when he found himself suddenly thrust into power. The shock of his father's brutal assassination must have been made worse by his own lack of training. As a second son, he had not been brought up expecting to become tsar. It was only when his elder brother Nicholas died in 1865 that he found himself heir to the imperial throne. His tutor, Konstantin Pobedonostev (1827–1907), had ensured that he understood the importance of autocracy and he was persuaded of the folly of 'dangerous advance' along Western lines. Alexander blamed his father's death on the reforms he had unwisely introduced. He lived in fear of the revolutionaries, preferring to stay away from St Petersburg in his fortifi ed castle at Gatchina, around 50 km (30 miles) to the south.

Alexander III (1845–94):

Alexander was a large, ungainly man, who stood 193 cm (6 feet 4 inches) tall. He was immensely strong and enjoyed demonstrating 'party tricks' such as bending an iron bar with his bare hands or tearing a whole pack of cards in two. He had a commanding appearance and looked every inch the autocrat that he always strove to be. However, after his father's assassination, he always feared revolutionary activity. For this reason, he preferred to live in the fortress of Gatchina, rather than the Winter Palace in St Petersburg where he felt vulnerable. Despite his strength and size, he died young at only 49.

SOURCE 4.1

Alexander Mossolov, head of the court chancellery from 1900 to 1916, made the following comments in his memoirs.

> He had had one idea instilled into him above all others – that of the omnipotence of the Tsars of Russia, and of the consequent necessity of maintaining the prestige of the Imperial authority. On this latter point the tradition inherited from his august father and his grandfather Nicholas I was maintained in its full grandeur and integrity. The doctrine was continually impressed on the future Emperor that the Russian Tsars are the masters whom God has willed to bestow on Holy Russia in her boundless immensity. The Tsar was his country's guardian and a symbol of the national unity: he stood forth as the last rampart of paternal benevolence and chivalrous justice.

From: www.alexanderpalace.org/mossolov and Mossolov, A. A. 1935. **At the Court of the Last Tsar.** *London, UK. Methuen.*

QUESTION

What does Source 4.1 suggest about the powers and authority of the Tsar of Russia?

Pobedonostev, who later also became the tutor of Alexander's son, the future Nicholas II, had a profound influence over these last two tsars. He ensured that they remained true to the principles of 'Autocracy, Orthodoxy and Nationality'. He himself was the over-procurator of the Holy Synod from 1880 to 1905. He was an extreme right-wing conservative, who held Slavophile, nationalist and strongly anti-Semitic beliefs. He spoke of the need for 'family, obedience and governmental coercion' and he described the idea that power came from the people as 'the great falsehood of our time'. According to the historian Hugh Seton-Watson, he imposed 'an overall attitude of nostalgia, obscurantist and narrowly bureaucratic paternalism' on Alexander's government.

Alexander III was never happier than when he was with his family at Gatchina. He was devoted to his wife, the Danish Princess Dagmar, who took the name Marie Fedorovna. They had five children, the eldest of whom, Nicholas, would become the last Russian tsar. However, in 1894, at only 49 years of age, Alexander began to suffer from migraine, insomnia and weakness. He soon died of nephritis (a kidney infection), brought on by bruising suffered when the royal train had been derailed six years earlier.

Theory of Knowledge

History, empathy and understanding

The novelist L. P. Hartley (1895–1972) wrote: *'The past is another country. They do things differently there.'* Most historians believe it is important to study the beliefs and motives of rulers. Is it possible to know what a person in the past thought, and/or why they thought the way they did? Do our present-day beliefs and attitudes make this impossible?

The autocracy in 1881

SOURCE 4.2

One of the first pieces of advice that Alexander received as tsar came from his tutor Pobedonostev, whose speech of March 1881, delivered just a week after his Father's assassination provided a warning:

> Your Majesty! By oath and by conscience I am obliged
> to express all that is on my soul. I find myself not
> only in a state of confusion, but also one of despair.
> In Russia people want to introduce a constitution. But
> what is a constitution? Western Europe provides an
> answer to this question. Constitutions existing there are
> in essence instruments for every kind of untruth, the
> source of all kinds of intrigue. Russia was strong thanks
> to autocracy, thanks to the unlimited mutual trust and
> close connection between the people and their Tsar.
> This connection between the Russian Tsar and his
> people is an incalculable good.

It was clear that Alexander III hardly needed reminding of the need for 'unshakable autocracy'.

Taken from a speech by Konstantin Petrovich Pobedonostsev delivered on 8 March 1881 in the Winter Palace, St. Petersburg. Originally printed in **Russkii Arkhiv no. 5** *(1907): pp. 103–105. Translated by Paul Werth, https://faculty.unlv.edu/pwerth*

Alexander III's sentiments were not entirely out of tune with public feeling. There was a widespread mood of revulsion at his father's untimely end and the tsar was still deeply venerated. Consequently, there was no public outcry when Alexander's first action was to abandon the Loris-Melikov proposals for constitutional reform. Alexander wrote on the front page of the draft: 'Thank God this over-hasty, criminal proposal was never realised and the whole crazy project has been rejected.'

SOURCE 4.3

In a manifesto called 'Unshakeable Autocracy', issued on 29 April 1881, Alexander III made a declaration.

> We trust that the fervent prayers of our devoted people, known throughout the whole world for their love and devotion to their sovereigns, will draw God's blessing upon us and the labour of government to which we have been appointed. Consecrating ourselves to Our great service, We call upon our faithful subjects to serve us and the state in fidelity and truth, for the eradication of the vile sedition disgracing the Russian land, for the strengthening of faith and morality, for the proper upbringing of children, for the extermination of falsehood and theft, and for the introduction of truth and good order in the operations of the institutions given to Russia by her benefactor, Our beloved Father.

Quoted in Holland, A. 2010. **Russia and its Rulers, 1855–1964***. London, UK. Hodder Education. p. 18.*

QUESTION

In what ways do the views expressed in Source 4.3 support those given in Source 4.2 about Tsarist autocracy?

In May, Loris-Melikov and two other reforming ministers, Alexander Abaza and Dimitri Milyutin, resigned in protest. Loris-Melikov was initally replaced as minister of internal affairs by Count Nikolai Ignatev, a staunch nationalist whose belief in the unity of the Slav peoples under Russian protection (known as pan-Slavism) had helped provoke the 1877–78 Russo-Turkish war.

A year later, an even more extreme conservative was brought in – Count Dmitri Tolstoy (see 3.2, The turning point 1866). Formerly Alexander II's minister of education, Tolstoy had served as over-procurator of the Holy Synod between 1865 and 1880, when Pobedonostev had taken over. Like Pobedonostev, he had a very strong influence over the tsar in the early years of the reign, encouraging Alexander's commitment to autocracy.

The right-wing journalist Mikhail Katkov, editor of the *Moscow News* from 1863 to 1887, was another powerful figure. He also gave his full support to the government's ultra-conservative policies, thereby delivering a clear message to the literate public.

KEY CONCEPTS ACTIVITY

Perspectives:

- Write an article as if you were Mikhail Katkov, arguing in support of government policies in 1881.
- Swop articles with a partner who should write a commentary on the article in the form of a letter from one Zemstvo member to another.

Repression and the police

In August 1881, the Statute on Measures for the Preservation of Political Order and Social Tranquility, sometimes referred to as 'exceptional measures', set out to eradicate the 'vile sedition disgracing the Russian land'. The statute declared that any area of the empire where trouble was suspected could be designated an area of 'extraordinary security'. It would then have a commander-in-chief appointed to it, to root out the troublemakers and ensure loyalty to the regime. These commanders-in-chief would have full power to search property and arrest, interrogate, imprison and exile suspects. The 'untrustworthy' (including those suspected of planning crimes) would have no right to legal representation. This 'temporary' measure was initially supposed to last three years, but in practice it was repeatedly renewed and was still in place in 1917.

Figure 4.2: The police raid the premises of a Nihilist group engaged in printing a dissident journal in St Petersburg in the 1880s.

The department of police was put in the hands of **Vyacheslav Konstantinovich von Plehve** from 1881 to 1884, and subsequently under Ivan Durnovo, working under the direction of the ministry of internal affairs. It supervised the gendarmerie, the security police and the secret police network (the *Okhrana*), which had offices in Moscow, St Petersburg and Warsaw.

Vyacheslav Konstantinovich von Plehve (1846–1904):

Plehve was of German descent but was raised in Warsaw and sent to Moscow University, where he trained in the law and subsequently entered the ministry of justice. He was responsible for the investigations into Alexander II's assassination in 1881 and was given new responsibilities as director of the department of police, which included control over the *Okhrana*. He became minister of internal affairs in 1902 and at first tried to adopt a conciliatory role, working with the *zemstva*. However, he changed his approach and abandoned the police-supported trade unions that he initially favoured. Several attempts were made on his life and he was eventually assassinated in July 1904.

In March 1882, the Statute on Police Surveillance permitted the police to conduct searches and monitor exiles' correspondence as well as expanding the secret police network. This statute signalled a drive to recruit spies, and counter-spies (to spy on the spies), to watch the factories, universities, army, civil service and central government. The *Okhrana* dealt with communists, socialists and militant unionists, using torture and execution. Thousands of suspected revolutionaries were sent to Siberia as a result. From 1886, the island of Sakhalin was also made a place of political exile. Even after they were released, ex-political prisoners were to be excluded from employment in government or public service or as lawyers, doctors or teachers.

The re-establishment of noble influence

In order to control the countryside, Alexander decided to create a new noble position – that of land captain. These land captains would be appointed by, and under the direct control of, the minister of internal affairs. The land captains were picked from eligible hereditary nobles (those who had sufficient land, education and length of government service) and they were made responsible for enforcing government orders in their areas. They were given wide-ranging powers to root out sedition (plotting against the regime). They could also override elections to the *zemstva* and village assemblies and overturn the decisions of local courts.

The land captains could even remove unreliable village elders, thereby undermining the tradition of self-government in the *mirs*. According to Richard Charques, 'no single act of government in the reign of Alexander II stirred the Russian peasant to more bitter resentment'.

Both Charques and E. A. Lutsky have suggested that this measure, in effect, created a state of 'semi-serfdom' in the countryside. It did this by re-instating the dominance of the nobility and removing some of the autonomy the peasants had enjoyed since emancipation.

Alexander III and his ministers were, in any case, suspicious of the elected *zemstva* and *dumas* created by Alexander II. The membership of these councils was overwhelmingly 'professional', but they contained some working-class and peasant representatives. Their political criticisms and support for Loris–Melikov's constitutional proposals suggested that they were centres for 'dangerous' liberal thinking. Consequently, although Alexander III did not abolish these institutions altogether, he tried to reduce their influence by adjusting their membership to give more weight to the nobility.

In 1890, the constitution of the *zemstva* was changed to give the nobles 57% of the places available. The ministry of internal affairs assumed direct control, the *zemstva*'s right to appoint magistrates was removed and any decisions made became subject to the veto of the local land captain. In 1892, the property qualification for voters to the municipal *dumas* was also raised. In St Petersburg, the electorate was reduced by two-thirds as a result. Mayors and members of municipal councils were also turned into state employees, who were directly responsible to the central government.

Such changes had the effect of channelling the energies of the *zemstva* and *dumas* away from political discussion and into social and community work, particularly in education, health, transport and engineering. The effectiveness of local government therefore came to depend upon the attitude of the land captains, some of whom became infamous – less for repressive behaviour than for their laziness and apathy. The land captains' activities were supposedly overseen by the district marshals. However, in practice the district marshal avoided interfering and so offending them, since the land captains had an influence over the marshals' election.

Judicial changes

While Alexander II had encouraged moves towards fairer trials and the use of the jury system, Alexander III's reign saw the partial reversal of such reforms. By a decree of 1885, the minister of justice was given greater control over the dismissal of judges whose decisions he disliked. 'Closed court sessions', where no observers or reporters were permitted, were made legal from 1887 for cases where the 'dignity of state power' was in question. Furthermore, jurors now needed more property and higher educational qualifications in order to serve on juries. In 1889, local magistrates disappeared and the central ministry of justice took control of the appointment of town judges. Meanwhile, the land captains assumed judicial powers in the countryside.

KEY CONCEPTS ACTIVITY

Change and continuity: Look back at the reforms made by Alexander II. List these on the left-hand side of a page. On the right, note whether each reform remained as it was, or was changed in the years to 1894 (Alexander III's death). Was there more change or more continuity?

Education, orthodoxy and intellectual life

Along with these administrative changes came a close supervision of intellectual life, ranging from control over schools and universities to the censorship of newspapers and books. The reactionary Ivan Delyanov was appointed minister of education. He ensured that what was taught, and to whom, was restricted at all levels.

In 1884, universities were deprived of their independence. Chancellors, deans and professors had to be approved by the ministry of education. They were to be chosen according to their 'religious, moral and patriotic orientation', rather than just their academic qualifications. The universities also had to undergo government inspection. From 1887, fees were raised and the separate university courts (established in 1755) were abolished. Only the upper classes became eligible for higher education, and students had to pay to attend lectures and to take examinations. Additional legislation (passed in 1882 and 1886) barred women from the universities altogether. Furthermore, all student organisations were suppressed and private meetings involving more than five students were strictly forbidden.

Delyanov also circulated a memorandum to all secondary schools, ordering them to stop accepting 'the children of coachmen, domestic servants, cooks, washerwomen, small shopkeepers and other similar persons… whose children should not be taken out of the social environment to which they belong'. Fees were raised for secondary education in 1887, in a bid to keep these 'lower orders' out. In addition, a quota system was introduced to control the intake.

The number of elementary schools increased, but they were put under the control of the Church. Lessons reinforced the value of humility and obedience, and there was constant religious indoctrination. Pupils were taught to read Slavonic texts and to accept that Russia was a 'holy land' chosen by God to save the world. It was thought that the 'lower orders' needed to receive only minimal education, in order to ensure religious observance. The educational budget was only a tenth of the amount allocated for defence. There were fewer pupils in elementary schools in 1895 than there had been in 1882, and the 1897 census revealed that a mere 21% of the population could read and write. By 1904, there were still only 27% of Russian children at school.

The moral domination of the Orthodox Church was seen as part of the constant battle against liberalism and secularism. Indeed, in many respects, the Church formed another arm of government. In 1893, Orthodox priests were made official state servants, with their salaries paid by the state. Priests had to read out imperial decrees and manifestos to their congregations, religious books were subject to censorship by the Church, and Church courts judged social and 'moral' crimes such as divorce.

DISCUSSION POINT

Is it better to separate knowledge from belief? What problems are posed by an educational system that is run by the Church?

Other religions were generally tolerated, but Orthodox priests had an important and overriding status. From 1883 onwards, members of non-Orthodox Churches were not allowed to wear religious dress (other than at their meeting place), spread religious propaganda or build any new places of worship. In addition, the crime of attempting to convert an Orthodox Christian to another faith was made punishable by exile to Siberia.

A new committee on censorship was established in 1882, under the direction of the minister of internal affairs, Dimitri Tolstoy. Pobedonostev was also a member. This committee issued a series of 'temporary regulations', giving the government the power to close offending publications and ban the editor and publishers from any future activity. Any newspaper that received three warnings had to present all their text to the Board of Censors the day before publication. Provincial reading rooms were controlled by local governors, and official approval had to be given before books could be purchased for these reading rooms. There was also censorship of the theatre, arts and culture, partly linked to the Russification campaign.

Russification

Russification involved trying to turn a multi-national empire into a single country, with a shared sovereign, language and nationality. This policy was pursued during the reigns of both Alexander III and Nicholas II, with Pobedonostev's encouragement. Pobedonostev suggested that 'the instinct of nationality serves as a disintegrating force'. He believed that the removal of the separate languages and cultures of the 40 million or so non-Russians (60% of the empire's population) would strengthen the tsar's autocracy and encourage stability. But nothing could have been further from the truth. Its effect was to turn non-Russian peoples, who had previously been unswervingly loyal, into opponents of tsarist rule.

Russification measures included the enforced use of the Russian language in schools in Poland, Finland, Lithuania and central Asia. The Ukrainian and Belorussian languages were forbidden and their churches persecuted. The publication of any literature in Ukrainian was outlawed in 1883 and all the theatres in five Ukrainian provinces were closed in 1884. In Livonia, Estonia and Courland, similar action was taken against the use of German. Local liberties were suppressed and there were some forced conversions from Lutheranism to Greek Orthodoxy.

In Poland, the national bank was closed in 1885. In Finland, which had its own constitution and parliament and regarded the tsar as a 'Grand-Duke', progressive steps were taken to diminish Finnish independence. In 1892, the Finnish Senate was reorganised in order to weaken political influence, the independent postal service was abolished and the use of Russian coinage was made compulsory. Under Nicholas II, the Finnish constitution was abolished altogether in 1899.

Accompanying such measures was the harsh repression of uprisings of ethnic peoples in Bashkira (1884), in the Uzbed district of Fegana (1886), Armenia (1886), Tashkent (1892) and Guriya (western Georgia, 1892). These actions were accompanied by deportations and imprisonments. Some non-conformist sects, such as the Doukhobors, Molokany and Stundists, were persecuted. In some areas, Roman Catholics were not allowed to hold government posts.

Jews

The group that suffered most acutely from enforced Russification was the Jews. Since 1736, Jews had been mainly confined to the area known as 'the Pale of Settlement' in the south and west of Russia. (Alexander II had allowed some movement, until the Polish revolt of 1863 led him to clamp down once more.) Jews worked within the local communities, pursuing a variety of trades and becoming involved in businesses, although anti-Semitic sentiment was never far below the surface.

Anti-Semitism was strengthened by the publicity given to the case of Hessia Helfmann, a Jewess convicted of involvement in Alexander II's assassination but reprieved because she was pregnant at the time. The government was happy to encourage anti-Jewish pogroms. (Pogrom was an old Russian word meaning 'a round-up' or 'lynching'.) Slogans such as 'Russia for the Russians' and 'Beat the Yids – Save Russia' were used to encourage attacks on Jewish communities. The first such pogrom occurred in April 1881, in the town of Elizavetgrad in Ukraine, and may have been deliberately sparked off by the tsar's secret police. Homes were set on fire, shops were destroyed and looted, women were raped and many Jews were murdered.

Figure 4.3: The pogroms of 1881 in south-western Russia; the area in orange shows the Pale of Settlement, but some Jews had moved outside the Pale so the pogroms extended well beyond it.

By 1882, the attacks had spread through Kirovi and Kiev in Ukraine, through 100 Jewish localities in southern Russia including Odessa, to Warsaw and Podolia in Poland. Over the next three years, well over 200 communities with a high concentration of Jews experienced similar violent outbursts.

In 1882, a series of Temporary Regulations, known as the 'May Laws', further reduced Jews' rights, even in the Pale of Settlement. Jews were not allowed to purchase 'immovable property' or live in rural areas. This had the effect of forcing them to live in ghettoes in large towns and villages.

The towns of Rostov-on-Don and Taganrog were removed from the Pale in 1887 and a quota was placed on Jews in primary, secondary and higher education. In 1889, they were excluded from the law and other professions such as medicine. The war ministry even limited the number of Jews in the medical corps to 5% and justified this by claiming that Jews lowered standards of sanitation.

In 1891, Jewish artisans were forbidden to live in Moscow, and over 17 000 were forcibly deported during the bitter winter of 1891–92. In 1892, Jews were prohibited from voting in local elections for the *zemstva* and the municipal *dumas*, despite their tax-paying status. Even worse, from 1894 onwards, they were no longer allowed to hold licences to sell alcohol. This deprived the many Jewish innkeepers of their means of earning a living.

Russification continued under Nicholas II, and a second wave of pogroms spread through Russia in the years 1903 to 1906. In total, 45 Jews died in Kishinev in 1903, 300 in Odessa, and 80 in Bialystok in 1905. Government propaganda associated Jews with revolutionary troublemakers. However, it was probably the government action that actually drove Jews into the revolutionary movement. Early 20th-century Russia did contain a disproportionate number of Jewish revolutionaries, including Leon Trotsky, Yuli Martov, Grigori Zinoviev and Maxim Litvinov. It also drove large numbers of hard-working and formerly loyal Jewish citizens to emigrate, thereby creating the Zionist movement in which Jews searched for a separate Jewish homeland.

What kind of ruler was Nicholas II?

Alexander III's death in 1894 brought his son, **Nicholas II**, to power. Nicholas was a much less imposing figure than his father. According to one of his ministers, Sergei Witte, 'His character is the source of all. His outstanding weakness is a lack of willpower.' Rasputin said, 'The Tsar can change his mind to the next; he's a sad man; he lacks guts.'

Nicholas II (1868–1918):

Nicholas grew up in the shadow of his father, Alexander III, who thought him a weakling and referred to him as slender, shy and not good at practical tasks. He had perfect manners and was able to speak several languages but he found politics boring. When he became tsar, he admitted that 'I never wanted to become one. I know nothing of the business of ruling. I have no idea of even how to talk to the ministers.' His inability to make balanced decisions, coupled with his determination to maintain autocracy, proved fatal.

Nicholas had a good education but it was controlled by the arch-conservative Pobedonostev. It was designed to instill in him a 'belief in the moral rightness of autocracy, and a religious faith that he was in God's hands and his actions were divinely inspired.' He was only 26 when he suddenly found himself on the throne, and had received little practical training in politics. He feared he would never be able to measure up to his father's standards, but he was determined to try.

Figure 4.4: Nicholas II, aged 13, in Russian military uniform.

This was a fatal combination – Nicholas tried to rule as an autocrat but did not possess the qualities of discernment and judgement that such a ruler desperately needs. According to Orlando Figes, 'It was not a weakness of will that was the undoing of the last Tsar but a wilful determination to rule from the throne, despite the fact that he clearly lacked the necessary qualities to do so.'

In 1894, he married Princess Alice of Hesse-Darmstadt (Queen Victoria's grand-daughter), who became Alexandra Feodorovna. She was a devoted wife but her influence over Nicholas was misguided. She kept urging him to stand firm and avoid making concessions that she thought would weaken the monarchy.

When a delegation of *zemstva* members came to Moscow in January 1895 to pledge their allegiance to the new tsar, they asked whether he might consider a small degree of democratic reform. Nicholas responded with a forceful speech, drafted by Pobedonostev.

SOURCE 4.4

I am pleased to see representatives of all estates who have journeyed here to profess their loyal sentiments together. I believe in the earnestness of these sentiments, that have been inherent in every Russian since time immemorial. But I understand that some people, carried away by senseless dreams, have been heard to suggest that local councils might be allowed to participate in the government of this country. I wish to make it clear that I, dedicating all my efforts to the well-being of the people, shall preserve the principle of absolute autocracy as firmly and resolutely as did my late lamented father.

Tsar Nicholas II, (partly quoted in Sixsmith, M. 2011. **Russia.** *London, UK. BBC Books. p. 157, extended by use of website http://allrussias.com/ tsarist_russia/romanovs_4.asp*

QUESTION

What is the significance of Source 4.4 for an understanding of the reign of Tsar Nicholas II?

The extent and impact of 'counter-reform' before 1905

By 1905, it looked as though the reforming impulses that had driven Tsar Alexander II had been completely forgotten. Russia's last two tsars, Alexander III and Nicholas II, appeared to be solely motivated by their belief in autocratic power. However, this interpretation is open to question.

The former serfs found that their position gradually improved. A law passed in 1881 reduced their land redemption payments and cancelled arrears in 37 of the central provinces of the empire. The salt tax was abolished in 1881 and the hated poll tax was phased out from 1886. In 1896, and again in 1899, some of the old redemption payments were deferred and debt arrears were cancelled. A number of commissions were also set up to consider the position of agriculture, such as the commission headed by Pyotr Stolypin in 1902.

New taxes helped to shift the burden away from the lowest classes, with the introduction of taxes on private businesses, the raising of taxes on urban property and the introduction of inheritance tax. Peasants gained the right to appeal to a higher court in cases where the peasants disputed the judgement of the land captain. They were also given the services of the peasants' bank in 1883, to enable them to borrow money to better themselves. Finally, the need to obtain a permit to leave the commune was removed in 1903, and this allowed the peasants greater freedom and mobility.

Town workers benefited from factory legislation, which helped to regulate child labour and reduce working hours, particularly women's night work. Legislation also ensured lower fines and less enforced payment in kind. In addition, an inspectorate was set up to check workers' living and working conditions.

Tsarist rule to 1905 cannot therefore be described as totally reactionary. Historians such as Bernard Pares, John Maynard, Frank Golder, Seton-Watson and Charques have traditionally dismissed later tsarist rule as inept. However, there has been a movement, over the last 30 years or so, towards a more 'optimistic' appraisal. For example, Robert Byrnes has reinterpreted the influence of Pobedonostev as a reformer. Meanwhile, David Saunders has emphasised the stability of this period and added, 'The traditional historians of late tsarism have been asking the wrong questions. Instead of asking why tsarism collapsed, the issues should have been, why was it so successful and why did it survive so long?' Peter Waldron's *The End of Imperial Russia* has also emphasised the degree to which Russia modernised itself under Alexander III and Nicholas II. However, Robert Service is less positive about these achievements and Figes has emphasised the inadequacies of the autocracy, so opinion remains mixed.

The real problem was the difficulty of reconciling the government's efforts to promote economic modernisation in Russia (which required an educated workforce and trained managers and bureaucracy) with the fear of 'undermining' society by promoting change. What *can* be said of the tsarist measures, whether reactionary or reformist, is that they failed to prevent unrest.

During the 1890s and early 1900s, the poor living and working conditions created by the growth of industrial cities, high taxes and land hunger gave rise to more frequent strikes and agrarian disorder. Opposition movements continued to flourish.

4.2 In what respects was Russia underdeveloped and what attempts were made at modernisation?

The need for economic modernisation

Despite the economic advances made during Alexander II's reign, Russia still lagged behind Western Europe economically. At the time of Alexander II's death in 1881, much of Russia's vast economic potential remained untapped. A major problem preventing the growth of industry was the relative lack of capital. Landowners (who had barely been able to keep out of debt since before emancipation) had limited capital to invest in industry, even if they wished to do so. In addition, there was no sizeable middle class to provide capital, direction or expertise. Furthermore, Russia's huge size and poor infrastructure made internal economic development difficult if not impossible. For all these reasons, there was little chance of industrial change driven 'from below'.

Alexander III's first finance minister (from 1882 to 1886), Nikolai Bunge, had begun a move towards greater state ownership of the railways. However, Bunge failed to balance the budget and was blamed for a fall in the value of the rouble. Following his 1887 replacement by **Ivan Vyshnegradsky**, a much-needed change in direction occurred.

Ivan Vyshnegradsky (1832–95):

Vyshnegradsky started out as a priest and subsequently taught mathematics and mechanics in St Petersburg. His entrepreneurial skills enabled him to make money through investments in joint-stock companies. In 1884, he was made a member of the Council of Ministers. Here, he drew up a new programme for technical education. In 1886, he was appointed a member of the Council of State and from 1887 to 1892 he was head of the ministry of finance. Vyshnegradsky succeeded in his aim of reducing the budget deficit. He encouraged the development of the railways under partial state control and supported the growth of domestic industry. But his methods – which involved increased indirect taxes and a massive grain export drive – attracted criticism, as they contributed to the 1891–92 famine.

Economic change under Vyshnegradsky

Vyshnegradsky accepted the need for government involvement to kick-start economic growth. He also recognised the importance of government capital for investment. This required a budget surplus, so his economic policies were based on a reduction in imports through the imposition of tariffs, coupled with a massive increase in exports (particularly of grain). He also believed in increasing indirect taxation and negotiating foreign loans in order to expand cash reserves.

Vyshnegradsky's policies appeared to be remarkably successful. By 1892, grain exports had increased by 18% (as a percentage of Russian exports) and the budget was in surplus. A valuable loan had been negotiated with the French in 1888. Furthermore, through the Medele'ev Tariff Act of 1891, the highest tariffs in Russia's commercial history (accounting for 33% of the value of all imports) were helping to protect developing internal industries, while contributing to the government's taxation revenue.

However, these positive-sounding statistics hid the suffering caused to the peasants. Exports of grain earned the gold and foreign currency needed to guarantee repayments on foreign loans, but they left many of the most vulnerable members of society on the edge of starvation. Peasants faced a growth in indirect taxation while struggling to buy goods, the prices of which were inflated by high import duties. To make matters worse, the grain requisitions often left the peasants without any reserves for the winter. Vyshnegradsky's motto, 'We ourselves shall not eat, but we shall export', was all too true for the peasants. The 1891 famine was partly caused by this ruthless policy and it led to Vyshnegradsky's dismissal in 1892.

Theory of Knowledge

History and emotion

Emotion is one of the four ways of knowing. Reading the above paragraph, you have probably formed a 'view' of Vyshnegradsky, but is your view an emotional response? Is it possible to form an objective opinion of people or events, without being swayed by emotion?

Industrialisation under Witte

Vyshnegradsky's replacement, **Sergei Witte**, came from a non-noble background. He was a railway administrator and, according to Seton-Watson, both a brilliant organiser and a man of broad ideas. Witte accepted that if Russia was to remain a great power it could no longer be a country of peasants and agriculture.

Sergei Witte (1849–1915):

Witte worked for the Odessa Railways between 1871 and 1877 and became an expert in railway administration, writing a book on rail tariffs in 1883. He joined the ministry of finance in 1889 to help develop a new railways department. In 1892, he was made minister of communications and, a few months later, minister of finance. He was a capable administrator, with some advanced ideas. However, he found himself in a prominent position at the time of the 1905 revolution, and his drafting of the 'October Manifesto' caused controversy. He became Russia's first constitutional prime minister in 1906, but was forced to resign after six months.

SOURCE 4.5

Witte made the following comment in a memorandum dated 1899.

> Russia was, and to a considerable extent still is, a
> hospitable colony for all industrially developed states,
> generously providing them with the cheap products of
> her soil and buying dearly the products of their labour.
> But there is a radical difference between Russia and
> a colony: Russia is an independent and strong power.
> She has the right and the strength not to want to be
> the eternal handmaiden of states which are more
> developed economically.

Quoted in Christian, D. 1997. **Imperial and Soviet Russia.** *Basingstoke,
UK. Palgrave Macmillan. p. 106.*

QUESTION

What is Witte's message in Source 4.5?

Witte introduced a new vigour into Russia's economic development.
He encouraged close contacts between the state and business. He also
used government propaganda (through exhibitions, festivals, special
training programmes and the press), together with state subsidies, to
stimulate industrial development. Like Vyshnegradsky, Witte saw it as
the state's role to drive industrial change, although he hoped that private
entrepreneurs would eventually take the lead. To this end, he encouraged
private businessmen through the funding of credit institutions, the
encouragement of trade fairs, and by offering entrepreneurs protection
through tariffs.

Despite his belief in the need for economic modernisation, Witte
was politically conservative. He believed that state capitalism could
only be organised through an autocratic system and he wrote a book
defending tsarism. He also praised the peasant commune system,
on which his policy of heavy taxation and grain exports depended.
According to David Christian, 'Like Peter the Great, Witte hoped to use
Russia's traditional political and fiscal structures to pay for economic

modernisation.' He was well aware of the pressures on the peasants, but saw these pressures as unavoidable – a necessary evil.

Witte raised capital within Russia through taxation, loans and import tariffs, but also relied on foreign investment. To encourage this inward investment, he stabilised the rouble. He put the rouble on the gold standard (a fixed international value) in January 1897, so that foreigners would know the real value of the interest they would earn. Foreign investment, particularly from France and Belgium, subsequently grew from 98 million roubles in 1880 to 911 million in 1900.

The amount of foreign capital invested in Russia's industrial companies therefore rose from 26% in 1890 to 41% by 1915. With this foreign investment came foreign expertise. Managers, engineers and workers were attracted from France, Belgium, Germany, Britain and Sweden to provide the managerial and technical skills needed to develop Russian industry.

Heavy industry

Witte achieved rapid industrial expansion, particularly in heavy industry. During his time in power, coal production doubled and iron and steel increased seven-fold. By 1900, Russia had replaced France as third-largest global producer of iron. Indeed, Russia's growth rate (more than 8% per year between 1894 and 1904) was the highest in the world, although it had admittedly started from a low base. Nevertheless, it is impressive that Russia was the world's fourth-largest industrial economy in 1897.

Newer industries using modern technology (such as the oil and chemical industries) were also established and oil soon became the fastest-growing sector of the Russian economy. Production at the Baku oilfields in Georgia, on the western coast of the Caspian Sea, was greatly expanded.

By 1900, Russia was entirely self-sufficient in petroleum products and beginning to outstrip the US – its oil production almost trebled between 1885 and 1913. Baku was also ranked third in the Russian Empire, after St Petersburg and Moscow, for its electric power plant output. Only 5% of the electricity being produced was used for domestic lighting; 95% was used by industrial enterprises.

Other industrial development

Although the government mainly focused on heavy industry, consumer and domestic goods industries probably had an even greater impact on the economy as a whole. For example, the textile industry (which led the way in the earlier stages of industrial growth until the 1880s) still represented 40% of industrial output in 1910. Production of foodstuffs made up a further 10%.

Figure 4.5: A textile factory in Moscow in 1887.

As a result of deliberate government policy to concentrate production and maximise output, industry was largely centred on eight main areas (see Figure 4.6): textiles in Moscow, which overtook St Petersburg in size because of its position at the hub of the rail network and between Europe and the East; metal processing and machines in St Petersburg, where the Putilov metal works led the production of rails, machinery and artillery; textiles, coal and chemicals in Poland; coal, iron ore and basic chemicals in Krivoy Rog and Donetz; mines in the Urals; oil on the Caspian Sea at Baku; sugar beet processing in the south–west; and manganese production in Transcaucasia.

The table in Source 4.6 shows the speed of economic growth after 1861. The increase in total industrial production is impressive, and the growth of the iron industry and the spread of the railways even more so. When the figures for production are compared with the growth of the urban population, it can be seen that the productivity of the urban workforce must have also increased, since the rise in production exceeds urban growth rates.

The numbers of industrial workers grew from 1 to 3 million between 1887 and 1897. However, labour costs were kept low because of the encouragement given to large factory units. Over one-third of the 1900 workforce toiled in units of more than 1000 workers, and some slept at their workplace too. However, smaller-scale enterprise also flourished. There were around 800 000 people working in small domestic industries in 1861, and about 3 million by 1913.

SOURCE 4.6

	Total	Total	Overall	Growth of urban			Iron	
1861	1.00	1.00	1.00	1.00	1.00	1.00		1.00
1871	1.49	1.11	1.16	2.12	2.42	6.18		1.25
1881	2.52	1.12	1.36	–	3.59	10.50		1.60
1891	3.99	1.17*	1.62	–	5.04	13.95		2.19
1896	5.33	1.96	1.70	4.25	6.47	17.95		3.36
1901	7.50	1.81	1.83	–	7.40	25.64		4.41
1906	8.10	1.89	1.99	–	7.25	28.91		5.57
1913	11.65	3.09	2.32	6.96	7.83	31.91		8.38

Table showing Russia's economic growth 1861–1913.

Notes: * A famine year (1890 = 1.49; 1892 = 1.43) ** Figures for 1861–65, 1871–75, 1881–85, 1891–95, 1896–98, 1901–05, 1906–10, 1911–13

This table, based on statistics from a mixture of Soviet and British sources, shows how much economic growth there was after 1861, which is used as a 'base year' and given the value '1'; the subsequent index numbers show the ratio of increase after 1861.

Source: Christian, D. 1997. Imperial and Soviet Russia. Basingstoke, UK. Palgrave Macmillan. p. 111.

SOURCE 4.7

Years	Average annual rate of growth of industrial production (%)
1885–89	6.10
1890–99	8.03
1900–06	1.43
1907–13	6.25

Table showing Russia's rates of industrial growth 1885–1913.

Source: Christian, D. 1997. **Imperial and Soviet Russia**. Basingstoke, UK. Palgrave Macmillan. p. 113.

QUESTION

How far do sources 4.6 and 4.7 support the view that Russia had steady and impressive economic growth in all sectors in the years 1881–1913?

The railways

Industrial expansion was underpinned by a huge expansion in the railways. In the 1880s, the state bought many private railway companies, using loans with guaranteed interest payments, and began to build new state-owned, long-distance lines.

By the mid 1890s, 60% of the whole network was state owned. The amount of railway track increased from 14 000 km (9000 miles) in 1860 to 30 000 km (19 000 miles) in 1890. Whereas before 1892, Russian railway building progressed at less than 640 km (400 miles) per year, it increased to 2200 km (1400 miles) annually thereafter. By 1901, Russia had 53 000 km (33 000 miles) of track.

The building of the railways was an industrial stimulus in itself, while the government gained valuable revenue from freight charges and passenger fares along the new lines. The railways also opened up the Russian interior, allowing more intensive exploitation of Russia's raw materials. For example, a rail link was built between the Donbass coalfields and the iron ore deposits of Krivoy Rog, and another between Batum and Baku. This railway linked the Caspian and Black Seas, and permitted the export of Baku oil.

Perhaps most importantly of all, the railways reduced the cost of transporting grain and therefore aided the huge growth in exports. In the mid 19th century, less than 2% of the grain harvest was exported. But by the early 1880s the figure had risen to 6%, and by the late 1890s around 18%.

The most widely acclaimed transport development was the building of the 7000 km (4300 mile) Trans-Siberian Railway linking central European Russia with Vladivostok and the Pacific. Many labourers died from plague, cholera, hunger, cold, influenza and accidents while building this mammoth line in freezing conditions, between 1891 and 1904. Nevertheless, it helped open up western Siberia and increased migration to the area. It was also strategically useful for transporting troops to the outlying parts of the Russian Empire. But whether the benefits warranted the enormous human cost is far from certain.

Foreign involvement

Many of the new industrial enterprises were managed by foreigners. One example was the New Russia Company, founded by the Welsh ironmaster John Hughes. On the tsarist government's invitation, Hughes built factories and a modern ironworks in the Donetz valley. The Welshman transformed iron and steel production at Ekaterinovslav, and his company became the largest producer of pig iron and railway track in the Russian Empire. Together with his associates, Hughes was responsible for about half of Russia's total steel production.

The oilfields at Baku were also built on foreign capital, principally that of the Nobel brothers, the Rothschilds and the Vishau family. A government resolution to promote investment in this area was adopted in May 1880.

SOURCE 4.8

In 1880, Grigori Golitsyn, who became governor-general of the Caucasus in 1896, wrote the following letter.

> The situation in the Caucasus is unique. Without participation of Russian capitalists, it is difficult to solve. The lack of free capital, the limited industrial infrastructure, the low level of agriculture, the lack of technical knowledge and weak business initiative of the resident population are long-term obstacles to the economic growth of the region. Under such circumstances, the participation of foreigners in the economy in the Caucasus should not be rejected. In addition, the prohibition on purchasing real estate could lead to a stoppage of foreign capital inflow, and to unavoidable damage to its economic interests.

From: http://azer.com

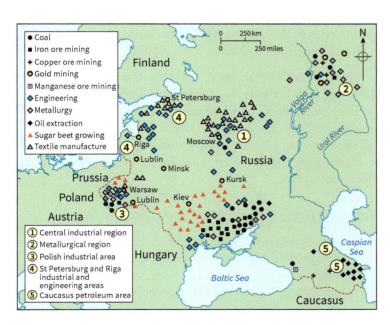

Figure 4.6: The concentrations of Russia's industry in 1880–90.

Foreign capital also supported the growth of industries supplying services to the oilfield and oil-refining sectors, such as new ports and electric power stations. Moreover, it was British textile companies, such as Mather and Platt of Oldham, who set up the leading steam-powered spinning mills near Moscow, while firms such as the Jerseys and Ludwig Loop of Manchester dominated textile production.

Agriculture

Despite the massive industrial changes, Russia still remained primarily an agricultural economy. Only 30% of national production came from industry, as opposed to 75% in Britain and 70% in Germany. Although the urban working class more than doubled between 1865 and 1890, still only 12% of the Russian population lived in towns in 1900. In Germany, the figure was 55%. It would not have been possible to import the machinery and goods needed to fuel this industrialisation without the income from Russia's huge grain exports. Nevertheless, agriculture was largely neglected. Despite the emancipation of the serfs, productivity remained low because the peasants received only small landholdings and continued to rely on traditional farming methods. This meant that the fields produced only around half as much grain per acre as in the richer agricultural countries of Western Europe. At the same time, the growing population placed immense pressure on food supplies.

During the regular periods of famine that followed bad harvests (as in 1891–92, 1898 and 1901), hundreds of thousands died of starvation. Rather than improving, the situation of the peasantry gradually worsened in the late 19th century. For example, the average size of landholdings shrank when plots were subdivided to provide for all male peasants. In addition, the gap between the *kulaks* (rich peasants) and the poor peasants grew wider.

The consequences of Witte's reforms

The traditional view was that the peasants suffered from Witte's approach to industrialisation because his state-sponsored policies depended on taking money from them. However, some historians, notably Paul Gregory, questioned the idea of a decline in rural living standards. Gregory argued that the economy was growing marginally faster than the population was rising. He therefore believed that output rose fast enough to feed most of the population most of the time.

He also suggested that opportunities for additional paid work helped supplement peasant incomes.

This argument was taken further by James Simms. Since peasant tax revenues were rising, he suggested that the peasant sector must have been prospering to enable them to pay these higher taxes. Finally, in 1986 Peter Gatrell calculated that there was a small overall growth rate in the Russian economy at this time, which resulted in slowly rising living standards in all sectors.

Whatever the arguments of the economic historians, life in rural Russia remained grim, with an average life expectancy for males of only 27.25 years and for females of 29.38. (In England at the time, the average life expectancy was 45.25.)

In order to ensure that the peasants paid their taxes, the commune remained a powerful influence and peasants stayed in a state of semi-servitude. Not surprisingly, the countryside simmered with resentment and the famine of 1899 caused widespread unrest.

Witte's reforms brought the rapid rise of the urban proletariat – comprising 4% of the population in 1897 and 12% by 1914. Poor town-dwellers suffered overcrowding and a lack of electricity, lighting, sanitation and even clean water. They were easy prey for opposition agitators. Even though workers were not officially able to join trade unions or engage in strike action (although some did so illegally), they grew more politically conscious.

The industrial changes also brought into being a small middle class of factory owners, managers and other professionals (such as bankers, doctors, teachers and administrators), who served the needs of the changing society. This group was still no more than 500 000-strong in 1897. However, these people increasingly demanded political change, through the provincial *zemstva* and town *dumas*. Witte's reforms had the unintended effect of breaking down the old social structure and also providing a forum for new evolutionary thinking in these councils.

Figure 4.7: Penniless Russians in a workhouse (a charitable institution), photographed around 1900.

Some historians, such as Alexander Gerschenkron, have accused the government of forcing through industrialisation with little regard for the Russian people. Yet, more recent research (for example, by Peter Gatrell, Hans Rogger and Thomas Owen) suggests that Russia's economic development and its impact were largely beyond government control. Nevertheless, there was still a contradiction between Witte's support for a government that preserved traditional attitudes to ruling and his attempts to promote economic modernisation.

4.3 Why and how did opposition movements grow?

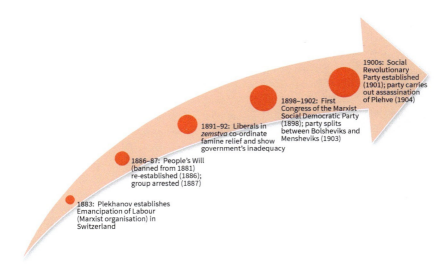

Figure 4.8: The development of opposition 1883–1904.

The 1880s

The failure of the Populist movement and the lack of change following Alexander II's assassination did nothing to reduce revolutionary zeal in Russia. The opposition movements may have adjusted their views and tactics in response to the problems caused by rapid population growth, the tension in the countryside, and the crises surrounding the growing pace of industrialisation. However, the revolutionaries grew tougher and even more determined. Industrial growth also brought greater contact with Western ideas and this led to new theories about Russia's economic and political future.

In 1883, four exiled ex-Populists met in Geneva, Switzerland, to found the first Marxist revolutionary group, known as The Emancipation of Labour. The founder members were Georgi Plekhanov (1856–1918), Pavel Axelrod (1850–1928), Lev Deutsch (1855–1941) and Vera Zasulich (1849–1919). Their declared aims were: to assess Russia's position in relation to Marxist theory; to spread knowledge of Marxism more widely in Russia through propaganda and agitation; and, by translating Marxist texts and smuggling them into the country, to establish a Marxist–Socialist party dedicated to bringing about a proletarian (workers') revolution. Their ideas were based on the writings of **Karl Marx**.

Karl Marx (1818–83):

Marx was a German philosopher and historian. He argued that class struggle and conflict were the most (but not the only) important factors behind social and economic – as well as intellectual and political – change. He also identified stages in the development of human societies. He worked closely with his friend, Friedrich Engels (1820–95). Together, in 1847, they wrote *The Communist Manifesto*. Marx wrote a study of the workings of capitalism, entitled *Das Kapital* ('Capital'). His ideas inspired many revolutionaries, including Vladimir Lenin and Leon Trotsky, who first attempted to put Marx's ideas into practice in Russia, following the Bolshevik Revolution. However, practice turned out to be very different from theory – and many have argued that true communism has never yet been implemented anywhere.

Their plans were certainly ambitious, given that Russia had no politically conscious middle class and only a tiny industrial working class to lead a Marxist revolution. Furthermore, with no free press or representative institution, and with the *Okhrana* watching out for subversion, advancing such a cause would be extremely difficult. However, Plekhanov wrote works such as *Socialism and the Political Struggle* in 1883 and *Our Differences* in 1885, which demonstrated that Marxist–Socialism could work in Russia. He argued that the way forward was through the growing industrial working class, not the peasant commune. He developed a following among committed intellectuals who read his smuggled works and town-dwellers who studied ideas through self-education circles. He therefore became known as 'the Father of Russian Marxism'.

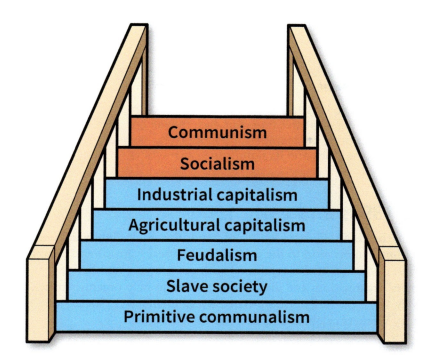

Figure 4.9: Diagram of Marxist Stage Theory.

The last flourish of Populism occurred in the universities in 1886, when the People's Will was re-formed among students in St Petersburg. Its activities were curbed when students preparing bombs (including Lenin's brother, Alexander Ulyanov) were arrested and hanged in March 1887. There was some attempt to keep the movement alive in small underground groups. However, infiltration by spies, direct suppression by the police, and lack of enthusiasm from the peasants (whose concerns were ever more non-political in the wake of famine) meant that this branch of the opposition movement made little progress.

Yet another opposition group – made up of liberals seeking moderate reform and 'moral regeneration' – flourished in the *zemstva* and town *dumas*. Despite the new political curbs, which reduced some of their power, professionals and educated Russians in these councils remained critical of the central government. They also used their own initiative to address some of the social problems. During the famine, for example, it was the *zemstva* representatives who did the most effective relief work, thereby highlighting the relative incompetence of the tsarist government.

ACTIVITY

Make a chart to illustrate the various opposition movements that emerged in Russia at this time. For each movement, give the name of its leader/principal members, its supporters, its ideology or beliefs, its methods and its significance at the time.

The 1890s and early 1900s

During the 1890s, all three strands of opposition took slightly different directions – in reaction to the continuing political stagnation in Russia. Marxist discussion circles combined with the growing number of workers' organisations and illegal trade unions, to help organise strikes. In May 1891, the St Petersburg-based Social Democratic Society of Factory Workers celebrated its first May Day festival.

Vladimir Lenin was one early convert to the Marxist cause. He had read law at the University of Kazan, although he had been expelled in 1887 for attending a student demonstration. He was sentenced to three years' exile at the village of Shushenskoe, in western Siberia. Nevertheless, he went on to graduate with top honours from the University of St Petersburg. In 1895 he helped to found the Union of Struggle for the Liberation of the Working Class.

Vladimir Lenin (1870–1924):

Lenin's real name was Vladimir Ilyich Ulyanov but he took the name 'Lenin' after a period of exile by the River Lena in Siberia. Lenin became a revolutionary after his brother's execution in 1887 and joined the Marxist RSDLP (Russian Social Democratic Labour Party) when it was formed in 1898. Lenin believed that a small group of fully committed revolutionaries was necessary to drive the proletarian revolution. His disagreement with Martov on this issue led to a party split between Bolsheviks and Mensheviks in 1903. Lenin lived in exile until April 1917, when he returned to Russia after the tsar gave up the throne in the February/March 1917 revolution. Lenin led the Bolshevik Revolution in October/November 1917 and dominated Russian government until his death in 1924.

In 1898, the first congress of a new Russian Social Democratic Labour Party was held in Minsk in Belorussia, in an attempt to bring these various groups together. Although only nine delegates attended, the meeting was broken up by the *Okhrana* and two of the three-man central committee were arrested. Nevertheless, the meeting produced a manifesto drawn up by Pyotr Struve, emphasising the proletariat's leading role in the revolutionary struggle. The group continued organising in secret. From 1900, Plekhanov and others – such as Lenin, who joined him in exile after his release from Siberia – founded the revolutionary newspaper *Iskra* ('The Spark'). This was printed abroad and smuggled back into Russia.

In 1902, Lenin produced a pamphlet called *What is to be Done?* to argue against those who had begun to question the need for a proletarian revolution. He wanted to divert the working class away from trade union activity and guide them into the wider political struggle. The Social Democrats (SDs) were committed to the nationalisation of land and industry, and Lenin thought that the Democratic Party should lead the struggle. He believed that success would only come through discipline and organisation. This led to a split in the party when its second congress met, first in Brussels and subsequently in London, in July 1903. There were disagreements between the 51 voting members over party membership. Yuli Martov led the group that wanted a wide membership of sympathetic followers. Lenin led those who wanted all party members to be disciplined, dedicated activists. Lenin lost this vote, but later disagreements led some to withdraw from the meeting. Lenin then found his supporters in the majority when votes were taken on another composition of the party.

Figure 4.10: Lenin's article, entitled 'Urgent Tasks of Our Movement' in the first issue of *Iskra*, December 1900.

Having won support for a smaller, more centralised structure, Lenin referred to his supporters as the Bolsheviks (meaning 'Majority-ites'). Martov's group were known as the Mensheviks (or 'Minority-ites'). The name Bolshevik stuck. However, until 1917 the Bolsheviks remained the minority in the party as a whole.

In the 1890s, some veterans of the Populist movement and especially People's Will returned from exile in Siberia. At the same time, the Great Famine revived interest in the position of the peasantry, and another new political force was born. The Social Revolutionary Party (whose members were known as 'the SRs') was established in 1901. This party wanted to encourage the peasantry to take action, by holding out the promise of land redistribution. It was an 'umbrella party' of the left, embracing a variety of views, from those who favoured democratic reform to more extreme socialist–terrorists. However, its members were non-Marxist. They favoured decentralised workers' cooperatives and small peasant communes organised under collective ownership, rather than the development of a vast industrial proletariat.

The SRs, like the SDs, were committed to changing or completely removing the tsarist regime, but the authorities feared the SRs more than the SDs. This was particularly true when Victor Chernov set up a special combat detachment in Berlin in 1901, to arrange a renewed campaign of terrorism and assassination. The same group was also behind large-scale rioting in the Russian countryside in 1902. Among its 'successes' in the early 20th century were the assassinations of the governor-general of Finland, two ministers of internal affairs (Plehve and Stolypin) and the tsar's uncle, Sergei.

Another more moderate strand of opposition, based on the *zemstva* established by Alexander II, was also growing in Russia. The first annual Congress of *Zemstva* Presidents was held in 1896. This organisation passed resolutions in favour of political liberty, constitutional reform and a National Assembly, but it was banned after its second congress in 1897. Some members continued to meet abroad and in 1902 formed the Union of Liberation, in Germany, aiming to unite the moderate opposition. In 1904, they refounded the union in St Petersburg, drawing up a manifesto for action.

In any consideration of opposition movements in Russia in this period, the various ethnic minorities within the Russian Empire should not be ignored. In response to government Russification policies, the ethnic minorities became more organised and determined. The Poles wanted their own kingdom, while the Armenians formed the Armenian Revolutionary Federation in 1890.

Both Alexander III and Nicholas II took the view that all opposition groups were equally dangerous, and an official ban on political parties remained in place until 1905. There was no attempt to distinguish between those who wanted to work within the tsarist system and those who wished to overthrow it. By taking measures to reduce the power of the *zemstva* and town *dumas*, and by using the *Okhrana*, the last two tsars appeared to have successfully avoided any weakening of the autocracy before 1904.

However, as Stephen Lee has written, the 'combination of frustrated constitutionalism and repressed radicalism weakened any scope for evolution through constitutionalist parties and strengthened that for more dramatic change at the hands of revolutionary parties.' The older historical view, as expressed in *The Russian Autocracy in Crisis* by Peter Zaionchkovsky (1979), emphasised the inevitability of tsarist failure – thanks to the growth of opposition movements. Nevertheless, more recent historians have tried to suggest that there was nothing inevitable about the collapse of tsardom.

DISCUSSION POINT

Is it possible to distinguish between pressure 'from below' and 'from above'? Is it important to try to identify where the forces that promote change in history come from, and can we ever be sure?

Paper 3 exam practice

Question

To what extent was Alexander III successful in upholding the tsarist autocracy in the years 1881–94? **[15 marks]**

Skill

Writing an introductory paragraph

Examiner's tips

Once you have decided on your argument (or thesis) and planned your answer to a question (as covered by Chapters 2 and 3), you should begin by writing a clear introductory paragraph. This needs to set out your view (what you will argue in response to the question) and to outline **briefly** the key points you intend to make, and will be going on to support with relevant and precise own knowledge, in the main body of your essay. Remember, '*How successful*' questions (like others you will meet on Higher-level history papers) require analysis of differing interpretations. Your introduction should show an awareness of the interpretations you will consider, and make clear what overall line of argument you intend to follow.

Depending on the wording of the question, you may also find it useful to define in your introductory paragraph what you understand by the question, and make its parameters clear. You may also want to show that you understand what any 'key terms' (such as 'autocracy') mean, although you should never simply give a dictionary definition. The purpose of an explanation is to make clear to the reader what you understand by the term as you use it in your essay. For example, you might want to make it clear that 'autocracy' refers not simply to Alexander's own power but to the whole system of tsarist government.

For this question, you should:

- consider what the tsarist autocracy was like in 1881 and 1894, and observe what was the same and what was different

- consider Alexander III's successes in his measures to uphold autocratic government, and also his failures (which would include the growth of opposition movements)
- write a concluding paragraph that sums up your judgement.

You need to cover the following aspects of Alexander III's rule:

- the abandonment of the Loris-Melikov reform proposals and Alexander III's change of ministers
- the re-establishment of noble power, the land captains, and the undermining of the *zemstva* and *dumas*
- changes in methods of control and repression, including the use of law courts, education, censorship and the police
- Russification and the treatment of ethnic minorities
- religious policies
- the growth of opposition.

In your introductory paragraph, it is important to provide an explanation of 'autocracy' together with an overview. You should also make it clear that you are aware of the main areas that need to be examined. However, always remember that the most important requirement of all is to set out your view or thesis. This method will give you a clear line of argument on which to base your essay.

Common mistakes

A common mistake – one that might suggest to an examiner a candidate who hasn't thought deeply about what's required – is to fail to write an introductory paragraph at all. This is the mistake of candidates who rush into writing **before** analysing the question and preparing a plan. The result may well be that they focus entirely on the words 'Alexander III' and 'success' and simply write an evaluation of the tsar's reign. Even if the answer is full of detailed and accurate own knowledge, this will not answer the question and so will not score highly.

Another common error is to use the introduction to provide a lot of irrelevant background detail (such as a brief history of the reign of Alexander II), which is unnecessary and suggests a lack of focus.

Equally unhelpful is an introduction composed of a series of rhetorical questions, such as 'Was Alexander III successful as an autocrat? This question has caused endless debate among historians. Can he be condemned for failing to see the tide of opposition that his reign was promoting? Alternatively, should he be praised for preserving the tsardom and passing it on to his son? How should history judge this ruler?'

Finally, try to avoid 'I', as in 'I think...' in the introduction and the essay as a whole. Since the whole essay should be what you think, there is no need to state this.

Remember to refer to the simplified Paper 3 mark scheme in Chapter 8.

Sample student introductory paragraph

Superficially, Alexander III was extremely successful in upholding the tsarist autocracy during his reign. It could even be suggested that he strengthened it. In 1881, he inherited an 'autocratic' governmental system in which all political authority was vested in his being. He held the supreme legislative, executive and judicial power and his imperial edicts were law. He was also nominal head of the Russian Orthodox Church and ruled the country as the embodiment of God on Earth. None of this had changed by the time of his death in 1894. The autocracy was seemingly as firm as ever, and by bringing back some of the powers of the nobility and weakening those of the zemstva and dumas, he had reversed some of the minor inroads into autocracy that had taken place during his father's reign. However, despite tightening tsarist control over the courts, education, free-thinking and the ethnic minorities, as well as promoting Orthodoxy as a support to autocracy, by 1894 tsarist autocracy had been fatally weakened by the rise of uncontrollable opposition movements. Alexander must therefore be judged unsuccessful in upholding the autocracy, even though this may not have been apparent to all at the time.

This is a strong introduction, as it shows a good grasp of the issues and is clearly focused on the demands of the question. It defines autocracy, shows a sound appreciation of differing interpretations and outlines the areas that will be subsequently discussed, so demonstrating to the examiner how the candidate intends to proceed. Above all, the introduction ends with a clear view, showing that the candidate has thought about what will be argued. This indicates that the answer – if it remains analytical and is well-supported – is likely to be a high-scoring one.

4 Imperial Russia and the Soviet Union (1855–1924)

Activity

In this chapter, the skills focus is on writing a good introductory paragraph. Using the information from this chapter and any other sources of information available to you, write introductory paragraphs for at least two of the following Paper 3 practice questions.

Paper 3 practice questions

1   To what extent was Alexander III 'a disaster' as tsar of Russia?

2   Discuss the view that 'The Great Reactionary' is an appropriate title for Alexander III.

3   Compare and contrast the domestic policies of Alexander II and Alexander III.

4   Evaluate the success of Russian governments in promoting economic modernisation in the years 1861 to 1905.

5   'Russia was a strong nation in the second half of the 19th century.' To what extent do you agree with this statement?

The 1905 revolution and its aftermath

TIMELINE

1904   **8 Feb:** Russo-Japanese War begins; Japanese attack Port Arthur

1905   **9 Jan:** Bloody Sunday – Father Gapon's marchers fired on by troops

27–28 May: Battle of Tsushima

14 Jun: Mutiny on battleship Potemkin

23 Aug: Treaty of Portsmouth brings Russo-Japanese War to an end

13 Oct: Formation of St Petersburg Soviet

17 Oct: Nicholas signs October Manifesto, including establishment of a State *Duma*

1906   **23 Apr:** First State *Duma* called

21 Jul: State *Duma* dissolved

9 Nov: Stolypin's decree on agricultural reform

1907   Russia, England and France form Triple Entente

1911   **5 Sep:** Assassination of Stolypin

1912   **4 Apr:** Lena goldfields massacre

1913   Celebration of 300th anniversary of foundation of Romanov dynasty

1914   **30 Jul:** Russia mobilised in support of Serbia

Aug: Germany declares war on Russia

Note: The Russian calendar was 13 days behind the one used in the West. The dates given here and in Chapter 6 are from the old (Russian) calendar that was in use until 1918.

KEY QUESTIONS
- What was the significance of the Russo-Japanese War?
- What brought about the 1905 revolution?
- How successful was Stolypin in bringing about change in Russia from 1906?
- What was Russia like in 1914?

In 1905, war with Japan brought the long-standing political and social tensions within Russia to crisis point. Trouble on the streets of St Petersburg rapidly spread to other major cities, causing new disturbances in the countryside and even in the military forces. Wartime disaster, a naval mutiny and striking workers forced Nicholas to make concessions. A manifesto in October 1905 promised constitutional reform. This appeased the moderates and appeared to give the masses some hope of better times ahead. Sadly for the Russian people, this hope turned out to be unjustified. Between 1905 and 1914, Nicholas and his ministers tried to take back much of what they had conceded. Russia therefore entered the First World War as an economically powerful but politically undeveloped state.

Overview

- War with Japan brought economic problems and further national humiliation, and highlighted government incompetence.
- The revolution that broke out in 1905 was the result of both long-term economic, social and political issues and more immediate factors relating to the war and conditions in St Petersburg.
- In January 1905, Father Gapon led a group of workers to the tsar's Winter Palace and they were shot at by the authorities (an event that became known as Bloody Sunday).
- Bloody Sunday led to a breakdown in order, including a mutiny on the battleship *Potemkin*.
- Liberals and revolutionaries pushed for change, and the revolutionaries created the first St Petersburg Soviet.
- The tsar's October Manifesto promised an elected State *Duma*. This, combined with repressive action, brought the revolution to a close.
- There were four State *Dumas* in the years to 1914 but their power was progressively reduced, leaving them unable to force through any fundamental changes.
- Stolypin began a new programme of reform in the countryside, but was assassinated in 1911.
- When Russia entered World War I in 1914, the country was politically weak, economically under prepared and still suffering acute social division.

Figure 5.1: Japanese troops storm a Russian-held fort during the Russo-Japanese War.

5.1 What was the significance of the Russo-Japanese War?

Despite the setback of the Crimean War, imperial Russia continued to regard itself as a major world power throughout the 19th century and kept looking for opportunities to expand its influence. For example, Russia had intervened in defence of breakaway Slav Balkan states in the 1877–78 war against the Turks. This was a rather more successful military campaign than that of 1853–56, but the intervention of the European powers in the 1878 Congress of Berlin deprived Russia of any gains in the Black Sea area. This caused Russian attention to be diverted to the Far East instead.

The Russians believed the decaying Chinese Empire offered opportunities for expansion and for obtaining more coastline and an ice-free port. Indeed, one of the aims behind the building of the Trans-Siberian railway was to give Russian soldiers access to northern China to aid Russian penetration. Meanwhile, Japan, with a growing population in need of more land and resources, also planned to attack China. In 1894–95, Japan defeated the Chinese in Korea. This war not only showed Chinese weakness but also revealed Japanese ambition. Japan secured a favourable peace treaty, as well as control of the Liaodong peninsula and Port Arthur. However, Russia expressed immediate concern, suggesting that such a concession would upset China's stability. With the support of France and Germany, pressure was placed on Japan, and Japan agreed to return the territory in return for monetary compensation.

Figure 5.2: The Trans-Siberian Railway with branch lines through northern Manchuria connecting it to the Chinese Eastern Railway.

The Russians were themselves interested in Port Arthur. In 1896, the weakened Chinese agreed that the Russians could build a railway through northern Manchuria, from Vladivostok to Harbin. In 1898, they went further, giving Russia a 25-year lease on the Liaodong peninsula, which lay to the west of the Korean peninsula. The Chinese also gave Russia the right to build a further railway from Harbin to the port at the tip of the Liaodong peninsula – the naval base of Port Arthur.

This excited the ambitions of some Russian ministers to press for further expansion – moving along the Yalu River (the modern-day border between China and North Korea), with a view to occupying the Korean peninsula itself. But Russia's presence in the Liaodong peninsula, coming so soon after the peninsula had been held by the expansionist Japanese in 1895, sparked conflict. The Japanese regarded the area as their sphere of influence. After some rather half-hearted negotiations on both sides, the Japanese attacked Port Arthur on 8 February 1904.

The subsequent Russo-Japanese War of 1904–05 proved catastrophic for the tsarist autocracy, both militarily and politically. There was an emphatic declaration from the minister of internal affairs, Vyacheslav von Plehve, that a 'short victorious war' would put a stop to the internal political opposition threatening tsardom and win back glory and loyalty. Yet, in the event, a long drawn-out defeat provoked the worst crisis that tsardom had faced in modern times.

The task of directing a war 9600 km (6000 miles) from the Russian capital was never going to be easy. Port Arthur was cut off by sea and the Russian Pacific fleet was unable to sail out. All troops and supplies therefore had to be sent along the single-track Trans-Siberian Railway, which took six days. This immediately put Russia at a disadvantage, compared with Japan. These difficulties were increased by ministers' ignorance, organisational confusion (which left ammunition in short supply) and a rapid loss of morale among the Russian troops as Port Arthur suffered a long siege.

The fleet's attempts to break out of the harbour in February and August only brought dramatic losses, and Port Arthur was eventually forced to surrender to the Japanese in December 1904. The Russian armies were defeated in April along the Yalu River and twice at Mukden (north of Port Arthur), in August 1904 and again in February 1905.

In desperation, the Russians sent their Baltic fleet on a 29 000 km (18 000 mile) journey halfway around the world to challenge the Japanese navy. It set sail in October 1904 and by the time it arrived in the spring of 1905, several months after the surrender of Port Arthur, the Japanese were waiting in the Tsushima straits between Japan and Korea. In the ensuing battle, the Japanese succeeded in destroying eight Russian battleships and four cruisers, leaving 4000 Russians dead and a further 7000 as prisoners. The Japanese lost just three torpedo boats. It was the worst naval defeat in Russian history.

A peace treaty was eventually signed in Portsmouth, New Hampshire (USA) in August 1905, and Russia agreed to a total withdrawal from Manchuria. The war had wasted precious resources and proved to be a gross national humiliation. Far more importantly, it stimulated – and provided the backdrop to – a series of political disturbances within Russia. Each defeat in the war strengthened the opposition and weakened the autocracy.

Plehve himself was assassinated by a Social Revolutionary bomb in July 1904, shortly after the defeats on the Yalu River. In Plehve's home town of Warsaw, crowds turned out to celebrate his death on the streets. The loss of Port Arthur, in December, triggered a huge wave of demonstrations. The economic disruption caused by the war, which drove up prices and forced factory closures, rocked the very foundations of tsardom.

DISCUSSION POINT

With hindsight, it seems that Russia was foolish to enter a war with Japan and that defeat was almost inevitable. Is this true? From what standpoint should we judge actions in the past?

5.2 What brought about the 1905 revolution?

Long-term factors

Economic and social factors

Tension had been building up in the Russian Empire for years as the process of industrialisation had changed Russia's social make-up, increasing pressure 'from below' and weakening the traditional élites. When a series of poor harvests between 1897 and 1901 and an economic slump ended the boom years, unemployment grew and industrial unrest increased.

In addition, an international monetary crisis made it harder for Russia to negotiate foreign loans, while tax income at home declined. The formerly impressive overall annual growth rate in Russia fell from around 8% to just 1% per year after 1899.

The slump was felt most by the urban working class. Although strikes were strictly illegal, there were 17 000 stoppages in 1894 and 90 000 in 1904. Marxists played a part in stirring up trouble. For example, both Vladimir Lenin and Yuli Martov helped organise textile workers' strikes in St Petersburg in 1896–97.

In an attempt to channel this working-class discontent, the Moscow police chief and head of the *Okhrana*, Sergei Zubatov, helped organise several large 'official' unions between 1901 and 1903. These unions were permitted by the minister of internal affairs, Plehve. They were designed to channel workers' grievances and prevent the infiltration of the working class by radical socialists. When the government had to send in troops to suppress activities, Zubatov was dismissed in June 1903. Yet the principle of allowing official workers' unions remained. In 1904 a priest, Father Georgi Gapon, organised an officially sponsored union, the Assembly of St Petersburg Factory Workers. It had the approval of Plehve and the support of the Orthodox Church, and soon acquired 12 branches and 8000 members. Its activities became central to the governmental crisis.

There was disquiet among the peasants too. Attacks on landlords' property increased from the late 1890s onwards. Sometimes military reservists (who had returned to their villages) played a part in leading these outbreaks. Increased peasant literacy also meant that revolutionary propaganda found more support in rural communities. Between 1902 and 1905, peasant revolts escalated. The years 1903–04 became known as 'the years of the Red Cockerel' because the arsonists' red flames resembled a rooster's comb. Disturbances were worst in the central Russian provinces but ranged from Ukraine and Georgia through to Poland.

To control the countryside, the tsar again relied on his local officials and the army. However, royal officials increasingly found that the local voices of authority (in the *zemstva* and town *dumas*) took the side of the peasants with whom they worked, in preference to that of the state.

Figure 5.3: Strike leaders being arrested in 1905.

Theory of Knowledge

History, theories and explanations

Marxist historians have claimed that history is determined by economic factors and that economic change plays a bigger role in shaping events than the actions of individuals. Do you agree?

Political factors

The intelligentsia and members of the *zemstva* continued to press for moderate liberal reform, including an advisory State *Duma*. The most extreme members of this group formed the Union of Liberation, led by Ivan Petrunkevich, Pavel Milyukov and Pyotr Struve, which was established in St Petersburg in 1904.

The Union of Liberation demanded a fairly elected National Legislative Assembly and they wanted autocracy to be replaced by a form of constitutional monarchy. They organised around 50 revolutionary banquets during the winter of 1904, at which speakers attacked the government and demanded constitutional change. In November 1904, a *zemstva* congress presented a petition to the tsar, who responded: 'I will never agree to the representative form of government because I consider it harmful to the people whom God has entrusted to me.' However, these liberals all hoped for 'reform from above' and were alarmed by the events that took place in 1905.

The radical socialists also increased in strength after 1900. Both the Social Revolutionaries (SRs) and Social Democrats (SDs) helped provoke unrest. However, many of the more radical leaders remained in exile and the 1903 split in the Social Democrats (between the Bolshevik and Menshevik factions) weakened the party. Nevertheless, the SRs appealed to the peasants' desire for more land, and the SDs' promise of power attracted the workers. The SRs assassinated many prominent officials (including the tsar's uncle, the Grand-Duke Sergei, in February 1905) and organised the All-Russian Peasant Union from July 1905. Meanwhile, the SDs encouraged strikes and confrontations and continued to argue that the answer to Russia's problems lay in Marxist revolution.

Short-term factors

By the end of 1904, Russia was in a state of disarray. The political violence was becoming steadily worse, and an economic downturn and harvest failure had brought unemployment, high food prices and disrupted electricity supplies in the cities.

In St Petersburg, a dispute at the Putilov metal works led to a strike, which rapidly spread to other factories. Within a month, 111 000 factory workers were on the streets, protesting over pay and conditions.

Matters came to a head when the priest and trade union organiser, Father Georgi Gapon, decided to defy a ban on demonstrations and organise a march to the Winter Palace in order to present a petition to the Tsar.

SOURCE 5.1

Father Gapon's petition of January 1905, which was intended for presentation to the Tsar:

> Sire! We working men of St Petersburg, our wives and children, and our parents, helpless and aged men and women, have come to you, our ruler, to seek justice and protection. We are in deepest poverty and oppressed with labours beyond our strength. We are treated like slaves who must suffer in silence. Despotism and arbitrary rule are suffocating us. Sire, our strength is exhausted and our patience has run out. Things have become so terrible for us that we would prefer death to the unbearable torment we are being forced to suffer…

Quoted in Sixsmith, M. 2011. **Russia.** *London, UK. BBC Books. p. 160.*

QUESTION

What does Source 5.1 suggest about the motives of Father Gapon's followers?

Gapon had informed the authorities and promised that the march would be peaceful. Crowds of several thousand gathered at different points around St Petersburg on the morning of Sunday 9 January. They carried icons (holy images of the saints), portraits of the Tsar and Tsarina, and sang patriotic hymns – including 'God Save the Tsar' – as they advanced towards the Winter Palace.

However, the police and the Cossacks (well-trained and highly disciplined cavalry soldiers from southern Russia, who traditionally served the tsar as special guards) were on edge. They fired on the masses at several points, including as they reached Palace Square.

The police later suggested that 130 had been killed and 450 wounded, but these figures are probably gross underestimates. The blood of the dead and dying stained the snow, and the massacre became known as Bloody Sunday.

It has been suggested that Father Gapon was actually a government agent. He is known to have been in communication with the secret police, reporting on the activities of the trade union that he founded and ran. The Social Revolutionaries certainly believed that he was a spy. After the massacre, Gapon fled abroad to Geneva and London. He returned to Russia in 1906 to try to clear his name, but he was given a 'revolutionary trial' by the SRs, condemned and hanged.

Figure 5.4: Mounted Cossacks attack crowds of peaceful demonstrators in St Petersburg on Bloody Sunday, 9 January 1905.

Nicholas reacted to these events with his customary indecisiveness. He agreed to meet a delegation of workers ten days later, but could only suggest they should have more patience. Nevertheless, the royal couple donated 50 000 roubles to the families of those who had died in the massacre. Three weeks later, the tsar's own uncle, the Grand-Duke Sergei, was blown to pieces against the Kremlin walls. Nicholas went into such a state of shock that he did not appear in public again for the next eight years.

KEY CONCEPTS ACTIVITY

Causation: Draw a spider diagram to illustrate the causes of the 1905 Revolution in Russia. Colour code your factors to show whether they are political, economic, social, military or the work of an individual or group.

Bloody Sunday had enormous repercussions throughout the Russian Empire. Two years of unrest involving workers, peasants, students, national minorities and the military followed. It gave a huge boost to the radical opposition for, as Lenin later wrote, 'Even those St Petersburg workers who had believed in the tsar started to call for the immediate overthrow of the regime.'

In St Petersburg, the Putilov strike escalated into a general strike, involving more than 400 000 workers. Worse still for the authorities, there were soon similar strikes elsewhere in the empire. By the autumn, around 2.5 million workers had laid down their tools. In May 1905 an elected strike committee, known as a *soviet* ('workers' council'), was established in the textile town of Ivanov, east of Moscow. This arrangement was soon copied in other towns, including St Petersburg, where the first soviet met on 14 October. The St Petersburg Soviet, led by the young Marxist, **Leon Trotsky**, who had just returned from exile in London, rapidly assumed leadership over all the other soviets in the Russian Empire. In October, a strike by railway workers quickly developed into a general strike in St Petersburg and Moscow, and showed the benefits of centralised Soviet control in terms of coordinating protests and distributing arms to workers. Although it ultimately failed, the St Petersburg Soviet showed that it was possible to challenge the government through workers' uprisings.

> **Leon Trotsky (1879–1940):**
>
> Born Lev Bronstein, Trotsky was a Jewish intellectual, who studied the writings of Marx, Engels and Plekhanov and became involved in revolutionary politics. He gained his name in 1902, when he escaped from exile in Siberia, using a passport belonging to a prison guard called Trotsky. He met Lenin in London. Trotsky did not readily accept either the Bolshevik or the Menshevik position but briefly returned to Russia to lead the St Petersburg Soviet in 1905. When the February 1917 revolution broke out, Trotsky was in exile in the USA. He returned in May, became a Bolshevik and worked with Lenin to lead the October revolution. He became commissar for foreign affairs in the new government. Many expected him to succeed Lenin as leader, but he was outmanoeuvred by Joseph Stalin.

Peasant revolts spread, land was seized and property was looted and burned. In July and August, a peasants' congress was held, which established an All-Russian Union of Peasants, the first central political body for the peasants. It set up branches all over Russia, calling for the redistribution of land and a Constituent Assembly. In areas of mass peasant uprisings, the local organisations of the union acted as revolutionary committees and took orders from the St Petersburg Soviet.

Students also went on strike. Universities were closed down in March and their buildings were used to host large public meetings, where both moderates and radicals demanded constitutional change and an elected State *Duma*. Professional groups, such as teachers, engineers, doctors and lawyers, formed their own unions and called for full political and civil rights. In May, these professional unions and the Union of Liberation came together in Moscow to form the 'Union of Unions', chaired by the liberal reformer, Milyukov.

National minority groups, including Georgians and Ukrainians, used the unrest as an opportunity to protest against the absolutism and oppression of the tsarist monarchy. Polish socialists called for a general strike and there were protests in Finland, Riga (in present-day Latvia), and in parts of Asia and the Caucasus. Here, inter-ethnic confrontation resulted in Armenian–Tatar massacres, which severely damaged the cities and the Baku oilfields.

Unrest reached a peak in early summer and autumn. There were naval mutinies at Sebastopol, Vladivostok and Kronstadt, and on 14 June in the Black Sea fleet. These mutinies began on the battleship *Potemkin*, where the sailors protested against the maggot-infested meat they were served. The mutineers sailed to Odessa, where the whole town was briefly swept up in the revolutionary fervour, providing the historical basis for a later (and partly fictitious) communist film made by Sergei Eisenstein, *Battleship Potemkin*.

Constitutional change

In August 1905, in an attempt to halt the rising revolutionary movement, the tsarist government agreed to set up an elected, but purely consultative, National Assembly. However, none of the opposition leaders trusted the tsar's intentions. They were determined to press for more far-reaching constitutional change that would include a representative assembly with legislative powers.

A printing workers' strike in September was followed by a railway workers' strike and a soviet-organised general strike in October. Communications came to a standstill, the government ground to a halt and even government staff − including those at the Treasury and the state bank − went on strike.

Although most tsarist military forces remained loyal, the best troops had been sent east to fight in the Russo-Japanese war. This meant that there were too few soldiers nearer home to control the disorder and keep essential services running. Consequently, on 17 October, following the advice of Sergei Witte, Nicholas issued his October Manifesto. In an attempt to split the radicals from the moderates and so weaken the opposition, he promised full civil liberties and the constitutional democracy he had previously resisted. He would establish a State *Duma* with legislative powers, elected by universal manhood suffrage (one man, one vote, for all adult males).

While the moderates embraced the announcement, the radicals (bolstered by their successes) continued to demand that the whole tsarist system be swept away. The St Petersburg Soviet encouraged workers to keep up the pressure and continue the general strike.

SOURCE 5.3

Trotsky denounced those who were prepared to cooperate in a constitutional monarchy as 'bourgeois' and 'capitalist lackeys'.

> Citizens! If anyone among you believes in the tsar's promises, let him say so! Look around you! Has anything changed? Have the gates of our prisons been opened? Have our brothers returned to their homes from the Siberian deserts? No! The dictator still rules over us with the aid of the army. The guardsmen covered in the blood of January the ninth are his support and his strength.

Quoted in Sixsmith, M. 2011. **Russia.** *London, UK. BBC Books. p. 167.*

QUESTION

What does Trotsky mean by, 'The guardsmen covered in the blood of January the ninth '? Was he correct to call the Tsar a 'dictator'?

Disorder in the countryside continued, peaking in November and December. Army mutinies also escalated in the final months of the year. Having lost control over the urban garrisons, including that of Moscow, the tsarist government was in a dangerous position. Yet, division between the opposition forces worked to the tsar's advantage.

In December, the moderate liberals, under Alexander Guchkov, formed the Union of October 17th (creating the Octobrist Party). They signalled their intention to work with the tsar. The more radical liberals had already formed the Constitutional Democratic Party (or Kadets) under their leaders Milyukov and Petrunkevich in October. They also agreed to work within the provisions of the tsar's October Manifesto, though only in preparation for further reform.

Such support spurred the tsarist government to action. On 3 December, troops were sent in to crush the St Petersburg Soviet. They stormed the building and arrested all 260 members present. The councillors were put on trial and Trotsky was sentenced to exile in Siberia (although he escaped after a few weeks and went to England). Lenin had been in exile since 1900, supposedly for plotting against the tsar. He returned briefly in November but he was also forced to flee in 1906, as the tsarist government regained control.

A Bolshevik-led rising in Moscow was suppressed by troops in December. With promises to the soldiers of better conditions, the mutinies died down and order was re-imposed. By early 1906, with more tsarist troops returning from Manchuria, and a new French loan of 2250 million francs, the government's situation looked a little more secure.

ACTIVITY

Create a timeline of the revolutionary events of 1905. Beside each event make a comment on its significance to the revolution.

The 'Fundamental Laws', by which the Russian Empire would henceforth be governed, were published in April 1906. They were rather more conservative than the revolutionaries had hoped for. Nicholas refused to drop the word 'autocratic' from the statement describing his power, although he did agree to remove the word 'unlimited'. Consequently, Article 1 stated, 'Supreme autocratic power belongs to the emperor of all Russia'.

Furthermore, the new electoral system discriminated against the town workers in favour of the more conservative landlords and peasants. A nominated Council of State, or upper house, was introduced, to counterpose an elected State *Duma*. It was stated that ministers remained responsible only to the tsar, that the tsar could veto the decisions of the *duma* and dissolve it when he chose, that freedom of speech was subject to regulation and that the *duma* had power to reject only parts of the state budget. Finally, Article 87 of the laws allowed the tsarist government to rule by decree when the *duma* was not in session. In short, there was a vast difference between the expectation of constitutional change and the reality that emerged.

The opportunity for the tsar to work with his educated élites to forge a new democratic future for Russia had been lost. Even Witte recognised that what had been achieved was 'too little, too late'.

Figure 5.5: The new Russian State *Duma* in the Tauride Palace.

5.3 How successful was Stolypin in bringing about change in Russia from 1906?

Stolypin and the *Dumas*

The first *Duma*, April–July 1906

The first State *Duma* (which became known as 'the *Duma* of the Lords and Lackeys') assembled in April 1906.

SOURCE 5.4

Maurice Baring, an English journalist who attended one of the early
Duma sessions, commented on the wide cross-section of members.

> One saw peasants in their long black coats, some of
> them wearing military medals and crosses, priests,
> Tartars, Poles, men in every kind of dress. You
> see dignified old men in frock coats, aggressively
> democratic-looking intellectuals with long hair and
> pince-nez; a Polish bishop dressed in purple, men
> without collars, members of the proletariat, men in
> loose Russian shorts with belts and men dressed in the
> costume of two centuries ago. Some of the peasant
> deputies threw their smoke ash onto the polished floors
> and spat out husks of the sunflower seeds they liked to
> chew.

Ryan, J. (ed). 1998. **The Russian Chronicles.** *Godalming, UK.*
Quadrillion Publishing Ltd. p. 329.

QUESTION

What is the significance of Source 5.3 in relation to the First
Duma?

The elections had been boycotted by the radical socialist parties (except
for the Mensheviks), which meant that the *Duma* representatives were
all moderate or left-wing. The Kadets dominated the assembly and
they soon demanded changes that were regarded as radical by the
establishment. These included the transfer of all agricultural land to the
peasants as well as further changes to the constitution.

The tsar refused to accept such proposals. As peasant disturbances
escalated in the expectation of change, and trouble recurred in the army
(with around 200 mutinies affecting over 20% of army units), the *Duma*
was rapidly dissolved on 9 July. It had sat for just 73 days. The same day,
Witte was dismissed and the tougher **Pyotr Stolypin** was appointed
chairman of the Council of Ministers.

Pyotr Stolypin (1862–1911):

Stolypin entered government service after university and became the youngest ever governor in Grodno in 1902. In the same year, he led a commission on agriculture, which investigated rural violence. He was moved to Saratov province in 1905, after an outbreak of trouble there. He was known for his ability to enforce laws in the countryside by means of an efficient police force and strict surveillance methods. This brought him to the tsar's attention, and Stolypin was appointed prime minister in July 1906. As prime minister, he carried through a major programme of land reform and controlled the *Dumas*. He was assassinated in 1911 while attending an opera.

In protest at the dissolution, about 200 members of the first State *Duma* moved to the Finnish town of Vyborg, where they continued to meet and called on the people of Russia to protest and refuse to pay their taxes. However, Stolypin used the court-martial system to put down any disorder and made use of the right-wing Black Hundreds (gangs that used violent tactics to attack protesters, Jews and activists). Stolypin made such frequent use of the gallows that the hangman's noose became known as 'Stolypin's necktie'. The government executed 2390 people on charges of terrorism, while the terrorists assassinated 2691 between 1906 and 1909.

Stolypin promised the tsar that he would fix the next round of elections to procure a more favourable *Duma*. But he did at least resist Nicholas's calls to get rid of the *Duma* altogether. He believed that a mixture of repression and landownership reform would remove any remaining discontent and enable Russia to move forward.

The second *Duma*, February–June 1907

The government's efforts doubled the number of Octobrists in the second *Duma*. However, the leading Kadets lost their power to vote (following the failed protest in Vyborg) and this reduced the size of the moderate–liberal centre. Furthermore, the Bolsheviks and Social Revolutionaries chose to participate – alongside the Mensheviks – in these elections. The radical left therefore increased its strength, leading this *Duma* to be nicknamed the '*Duma* of National Anger'. Only 30 representatives from the first State *Duma* were returned, and the mood was confrontational.

Stolypin desperately tried to win the second *Duma*'s support for the agrarian reform programme he had devised. Facing difficulties in gaining such support, he resorted to passing legislation under the powers granted by Article 87, while the *Duma* was not in session. When the second *Duma* refused to ratify the new laws, it was also dissolved.

The SD representatives were accused of plotting to assassinate the tsar. They were arrested and exiled, and the government issued a new electoral law – again under Article 87. This new electoral law favoured the landowners and peasantry at the expense of the urban workers and national minorities. Such an action was technically illegal (since it was a breach of the Fundamental Laws, which could only be changed with *Duma* and Council of State consent), but few were left to protest.

The third *Duma*, November 1907–June 1912

The new law had its effect and the third *Duma* proved far easier for the authorities to manage. This *Duma* was dominated by the moderate Octobrists, and the number of Socialist representatives fell. The third *Duma* agreed to carry through major agricultural reform proposals but there were still some clashes, particularly over Stolypin's proposed changes to primary education and local government. This *Duma* was therefore suspended twice, while the government carried through measures under Article 87. By 1911, even some Octobrists had become government opponents.

Stolypin was assassinated on 5 September 1911 at the Kiev Opera House by an anarchist revolutionary (possibly a police agent). This left the tsarist government without an effective leader. Stolypin's death brought an end to reform and signalled the return of reaction. The Octobrists split into factions and Stolypin's successor, Vladimir Kokovstov, simply tried to ignore the *Duma*.

The fourth *Duma*, November 1912–February 1917

A fourth *Duma* was elected after the third had run its course. Apart from a reduction in the size of the Octobrist grouping, it was broadly similar to the third *Duma*. But it was allowed little influence and was too divided to be effective. It refused to disband when Nicholas ordered it to do so on 26 February 1917, and continued to meet as the Provisional Government (see Chapter 6). However, it was clear, long before this, that the *Duma* experiment had failed. The initiative had moved instead to the workers in the towns and cities.

ACTIVITY

Divide a page into four, with one section for each of the four State *Dumas*. In each section note the dates, composition, measures and issues which affected that *Duma*. Consider the question: were the *Dumas* of significance in the government of Russia between 1906 and 1914?

Stolypin and the peasantry

The position of the peasantry had gradually begun to improve, as the government relieved the peasants of some of their financial burdens. For example, in 1902 the regime abolished the collective responsibility of the commune for the collection of all the community's taxes. The same year saw the end of corporal punishment and another cancellation of debt arrears. This was followed, at the height of the troubles of 1905, by a law in November 1905 that cancelled remaining redemption payments. However, this cancellation did not come into effect until 1 January 1907.

These fiscal changes were accompanied by discussion of further changes to land ownership. Stolypin believed that the way forward was to abandon the commune altogether and allow the peasants to own and farm land privately. He argued that this would create a class of prosperous and independent peasants, who would farm more efficiently, using more modern methods of production. Since their surplus wealth would be spent on consumer goods, they would also act as a stimulus to industry. Some peasants of this type, known as *kulaks* (whom Stolypin referred to as the 'sturdy and strong'), had already shown what could be achieved using the opportunities offered by emancipation. Stolypin believed that such peasants would be hostile to revolutionary change, and would provide the stability the state so badly needed.

Figure 5.6: Policemen questioning a Russian peasant to check on land ownership, following Stolypin's agrarian reforms.

In November 1906, Stolypin introduced the first stage of land ownership reform under Article 87. It was supplemented by further legislation in 1910 and 1911, when the laws were approved by the third *Duma*. Collective ownership of land within a family was abolished, and a peasant landholder could apply to take his land out of the commune and farm it privately. He could also request a consolidated block of land, rather than separate strips. Special land settlement commissions (containing representatives elected by the peasants) were set up to negotiate and implement these reforms. In addition, a new peasant bank was established to help peasants fund the changes. In June 1910, all communes that had not redistributed their land were dissolved. Government subsidies were then increased to raise the productivity of the peasants, as well as to encourage migration and settlement in Siberia.

The legislation began the slow emergence of larger, peasant-owned farms. Stolypin is said to have claimed that the reforms would need 20 years of peace to take effect. (In the event, the coming of war prevented a 20-year period of calm.) Peasant proprietorship grew, increasing peasants' hereditary ownership of land from 20% in 1905 to nearly 50% by 1915, and several good harvests aided their prosperity. Meanwhile, 3.5 million peasants left the over-populated districts of western and southern Russia to make the government-sponsored journey to Siberia, which was transformed into a major agricultural centre for dairy farming and cereal production.

Yet, change was slow and the conservative peasantry proved reluctant to abandon the security provided by the communes. Few peasants possessed the education, the desire for self-improvement, or the ability to think and plan ahead that the reforms required. In addition, some landowners were unwilling to accept the changes. McCauley has suggested that the reforms made life easier for the peasants, but they did not go far enough in creating the prosperous *kulak* class that Stolypin wanted.

DISCUSSION POINT

If war had not come in 1914, could Stolypin's reforms have brought peaceful change to the Russian agrarian economy?

KEY CONCEPTS QUESTION

Change and continuity: To what extent did the years 1906 to 1914 show more continuity than change from those between 1894 and 1905?

5.4 What was Russia like in 1914?

Russia in 1914

In the years between 1905 and 1914, Russian industry enjoyed a brief period of success as the economy recovered. Factory output grew at 5% per year. (Although the level of production was lower than it had been in the 1890s, it was still impressive.)

When Nicholas II celebrated the 300th anniversary of Romanov rule in Russia in 1913, he wrote in his diary: 'Thank Lord God who shed his grace upon Russia and us all so that we could joyously celebrate the days of the tercentenary of the Romanovs' accession'.

As part of the celebrations, the royal family made a tour of Russian towns and villages. Wherever they went, peasants came out with their precious holy icons and bread and salt (the traditional Russian welcome) to offer greetings to their tsar. Alexandra was so overjoyed, she said to Nicholas: 'Now you can see for yourself what cowards those state ministers are. They are constantly frightening the Emperor with threats of revolution and here – you see it for yourself – we need merely to show ourselves and at once their hearts are ours.'

Nevertheless, Russia still had massive social problems, with 60% illiteracy and widespread poverty in both towns and the countryside. In addition, the tsarist government was still trying to rule in the reactionary, repressive way it had done for centuries. In 1912, for example, a strike at the Lena goldfields in Siberia was suppressed by the police and 270 miners were killed. This provoked a series of 'sympathy strikes'. In the summer and autumn of 1913, when Nicholas and Alexandra were enjoying their tercentenary celebrations, there were more workers on strike than in 1905.

Nicholas remained hopelessly detached from such developments – partly because he was preoccupied by the illness of his son, Alexei, who suffered from haemophilia (a disease that causes uncontrolled bleeding). In 1905 Alexandra had met **Grigori Rasputin**, a peasant faith-healer, who seemed able to stop the boy's bleeding. This healer had since become close to the royal family and Nicholas referred to him as 'our friend' and 'a holy man'. When the president of the *Duma* tried to complain about Rasputin's wild behaviour, Nicholas countered, 'I will allow no-one to meddle in my affairs'.

Grigori Rasputin (1869–1916):

Rasputin was a peasant from western Siberia who joined a mystical sect, the Khlysty, and spent time wandering through Russia preaching and using his hypnotic eyes to carry out faith-healing. He arrived in St Petersburg at a time when spiritualism, astrology and the occult (the study of magic and the supernatural) were exerting a particular fascination among Russian aristocrats. Rasputin was introduced to the royal family in November 1905. He soon gained influence, particularly over Alexandra, as he appeared to be able to stop the bleeding of her haemophiliac son, Alexei. The royal family regarded him as 'God's messenger' and he was given exceptional power and influence for a man of his background. This provoked public hostility and Rasputin was eventually murdered in 1916.

Historians' views of Nicholas II are divided. Pyotr Multatuli has referred to Nicholas II as an example of 'a moral politician', who simply 'wanted his subordinates to be equally responsible for the destiny of their Motherland'. Similarly, Archbishop Vikenty of Yekaterinburg said, in an interview, 'Emperor Nicholas II was an example for politicians of his time. When we study his state activity, we see that he applied the Christian values he had been educated in as his policy.' However, there has been some debate as to whether the autocracy could have survived – even if the First World War had not started in 1914.

Alexander Gerschenkron has suggested that tsardom could have continued because Russia's industrial progress had placed it on the path towards Westernisation, which meant democratisation would inevitably have occurred. Donald Treadgold holds a more pessimistic view of the tsar, based on Nicholas's absolute refusal to consider any compromise to the autocratic system. The consensus among most recent historians, including Gregory Freeze, Geoffrey Hosking, Robert Service and Orlando Figes, is that – war or no war – the system that Nicholas was trying to preserve could not have survived without at least some change.

Figure 5.7: This cartoon reflects the popular view of Rasputin, showing Nicholas and Alexandra as puppet-like figures in his hands.

In the years before 1914, many strikes were organised by the Bolshevik Party. This party had grown considerably since 1905, and was particularly active in recruiting peasants who had recently moved to the towns. The Bolsheviks had come to dominate the largest trade unions in St Petersburg and Moscow and their newspaper, *Pravda*, was selling around 40 000 copies a day. In July 1914, the Bolsheviks helped organise a general strike in St Petersburg. Even some of the intelligentsia supported the strike, in the hope of forcing further constitutional change. However, we can only speculate on what the outcome might have been, since these troubles ended when a far greater threat presented itself – the outbreak of the First World War.

Imperial Russia and the Soviet Union (1855–1924)

Paper 3 exam practice

Question

'By the eve of war in 1914, Russia was well on the way to becoming an economically prosperous and politically stable country.' To what extent do you agree with this statement? **[15 marks]**

Skill

Avoiding irrelevance

Examiner's tips

Do not waste valuable writing time on irrelevant material. By definition, if it is irrelevant, it will not gain you **any** marks. Writing irrelevant information can happen because:

- the candidate does not look carefully enough at the wording of the question (see Chapter 2)
- the candidate ignores the fact that the question demands a response that conveys a view, an argument, a selection of facts to support that argument and show balance and a clear, sustained judgement; instead the candidate just writes down all that they know about a topic (relevant or not) and leaves the examiner to draw conclusions from it
- the candidate has unwisely restricted their revision; so, for example, if a question is set, as here, requiring knowledge of both economic and political developments, half the question is ignored. This might produce a feeble attempt to assert a view on one side, within an essay that deals only with the other side in depth.

Whatever the reason, such responses will fail to address the demands of the question asked.

For this question, you will need to:

- consider the details of the economic and political developments that took place in Russia down to 1914
- assess the actual results of those various developments
- provide a judgement as to whether Russia, in 1914, *was* 'economically prosperous' and another as to whether it was

'politically stable', or whether the picture was more mixed in one or both areas.

Common mistakes

One common error with questions like this is for candidates to write from a very long-term perspective. Although there is no start-date provided in this question, there will obviously need to be an emphasis on the shorter-term developments here, in order to give an accurate picture of Russia in 1914. General descriptions of tsardom, or the beginnings of industrialisation in the mid 19th century, will not be relevant to an explanation of the condition of Russia on the eve of war, and it would be a mistake to devote a lot of space to them.

Another mistake would be to treat the quotation as a single statement. Remember what was said in Chapter 3 about Higher-level questions often having more than one argument in them. Economic prosperity and political stability do not necessarily go hand in hand, although a thoughtful candidate would point out the links between the two. If the statement is not pulled apart for analysis, there is a danger that the essay could become over-generalised, vague and unconvincing. An unthinking candidate might, for example, assume that growing economic prosperity meant stability (without necessarily focusing on 'political stability'), whereas in fact the reverse seems to have been the case in pre-war Russia.

Writing in a generalised way is another form of irrelevance, which will lead to very low marks (see the guidance in Chapter 5).

Remember to refer to the simplified Paper 3 mark scheme in Chapter 8.

Sample paragraphs showing irrelevant focus/material

Russia was well on the way to becoming an economically prosperous and politically stable country by 1914. The transformation of the Russian economy had begun in the reign of Alexander II. This followed Russia's humiliating defeat in the Crimean War when Russia's transport system failed to support the movement of troops and the manufacture of ammunition was inadequate. Alexander's minister, Mikhail von Reutern, saw the importance of restoring Russian prestige and produced a series of reforms to help the military and promote industry. He was particularly interested in the development of the railways…

[There then follows a section on the development of the economy under Alexander II and Alexander III.]

The tsarist political structure was based on the idea of an autocratic emperor who ruled according to his own sense of right and wrong, guided by God. The Russian Orthodox Church acted as support for the tsar and he was its secular head. The tsar ruled as a 'father to his children' and regarded the land of Russia as his private property. Traditionally there was a 'bond' between the tsar and his people, who owed him complete loyalty…

[There then follows a section on the political structure of tsarist Russia, including the ministers, civil servants, police, army and finance.]

Gradually Russia became economically more prosperous and politically stable. In the early 20th century the economy began to grow faster, thanks to the work of Sergei Witte, and agriculture was transformed by Pyotr Stolypin. All this helped to create a more stable country…

[There then follows details of economic developments to 1914, with assertions of political stability and a very brief mention of the *Dumas* in the discussion of Stolypin. The final paragraph asserts that Russia was on the way to becoming an economically prosperous and politically stable country by 1914, and comments on the degree of change experienced since 1853.]

EXAMINER'S COMMENT

This is an example of a weak answer. Although the opening sentence suggests a view, the candidate merely agrees with the whole quotation and makes no attempt to unravel it or show an awareness of its constituent parts. The section that follows takes the reader back to the mid 19th century and offers too much detail on developments in that era, which are of limited relevance to the question asked. In considering the more short-term developments, economic growth and political stability are falsely merged and there is no depth of analysis focusing on 'by 1914'. Virtually all the underlined material is therefore irrelevant, and would not score any marks. In addition, the candidate has used up valuable writing time, which should have been spent providing relevant points and supporting knowledge about Russia in 1914.

Activity

In this chapter, the skills focus is on avoiding writing answers that contain irrelevant material. Using the information from this chapter and any other sources of information available to you, write an answer to one of the following Paper 3 practice questions, keeping your answer fully focused on the question asked. Remember – writing a plan first can help you maintain this focus.

Paper 3 practice questions

1 Evaluate the success of Nicholas II as tsar between 1894 and 1914.

2 Examine the long-term and short-term causes of revolution in Russia in 1905.

3 'The 1905 revolution changed nothing; in 1914 the tsarist autocracy was still intact.' To what extent do you agree with this statement?

4 To what extent did the outbreak of war in 1914 merely delay the fall of tsardom in Russia?

5 Discuss Pyotr Stolypin's success in improving the position of the peasants in Russia after 1906.

The Impact of War and the revolutions of 1917

TIMELINE

1915 **Sep:** Tsar Nicholas II assumes active command of military operations

1916 **16 Dec:** Assassination of Rasputin

1917 **23 Feb:** International Women's Day demonstration in Petrograd

24 Feb: Massive strikes and demonstrations throughout Petrograd

25 Feb: Nicholas II orders military to stop riots

26 Feb: Troops fire on crowds; mass mutiny begins in local army regiments

27 Feb: Provisional Committee of *duma* formed

1 Mar: Petrograd Soviet meets

2 Mar: Nicholas II forced to abdicate; Provisional Government formed

3 Apr: Lenin arrives in Petrograd; Milyukov resigns from government

7 Apr: April Theses are published in *Pravda* newspaper

3 Jun: First All-Russian Congress of Soviets opens in Petrograd

18 Jun–mid Jul: Brusilov Offensive in Galicia

3–7 Jul: July Days – unsuccessful Bolshevik rising

8 Jul: Prince Lvov resigns and Kerensky becomes prime minister

25 Aug–1 Sep: Kornilov attempts coup but is defeated

9 Sep: Bolsheviks achieve majority in Petrograd Soviet

10 Oct: Lenin persuades Bolshevik Central Committee to proceed with revolution

23 Oct: Provisional Government shuts down Bolshevik newspapers

24 Oct: Bolshevik troops take over government buildings in Petrograd

25 Oct: Kerensky escapes and Bolsheviks capture Winter Palace; Second Congress of Soviets meets

26 Oct: Remaining members of the Provisional Government arrested

KEY QUESTIONS

- What was the impact of the First World War on Russia?
- Why did revolution break out in February 1917?
- Why were the Provisional Government and Dual Power overthrown in October 1917?
- What roles did Lenin and Trotsky play in the events of 1917?

The moment feared by every 19th-century Russian tsar eventually came in 1917. The experience of the First World War unleashed forces that had been building up for decades. The inadequacies of the autocracy were highlighted and the military death toll, combined with shortages of food and essential items both at home and on the front line, angered people to the point where they were ready to rise up against the regime. The Romanov dynasty finally came to an end in February 1917. It was replaced by a Dual Power arrangement, made up of a Provisional Government and a Workers' Soviet. This compromise failed to work; with continuing wartime disasters, the Bolsheviks under Vladimir Lenin grew stronger. In October 1917, the Bolsheviks seized power in Russia and opened the way for a new communist future.

Overview

- The coming of the First World War in 1914, combined with military failures and the tsar's decision to take command on the front line in 1915, weakened the tsarist government. Rasputin, hated by many nobles for his influence over the royal family, was assassinated in 1916.
- Wartime economic and military problems exacerbated existing political issues and caused the tsarist system to break down.
- Riots in Petrograd in February 1917 turned into revolution, when soldiers refused to fire on the crowds and joined them instead.
- The tsar was forced to abdicate (give up the throne) and the Provisional Government took control, working alongside the Workers' and Soldiers' Soviet in a system of Dual Power.

- The Provisional Government's inadequacies (particularly its continued involvement in an unsuccessful war) enabled Lenin, who returned to Russia in April 1917, to build up support for the Bolshevik Party. Other socialist radicals (the Socialist Revolutionaries and the Mensheviks) were also strong forces within the Petrograd and Moscow Soviets.

- The Bolshevik cause was almost destroyed in the July Days, when an early coup (attempted seizure of power) was crushed. But Kornilov's attempt to lead a right-wing coup in August 1917 increased support for the Bolsheviks.

- Against the wishes of the Central Committee, a Bolshevik Revolution in Petrograd was organised on 25 October by Lenin (in exile until the outbreak of the revolution) and Trotsky (in charge of the Red Guards).

Figure 6.1: Lenin addresses workers outside the Putilov metal works in April 1917.

6.1 What was the impact of the First World War on Russia?

After Russia's humiliation by the Japanese in 1905, the tsar's Slavophile ministers again turned their attention to the Balkan area. In this region, Russia supported Serbia, which wished to create a new southern Slav state. This brought the tsarist empire into conflict with the Austro-Hungarian Empire, which was hostile to Serbia's ambitions and wanted to exert its own influence over the area. In July 1914 there was a crisis, when the Austrian Archduke Franz Ferdinand was assassinated in Sarajevo by Bosnian Serb nationalists. When the Austrians turned on Serbia, Russia leapt to Serbia's defence and declared war on Austria-Hungary and its ally Germany. Within weeks, the unravelling of treaties and alliances led to conflict in Europe. Many within the Russian political and military élites warned Nicholas of the dangers of embarking on a war.

There were a number of factors pushing Russia towards war. Quite apart from the pan–Slavist sentiment and Russia's 'understandings' with France and Britain, there were those who saw war as a useful way of diverting attention from Russia's internal troubles. Nicholas was uncertain, as always. In the confused days at the end of July 1914, he ordered the mobilisation of Russian troops, and then temporarily suspended the order in the hope of reaching some last-minute agreement with the Germans. However, it was difficult to stop the mobilisation machine once it was underway and the generals argued that Russia needed to be prepared – if and when war eventually broke out.

SOURCE 6.1

From a letter from Pyotr Durnovo (minister of internal affairs) to Nicholas II in February 1914. This document was found among Nicholas II's papers after the 1917 revolution.

> In the event of a defeat, the possibility of which in a struggle with a foe like Germany cannot be overlooked, social revolution in its extreme form is inevitable. It will start with disasters being attributed to the government. In the legislative institutions a bitter campaign against the government will begin, which will lead to revolutionary agitation throughout the country. Socialist slogans will immediately ensue. The defeated army will prove to be too demoralised to serve as a bulwark of law and order. The legislative institutions and the opposition intelligentsia parties will be powerless to stem the rising popular tide, and Russia will be flung into hopeless anarchy, the outcome of which cannot even be foreseen.

Quoted in Waller, S. 2009. **Tsarist Russia 1855–1917.** *Cheltenham, UK. Nelson Thornes. p. 112.*

QUESTION

With reference to origin, purpose and content, what are the value and limitations of Source 6.1 for historians studying Nicholas II and the First World War?

As elsewhere in Europe, the declaration of war (on 20 July 1914) was greeted in Russia with an outburst of patriotic enthusiasm. Demonstrations and strikes came to a sudden halt. Crowds gathered in Moscow and St Petersburg (which was renamed Petrograd to avoid German connotations) to sing hymns and celebrate Russia's opportunity to restore its international prestige. The French ambassador remarked, 'To those thousands the tsar really is the autocrat, the absolute master of their bodies and souls'.

The *Duma* met on 8 August and voted for war credits (the raising of money to pay for war by the issuing of government bonds). The five Bolshevik representatives opposed this measure and the moderate socialists did not vote, but all others abandoned their criticisms and voted in favour. A provisional committee of *duma* members, chaired by **Mikhail Rodzianko** (the *Duma* president), was also set up to organise aid for victims of war.

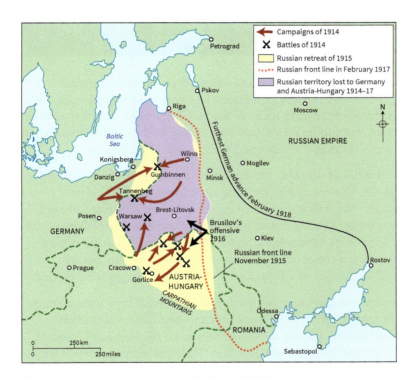

Figure 6.2: The Eastern Front in the First World War.

> ### Mikhail Rodzianko (1859–1924):
>
> He came from a land-owning family and had served as a senior army officer before being elected to the third *Duma*. He assumed leadership of the *Dumas* from 1911 and, although loyal to Nicholas II, opposed Rasputin and tried to persuade the Tsar of the need for constitutional change to avert revolution in 1917. He supported the subsequent Provisional Government but disliked Alexander Kerensky and encouraged the Kornilov coup. Following the October Revolution, he fled to Yugoslavia.

The public enthusiasm for war lasted around six months. Russian soldiers, whose training and conditions had greatly improved since 1905, set off to the front, bearing icons of the tsar. Patriotism soared as news of the 'Russian steamroller's' swift advance (as the British and French called the vast army) into East Prussia and Galicia was relayed home.

Then the Germans defeated the Russians at the Battle of Tannenberg in August 1914. In total, 300 000 Russian soldiers were killed or wounded and thousands more were taken prisoner. This was followed, in September, by another disastrous battle by the Masurian Lakes, which forced a temporary retreat from East Prussia. Although Russia gained some successes in the south, the initial enthusiasm for war quickly evaporated and hopes of a short and victorious campaign were dashed.

The Russian economy soon showed signs of strain. There were disputes about the organisation of the war effort and complaints of military incompetence. The *zemstva* came together in an All-Russian Union of Zemstvas for the Relief of the Sick and Wounded in August 1914. In May 1915, representatives of industry set up the Central War Industries Committee – with workers' *dumas* and industrialists' representatives – to coordinate war production. In June 1915, *zemstva* and municipal *dumas* merged to form the All-Russian Union of Zemstvas and Cities (ZemGor). This was chaired by Prince Lvov and claimed the right to help the government in the war effort, though it never had any official standing. These organisations did much to direct wartime Russia. Nevertheless, rather than cooperating with them, Nicholas tended to view them as centres of unwanted liberal ideas.

By mid 1915, the mood of national unity had been shattered by political incompetence and military defeat. A combined Austro-German offensive had pushed the Russians out of Galicia. In addition, a powerful

German attack along the front line had driven the Russians back about 400 km (250 miles) along the whole front, from Latvia in the north to Ukraine in the south, losing Poland, Lithuania and parts of Ukraine. Nearly 4 million Russian troops had been killed, captured or wounded or reported missing. Most of the officers, as well as many men from those initial armies, were dead.

Critical press reports about the lack of rifles and shells at the front provoked a bitter mood among the intelligentsia. When the *duma* met in August 1915, it was once again ready to challenge the tsarist regime. Octobrists, Kadets and some right-wing progressives (many of them members of the Central War Industries Committee) joined forces and created the Progressive Bloc. This bloc formed a majority in the *duma* and it demanded that the State *Duma* should be given real power so that the public would have confidence in government.

The Progressive Bloc's proposals had the support of the other professional groups such as ZemGor. Nevertheless, Nicholas rejected the demands and suspended the sittings of the *Duma*. He also dismissed his more liberal ministers, who opposed his decision to take up the position of commander-in-chief of the Russian Army and Navy and travel to the front line himself. The Council of Ministers feared that Nicholas was laying himself open to blame for every reverse the army suffered. However, since the army leadership was crumbling and many peasant soldiers still revered the tsar, there was some logic to the decision. He was fortunate in taking control just as the Germans decided to suspend offensive operations in the East. But by going to the front, Nicholas placed himself physically (as well as mentally) even further from the centre of government at home.

Unofficial *Duma* meetings continued and hostility mounted in the tsar's absence, with complaints directed against the 'German woman' (meaning the Empress Alexandra) and Rasputin, whose dissolute lifestyle exasperated the political élites. During the year of 'tsarina rule', thanks to Rasputin's interference, there were four prime ministers, five interior ministers, five agricultural ministers and three each of foreign, war and transport ministers. All administrative continuity was lost and Russia's future seemed to be in the hands of a degenerate mystic.

173

KEY CONCEPTS ACTIVITY

Significance: Empress Alexandra has often been blamed for the events that led to Nicholas II's abdication. Try to find out a little more about Alexandra, particularly her influence in the 1914–17 period. Has history judged her too harshly?

SOURCE 6.2

In November 1916, Milyukov, the leader of the Kadets and a former loyal moderate, gave a speech to the Duma:

> The regime does not have the wisdom or the capacity to deal with the current situation! Gentlemen! This regime has sunk lower than ever before! The gap between it and us has become a yawning chasm that can never be bridged! A handful of shady personalities are manipulating the affairs of state with treacherous intentions: the so-called 'court-party' grouped around the empress – are they motivated by treachery or by stupidity? You can take your pick – the results are the same!

Quoted in Christian, D. 1997. **Imperial and Soviet Russia.** *Basingstoke, UK. Palgrave Macmillan. p. 181.*

QUESTION

What does Source 6.2 suggest about attitudes to the autocracy in 1916?

Although Rodzianko warned Nicholas of the strength of feeling against Rasputin, the tsar did nothing. In desperation, three members of the 'inner circle', Prince Yusopov, a rich landowner; Vladimir Purishkevich, a right-wing *duma* deputy; and Grand-Duke Dmitri Pavlovich, one of the tsar's uncles, murdered Rasputin in December 1916. Nevertheless, this action achieved little, apart from enabling Rasputin's enemies to vent their frustrations. Hostility to the tsarist government remained, and even some of the army generals declared their support for an abdication.

Nicholas himself seemed blissfully unaware of all the mounting tensions. In his letters to his wife at this time, he was far more concerned about the fact that his children had measles.

Military issues

In 1914, Russia had a peacetime army of 1.4 million men; 4 million more were rapidly added by mobilising the reserves. However, the country struggled to equip and provide for so many soldiers. In December 1914, only 4.7 million rifles were available for 6.5 million men. Vital imports had been disrupted by Turkey's entry into the war on the German side in October 1914, and Russian industry proved incapable of producing sufficient munitions, clothing or footwear.

By 1916, some of these difficulties had been removed, as industry reorganised itself to produce rifles at the rate of 10 000 per month. But by this time the army was suffering from a lack of experienced officers (after many early deaths) and new recruits were receiving hardly any training. Although basic discipline was maintained in the front lines, it was sometimes a struggle. As a result of changes in the make-up of the army, revolutionary propaganda found a ready ear among the soldiers – officers as well as ordinary troops.

The Brusilov Offensive, when the Russians advanced for ten weeks over a 300 km (200 mile) front, brought the Austrian army close to collapse in the summer of 1916. When the Germans sent reinforcements, the over-stretched Russian communication lines failed and the advance was called off. This was a major blow to the Russian soldiers, who had been led to believe that they would be able to claim large new sections of territory for their country.

The soldiers' morale was damaged by heavy casualties on the front lines, combined with news of trouble at home. From October 1916 onward, desertions from the army increased. The peasant soldiers began to return to their farms, intent on taking advantage of the internal turmoil to seize land.

Figure 6.3: Russian prisoners of war, photographed in May 1915.

Theory of Knowledge

History and the importance of individuals

In deserting the army, the Russian peasant soldiers affected the course of history. Is history determined more by the actions of 'ordinary men and women' or by 'great and important individuals'?

Economic and social problems

The war was a financial disaster. Although government spending increased more than four-fold between 1913 and 1916, income from customs duties (much of which had previously come from Germany) declined. In August 1914, Nicholas prohibited the sale of alcoholic drinks for the duration of the war. This drastically reduced government income (30% of which had come from the government monopoly on liquor sales) and encouraged peasants and workers to brew their own illicit vodka, known as *samogon*.

There was an attempt to meet the huge costs of the war by raising money from income taxes and excess profits taxes (introduced in 1916), but these contributed very little. Russia relied mainly on borrowing and increasing the money supply. This was a form of indirect taxation because it brought inflation and a rise in the cost of living, which put pressure on the town workers in particular.

Army recruitment (and the loss of land to the Germans) reduced industrial production and agricultural output. Women and children were recruited to work in factories, but living conditions worsened – with insanitary lodgings, fuel shortages, totally inadequate diets and low wages. Many lived, according to a police department report, a 'half-starved existence', which made them receptive to revolutionary talk. Strikes and lock–outs spread and were sometimes encouraged by German saboteurs attempting to weaken Russia from within.

The peasants did better, selling their horses to the army, charging high prices for their labour (which was scarce because of conscription), and supplying grain to the government. Several good harvests also meant that there was plenty to sell. In the autumn of 1916, the department of police reported that rural areas were 'contented and calm'. However, some peasants were reluctant to sell at the low prices offered by the state, when there was little to buy with their money. They preferred to use their surplus grain to feed livestock or would simply hoard it, in the hope of prices rising later. Transport was also disrupted, so trade between country and town broke down. Whereas 25% of the grain harvest was sold on the market in 1914, the figure was only 15% in 1917.

By 1917, any hopes that the tsarist regime could redeem itself had gone. A total of 1.7 million soldiers had died, 8 million were wounded and 2.5 million were prisoners of war. The war had altered everything. Even the tsar was a changed man.

SOURCE 6.3

Paul Benkendorff, the Grand Marshal of the Court, wrote a melancholy description of Nicholas in the autumn of 1916.

> His Majesty is no longer seriously interested in anything. Of late, he has become quite apathetic. He goes through his daily routine like an automaton, paying more attention to the hour set for his meals or his walk in the garden, than to affairs of state. One can't rule an empire and command an army in the field in this manner. If he doesn't realise it in time, something catastrophic is bound to happen.

Quoted in Lieven, D. 1993. **Nicholas II.** *London, UK. John Murray.*

QUESTION

Using Sources 6.2 and 6.3 and your own knowledge, explain the breakdown of Tsarist authority in Russia in the years 1915–16.

KEY CONCEPTS ACTIVITY

Causation: Create a mind map to explain the long-term reasons for the final crisis of autocracy in February/March 1917. Using a different colour, add some short-term factors to your mind map after you have read the next section.

6.2 Why did revolution break out in February 1917?

By the third winter of the war, the atmosphere in Petrograd was tense. In January, 145 000 workers were on strike. On 22 February, 20 000 were locked out of the Putilov metal works after a dispute with their employers. The frustrations of yet more unemployed workers were added to those of the men and women from the 58 Petrograd factories where strikes had broken out. The citizens were suffering from constant food shortages, and rumours that bread would be rationed from 1 March angered the crowds of desperate, starving people on the streets. Women set up beds on the pavements by the bakeries and waited through the freezing night to buy the bread they needed to feed their families. Nerves were at breaking point, and the police struggled to keep order as crowds jostled for limited supplies.

On 23 February, events turned particularly sour. Thousands of militant women (many of whom had been conscripted into textile and armament factories because of the war) marched through Petrograd to show their solidarity (unity) on International Women's Day. They had plenty to protest about – exploitation, the war and the lack of bread – and their cries attracted others. They were joined by men from the Putilov metal works, militant students, women from the bread queues and other workers who abandoned their own jobs to join in the general demonstration. In the course of the day, the entire city fell into chaos. Female tram drivers abandoned their vehicles, leaving them to block busy roads. Other people took the opportunity to loot whatever they could, while the police were busy elsewhere.

SOURCE 6.4

One witness, Dr E. M. Herbert, described what he saw on the streets of Petrograd.

> People were smashing up shops, looting bread shops; women particularly. Tramcars were being overturned, barricades were being built out of wood blocks and paving stones.

Quoted in Sixsmith, M. 2011. **Russia.** *London, UK. BBC Books. p. 183.*

The protest was initially quite unplanned, and the rioting was uncoordinated. (Some Bolshevik agitators actually tried to stop the demonstrators, fearing that their premature action might put at risk a Bolshevik day of action that had been planned for 1 May.) Nevertheless, as many as 240 000 protesters came out onto the streets of Petrograd that day, and the police were unable to restore order until the evening.

Daily demonstrations continued, each one becoming more violent than the last. Socialists of all types tried to harness the agitation to more political goals – rather than simply demanding jobs and food. Agitators waved red flags, demanded an end to the war and sang a Russian version of the *Marseillaise*. This was the French national anthem, which had long been associated with 'liberty and equality', the motto of the French Revolution.

Protesters brought the transport network to a standstill. They halted the publication of newspapers and forced the closure of shops and restaurants in the city. They tore down tsarist statues and symbols, released prisoners from jails, and attacked the police who were trying to keep order. Over half the capital's workforce came out on strike and the city of Petrograd was virtually immobilised.

There were bloody scenes on both sides. The leader of a police charge was set upon, dragged from his horse, beaten and shot. On Sunday 26 February, around 200 men, women and children were slaughtered by a group of Cossacks who sent a volley of shots into the crowds. Following another clash, the same day, one eyewitness wrote that 'People fled, slipping in pools of blood, stepping across the bodies of the dead and dying sprawled in the roadway. Their faces were full of bitterness and anger.'

According to the historian Orlando Figes, 'Even at this point, the authorities could have still contained the situation'. Figes quotes a leading Bolshevik, Alexander Shliapnikov, who asked a local meeting of the party leaders in Petrograd on 25 February: 'What revolution? Give the workers a pound of bread and the movement will peter out.' Certainly, Mikhail Rodzianko believed that it was possible to maintain control by means of prompt action. However, he was well aware of the possible consequences of continued disorder in the streets.

SOURCE 6.5

On 26 February, Rodzianko sent the tsar a telegram about events in Petrograd.

> The situation is serious. The capital is in a state of anarchy. The government is paralysed. The transport system has broken down. The food and fuel supplies are completely disorganised. Discontent is general and on the increase. There is wild shooting in the streets. Troops are firing at each other. It is urgent that someone enjoying the confidence of the country be entrusted with the formation of a new government. There must be no delay. Hesitation is fatal.

Quoted in Golder, G. A. 1927. **Documents of Russian History 1914– 1917.** *New York, USA. The Century Co.*

QUESTION

In what ways does Source 6.5 support the picture given in Source 6.4?

Nicholas ignored the message and wrote in his diary: 'That fat-bellied Rodzianko has written some nonsense to which I shall not even bother to reply.' However, Rodzianko's words must have had some effect, since Nicholas decided to order the commander of the Petrograd Military District, Major-General Khabalov, to regain control using military force. Khabalov had been hoping not to receive such an order, because he knew his troops to be unreliable. Nevertheless, he accepted his duty and told his commanders, 'If the crowd is aggressive and displays banners, then act according to regulations: that is, signal three times and open fire.' The order from Nicholas therefore turned the demonstration into a revolution. As Figes writes, 'There could be no better illustration of the extent to which the tsar had lost touch with reality. Nor could there be any better guarantee of a revolution.'

DISCUSSION POINT

Is Figes right that what turns a demonstration into a revolution is the use of force against the demonstrators? Why do revolutions occur? Is it possible to identify the key factors?

Many of the soldiers called upon to shoot into the crowds were young and newly enlisted peasants or workers. These soldiers were waiting in the Petrograd garrison – possibly billeted with working-class families – before serving on the front line. Other troops had been rushed back from the front line, wounded or injured and tired of military discipline. All were disgusted by the order to massacre their fellow citizens. Some of the officers came from the middle classes, rather than the traditional noble classes. While they were prepared to fight for the Motherland, they were not ready to order their men to fire upon innocent civilians.

Consequently, the soldiers began to mutiny (rebel), refusing to fire on the protesters or follow any further orders. This started with the Volynski regiment and soon spread through the troops. By 27 February, more than 80 000 soldiers had joined the protesters, taking their weapons with them. Even the Cossack regiments changed sides and joined in attacks on the police.

By 28 February, the entire Petrograd garrison of 170 000 troops had mutinied; and any officers who tried to discipline them had been murdered. It is hard to be precise about how many died in the events of February 1917, but the figures have been estimated at around 1500 dead and several thousand wounded.

In despair, Rodzianko took matters into his own hands and set up a Provisional Committee of the *Duma* to assume control and demand the tsar's abdication. At the same time, a group of socialists recreated the Petrograd Soviet, with representatives elected from the factories, and took up residence alongside the *Duma* in the Tauride Palace. This Soviet expressed its willingness to recognise a *Duma*-led Provisional Government. Their promise was enough to persuade Mikhail Alekseev (the Army Chief of General Staff) and his officers that they should press Nicholas to step down from his military and imperial positions.

On 28 February, there was a mutiny among the sailors at Kronstadt, and the Petrograd Soviet voted to extend its membership to include representatives from the soldiers' regiments. The troops agreed to accept the authority of the Soviet 'in all matters political' and in this way some degree of order was restored. The Soviet renamed itself the Soviet of Workers' and Soldiers' Deputies, and Order No. 1 (a charter of soldiers' rights) was drawn up. This charter declared that troops should only obey orders that had been approved by the Soviet.

On the same day, Nicholas left his military base at Mogilev to return to Petrograd. No one can be sure what he intended to do when he arrived, because he never actually reached Petrograd. His train was diverted by rebellious railway workers and forced to stop at Pskov, 300 km (200 miles) to the south.

There he was joined by officers from the Army High Command. His wife Alexandra, who continually played down the events in Petrograd, had been sending him telegrams urging him 'not to sign any paper or constitution or other such horror'. Nicholas therefore put off making a decision until some *Duma* representatives, led by Vasili Shulgin and Alexander Guchkov, arrived at Pskov to put their case on the evening of 2 March. Moved by their description of the chaos and bloodshed, the tsar told them: 'There is no sacrifice I would not bear for the salvation of our Mother Russia. I am ready to abdicate the throne.'

The announcement was delayed while frantic discussions went on as to who should replace Nicholas. The Army High Command favoured the ex-tsar's son Alexei as his natural successor, with Nicholas's younger brother Grand-Duke Mikhail Alexandrovich acting as regent. But Nicholas feared for his son's health and nominated Mikhail Alexandrovich as the next Tsar, without even consulting him. However, Alexandrovich refused the tsardom. The Petrograd Soviet's newspaper, *Izvestiya*, therefore announced on 3 March, 'Nicholas II has abdicated the throne in favour of Mikhail Alexandrovich who has, in turn, abdicated to the people.' The tsar's portrait was hauled down from the wall of the Tauride Palace, where the *Duma* met. The deputies announced that there would be a Provisional Government until such time as elections could be called. The tsar and his family, along with most of their Council of Ministers, were placed under arrest. Nicholas wrote in his diary on 3 March, 'So Misha [Mikhail] has abdicated. His manifesto ends with a call for the election of a Constituent Assembly in six months. God knows what possessed him to sign such a vile thing!'

Figure 6.4: Nicholas II, photographed shortly after his abdication in March 1917.

ACTIVITY

Create a chart comparing the causes and significant developments of the 1905 revolution with those of February 1917. What did these revolutions have in common and in what ways were they different?

Theory of Knowledge

Patterns in history

It might almost seem that certain key factors will always produce similar outcomes. Is this true? Is it helpful to think in this way?

Problems of interpretation

Historians have offered different interpretations of the causes and developments of the February 1917 revolution. Western liberals have usually placed the blame on the war or Nicholas himself, or a combination of the two. For example, it can be argued that Russia was making real progress before 1914. There was economic growth in both industry and agriculture, as well as some (even if it was too little) political modernisation. Without the war, Pyotr Stolypin's reforms might have had time to provide noticeable benefits for the peasants, and Russia might have continued along an orderly path to constitutional monarchy.

Equally, it is possible to argue that the defects in Nicholas II's character were actually responsible for his fall. His weak grasp of politics, his reliance on Alexandra, his detachment (both in attitude and quite literally when he chose to lead his armies at the front) and his inability to understand the situation in Petrograd in February have all been variously blamed for the February revolution.

Soviet historians of the communist era saw events differently, arguing that the February revolution was the result of economic forces and the class struggle. This school of historians played down the importance of the war and emphasised the role of the oppressed working class (who had been politicised since 1905) and the Bolshevik Party. For them, the collapse of tsardom was part of an inevitable process of change. They argued that only the factory owners had benefited from industrial change, and that agricultural reforms had made no obvious difference to the peasants. Political change had also been very slight. While reforms might have briefly delayed the course of history, they believed the fall of tsardom was a natural progression that was bound to occur anyway.

However, both Western liberal and communist historians *did* agree that the February 1917 revolution in Petrograd was leaderless and spontaneous. In the first major Western study of the Russian revolution, published in 1935, William Chamberlin stated that the collapse of the tsarist regime in February 1917 was 'one of the most leaderless, spontaneous, anonymous revolutions of all time'.

Similarly, in his 14-volume *History of Soviet Russia* in 1951, the British historian Edward Carr wrote:

'The February Revolution of 1917 was the spontaneous outbreak of a multitude exasperated by the privations of the war. The revolutionary parties played no

direct part in the making of the revolution. They did not expect it and were at first somewhat nonplussed [confused] by it. The creation at the moment of the revolution of a Petrograd Soviet of Workers' Deputies was a spontaneous act of groups of workers without central direction.'

Communist historians wrote in similar terms. For example, Vsevolod Eikhenbaum (known as Voline) commented: 'The action of the masses was spontaneous, logically climaxing a long period of concrete experience and moral preparation. This action was neither organised nor guided by any political party.'

It was official Communist Party policy to view events this way, since all the major Bolshevik leaders, whose subsequent fame depended on their participation in crucial events, were absent at the time – Lenin and Yuli Martov in Zurich, Leon Trotsky in New York and Victor Chernov in Paris. It suited the authorities better to promote the idea of a leaderless revolution than to give praise to 'lesser leaders'.

In the post-communist era, revisionists from both East and West have reappraised events in the light of archival evidence that had been kept secret for years. James White, Professor of Russian History at Glasgow University, wrote an article in 1997 entitled 'The Russian Revolution of February 1917: The Question of Organisation and Spontaneity'. In this article, he produced some convincing evidence that the February revolution *did* have leaders. He identified a liberal group, which included Paul Milyukov, Alexander Guchkov, Alexander Konovalov and Michael Tereshchenko. This group was apparently planning to carry out a coup that would depose the tsar without involving the public at large. Its members were subsequently very alarmed by the turn of events in February. White also identified a revolutionary workers' group, led by men who took part in the 1905 rising in Nizhny Novgorod. This group was based in the working-class district of Vyborg in Petrograd. Its role has been traced through evidence that was not available when Chamberlin wrote his history in 1935.

Jason Yanowitz, author of *The Makhno Myth: Anarchists in the Russian Revolution*, published in 2007, wrote:

'February was the product of… concentrated effort by revolutionary socialist cadres [small bands of activists] from a number of groups. They planned for it. They agitated for it. They were accountable to each other. They tried to generalise and extend every action of workers. And they saw the combativeness and confidence of the Petrograd working class increase.'

The case is not yet closed, and various interpretations are still being offered. However, it is more common today to see the roots of the February revolution in the rise of the working-class movement before 1914, and to see the war as a catalyst that accelerated developments.

KEY CONCEPTS QUESTION

Perspectives: Analyse the disagreements between historians about the causes of the revolution of February 1917?

6.3 Why were the Provisional Government and Dual Power overthrown in October 1917?

The establishment of the Dual Power

The Provisional Committee of the *duma* appointed a range of ministers in order to create a new Provisional Government on 1 March. They included liberals, moderate socialists, Constitutional Democrats and others who had formerly favoured the idea of constitutional monarchy. Some had not been members of the fourth *duma* but together they represented a cross-section of influential society, bringing together landowners, industrialists and both moderate and radical members of the intelligentsia. The chairman was Prince **Georgi Lvov**, an aristocrat, wealthy landowner and *zemstvo* leader. Milyukov was made foreign minister, Guchkov became minister of war, Konovalov was appointed minister of trade and Alexander Kerensky became minister of justice.

> ### Georgy Lvov (1861–1925):
>
> He was an aristocrat who joined the Kadets and sat in the first *Duma*. He favoured constitutional reform and in 1915 became chairman of the All-Russian Union of Zemstvas. In March 1917, he became the head of the new Provisional Government. However, his determination to keep Russia in the war made him unpopular and he was forced to resign in July 1917. In October 1917, he emigrated to France.

When Grand-Duke Mikhail Alexandrovich rejected the offer of the tsardom on 3 March, he passed authority to the Provisional Government, thereby giving it some legitimacy – although he never intended to prolong the Provisional Government's rule. He made it clear that elections should be held as soon as possible, and a new Constituent Assembly should draw up a new constitution for Russia. Nevertheless, Mikhail's gesture enabled the Provisional Government to command the initial loyalty of the tsarist civil service, army officers and police, even though both the army and police force had been seriously weakened by desertions during the February crisis.

Being a self-appointed group, the Provisional Government was seen as undemocratic and untrustworthy by many workers, soldiers and peasants. The people believed it was dominated by rich landowners and tainted by its former cooperation with tsardom. Consequently, most workers, and many of the ordinary soldiers in Petrograd, had more faith in the alternative source of power – the Petrograd Soviet.

The Petrograd Soviet was largely made up of Mensheviks and Social Revolutionaries (together with a few Bolsheviks) and had never compromised with the old autocracy. While the Provisional Government had set itself up in the *duma* chamber in the east (right) wing of the Tauride Palace, the Soviet established its headquarters in the west (left) wing.

Figure 6.5: The leaders of the Provisional Government after the February revolution: Kerensky (standing, second right), Lvov (seated, second left) and Rodzianko (seated, first right).

Soviets (elected committees) of all types soon sprang up across Russia. Peasants organised themselves to take control of their own affairs and seize their landlords' land. Factory committees appeared in both large industrial enterprises and workshops. Soldiers along the front line created similar soviets, using them to nominate their own officers and dispose of those officers of whom they disapproved. By June 1917, when the first All-Russian Congress of Soviets met in Petrograd, 350 towns, villages and military bases throughout Russia were in a position to send representatives.

Although the Petrograd Soviet's meetings could be rough and disorderly, it could at least claim to have direct democratic authority and its members were united in wishing to bring about a true revolution and achieve workers' power. With the workers behind it, the Soviet had more support than the Provisional Government. Yet it made no attempt to take complete control, and was cautious in its approaches to the Provisional Government. It has been suggested that this was because the Soviet's leaders did not feel that capitalism was advanced enough in Russia for the country to become a socialist state.

SOURCE 6.6

Nikolai Sukhanov, an early Soviet leader, later gave his view on why the Soviet did not take control.

> Our revolution lacked both the material power and the indispensable prerequisites for an immediate Socialist transformation of Russia... The Soviet democracy had to entrust the power to the propertied elements, its class enemy, without whose participation it could not now master the technique of administration, nor deal with the forces of tsarism and of the bourgeoisie united against it.

Quoted in Christian, D. 1997. **Imperial and Soviet Russia.** *Basingstoke, UK. Palgrave Macmillan. pp. 181–82.*

QUESTION

Would you agree with Sukhanov's views in Source 6.6? Explain your answer.

This ideological explanation may well hide a more practical one: the Soviet leadership actually feared the responsibility of governing. As the Soviet was primarily composed of radical socialist intellectuals, and only seven of the first 42 members of the executive committee were workers themselves, the leaders may well have doubted their ability to control the strong forces they were representing.

Following negotiations conducted by **Alexander Kerensky** (who was the only member of both the Provisional Government and the Soviet), the Soviet agreed to cooperate with the Provisional Government – in return for several promised concessions. These included a general amnesty for political prisoners; the granting of basic civil liberties; the abolition of legal inequalities based on class, religion and nationality; the right to organise trade unions and to strike; and the promise of a Constituent Assembly.

Alexander Kerensky (1881–1970):

He joined the Socialist Revolutionary Party in 1905 and in 1912 was elected to the State *Duma*. He was regarded as a champion of the working class and in February, 1917 was appointed as Minister of Justice in the new Provisional Government as well as sitting in the Petrograd Soviet. He became Minister of War (May) and head of government (July). He supported the July Offensive but, on its failure, appointed Lavr Kornilov to replace Brusilov, leading to the 'coup' which endangered the regime. In October, he fled Petrograd on the eve of the Bolshevik takeover and his attempt to return with a military force was defeated. He hid in Finland until 1918 and subsequently moved to Western Europe and USA.

In line with its cautious approach at this stage, the Soviet made no attempt to gain concessions on land redistribution or the nationalisation of industry.

For its part, the Provisional Government welcomed the approval of the revolutionary Soviet, which at least had some control over the masses. Their agreement laid the foundations for the period of *dvoevlastie* (meaning 'Dual Power'), whereby Russia was governed by an alliance of the Provisional Government and Soviet. Between them, the two groups could claim to represent the whole spectrum of Russian society, except for the minority of extreme tsarists.

The Provisional Government's early decrees were popular. On 26 April, it promised that the power of the state would in future be based on the consent of the Russian people, rather than on violence and coercion (force). Freedom of religion and the press were proclaimed, the death penalty was abolished for soldiers who deserted from the front line, and the tsarist police force was replaced by a 'people's militia'. The tsar's provincial governors were also dismissed and their duties were handed over to the elected *zemstva*. Such changes suggested that the Provisional Government and Soviet would together be able to plan a better, fairer future for the Russian people.

The problems faced by the Dual Power system

Despite all the initial optimism, the Dual Power arrangement faced many problems. The Provisional Government and the Soviet had very different ideas as to what might bring about a 'better future' for Russia. The moderate, liberal Dual Power government that assumed control was therefore forced to rely on extreme radicals with whom it had little in common. As the Soviet was at first dominated by Social Revolutionaries and Mensheviks who did not agree with all that the Provisional Government wanted, the Dual Power arrangement was always bound to be difficult.

The removal of the tsarist police force and other instruments of coercion left the Provisional Government with none of the traditional means of disciplining disobedient troops or enforcing its will in the towns and countryside. The Soviet proved unhelpful and tended to encourage (rather than prevent) disturbances among peasants and workers. In March, there were peasant disorders in 34 districts; in April, there were 174 disturbances; in July, there were 325.

The supply of munitions was disrupted, as order broke down in the Petrograd factories, and large areas of the countryside were soon beyond the government's control. The problems were all made worse by the Provisional Government's determination to continue the war. Most ministers had seen the tsar's abdication as a way of improving Russia's chances in the war. Rather than seeking to end the fighting, they hoped the change of government would offer an opportunity to renew their efforts and fight more effectively.

However, the politicians' attitude was very different from that of the mass of the population. Most ordinary Russians believed the February revolution would mark the end of the problems – of tsarist control and also of wartime deprivation. But in April, Milyukov announced that the government would continue fighting until a 'just peace' had been won.

This led to a massive anti-war demonstration in Petrograd, which forced the resignations of Milyukov and Guchkov.

The peasants, who made up most of the conscripts, had no interest in fighting the Germans. They were far keener to return to their villages and seize land for themselves. Propaganda spread subversive ideas at the front, and the number of military desertions rose. There had been 195 000 desertions between 1914 and February 1917; between March and May 1917, there were over 365 000. General Alexei Brusilov undertook a major offensive in Galicia, in June, in the hope of rallying the nation. However, the Russian advance was beaten back (with heavy losses) and anti-war sentiment grew still stronger. Desertions reached a peak, and the death penalty was reinstated in an effort to control the troops.

Although the government tried to pass laws to satisfy both upper and lower classes, it proved unable to reconcile the two and instead ended up alienating both. The upper classes turned against a government that failed to maintain order, protect their property or achieve wartime success. A clear consensus emerged among the landowners, entrepreneurs and army officers that the country needed a stronger government.

The right-wing feared the Provisional Government had been hijacked by the left. Milyukov and Guchkov were replaced by socialists from the Soviet and Victor Chernov (founder of the Social Revolutionary Party) became minister of agriculture, Kerensky became minister of war and two further Mensheviks were added to the Cabinet. The replacement of Prince Lvov as chairman, with Kerensky in July 1917, further heightened the right-wingers' fear of a left-wing takeover.

There was an attempted coup in early July, which was blamed on the Bolsheviks. However, this was perhaps unfair, since the Bolsheviks did not organise the coup but only joined in so as to maintain their profile. After this, the élites increasingly pinned their hopes on General Lavr Kornilov, whom Kerensky appointed as commander-in-chief of the army on 16 July. Kornilov appeared a likely candidate to restore order and he had the support of Milyukov, Rodzianko and Guchkov, as well as the backing of the new Union of Army and Navy Officers.

Figure 6.6: General Kornilov inspecting the troops in August 1917.

At the end of August, Kornilov ordered six regiments of troops from the mighty Caucasian Native Division to march on Petrograd – presumably intending to crush the Soviet and establish a military dictatorship. However, Kerensky (who had at first supported Kornilov) panicked and asked the Soviet to help defeat the general. Kerensky released imprisoned Bolsheviks and provided the Soviet with weapons from the government's armouries. Kornilov (who, according to Alekseev, the former Army Chief of Staff, had 'a lion's heart and the brains of a sheep') found his supply lines cut. The coup failed, and Kornilov and his supporters were arrested for treason.

KEY CONCEPTS ACTIVITY

Change and continuity: Create a vertical timeline of the year 1917. On one side of your line indicate the key changes that occurred during the year; on the other indicate elements of continuity. Categorise these as political, economic, social and connected to the war.

The lower classes also became alienated from the government. The continuation of the war was a major issue, but the government's refusal to do anything about land redistribution was equally important. Even though the peasants were actively seizing land, it was argued that nothing could be done until after the election of the Constituent Assembly. However, immediate hopes for such an assembly were dashed, as the Provisional Government claimed it was impossible to organise elections in wartime conditions. An electoral commission was eventually set up in May, to arrange elections for November. But working people remained suspicious that the 'bourgeois' government was deliberately delaying a move to greater democracy in order to preserve its own power.

Workers were also disappointed to find that they experienced little real improvement in their conditions. Although the government granted an eight-hour day, the real value of wages fell even more rapidly than before, as prices rose. In January 1917 prices were 300% of 1914 levels. By October they had risen to 755%. Food supplies were also unreliable, with frequent shortages.

Furthermore, in August the government confirmed the right of factory owners to dismiss workers. It also banned meetings of factory committees during working hours (despite their previous acceptance of unions, factory committees and strikes). Not surprisingly, many workers claimed that the Provisional Government was not legitimate and said that they would only take orders from the Soviet.

The overthrow of the Dual Power in October 1917

The October revolution, which overthrew the Provisional Government, followed a Bolshevik coup. However, it is unlikely that this coup could have come about if there had not been profound disillusionment with the Provisional Government by that time.

In February 1917, the Bolsheviks were still only a small party of 25 000 members. They had just 40 representatives in the 1500-strong Soviet, and all their major leaders were living abroad or in exile. The likelihood of this group staging a coup must have seemed very remote in the early months of 1917. Although Lev Kamenev and Joseph Stalin returned in mid-March, they simply followed the other left-wing socialists in supporting the Provisional Government.

It was only after Lenin's return in April, with the new promises of 'peace, bread, land' and 'all power to the soviets' contained in his 'April Theses' – which the Party had initially rejected – that the Bolsheviks increasingly won over the workers, peasants and soldiers. As the Provisional Government grew weaker, so Bolshevik membership rose. By June, most factory committees in Petrograd, as well as the sailors at the Kronstadt naval base, were all supporting the Bolshevik cause. At the first All-Russian Congress of Soviets that month, the Bolsheviks had 105 delegates (though this was still fewer than the Mensheviks with 248, and the Social Revolutionaries with 285). Trotsky and his followers joined the Bolsheviks in July. On 3 July, pro-Bolshevik units in the army refused to be sent to the front. They joined other frustrated left-wing radical protesters on the streets, including the sailors from Kronstadt. A crowd of 250 000 people went to the Tauride Palace, demanding an end to the war and a handover of power to the soviets.

The riots, which were referred to as 'the July Days', were not organised by the Bolshevik leadership. However, after the disturbances were suppressed by government forces two days later, *Pravda* (the Bolshevik newspaper) was closed down and the Bolsheviks were blamed. Kerensky published letters showing that the Bolsheviks were receiving finance from the Germans. This undermined their popularity and several Bolshevik leaders, including Trotsky, were arrested (although Trotsky was soon released because insufficient evidence could be found against him). Lenin was accused of being a German agent. He chose to flee, along with Grigori Zinoviev, and eventually crossed into Finland.

The Bolshevik Party survived the damage. Although officially banned, it managed to hold a secret conference in Petrograd in mid-July. In early August, when Kornilov staged his coup, the Bolsheviks not only gained a pardon for their leaders (except Lenin) but also weapons, which their Red Guards used against Kornilov but subsequently refused to return.

By early September, the Bolsheviks had gained a majority on the Executive Committee of the Petrograd Soviet (and shortly afterwards in the Moscow Soviet too). They also won local government elections in several towns and cities. The Executive Committee therefore readily supported a Bolshevik resolution that power should be transferred to the soviets. Trotsky became chairman and on 16 October created a Military Revolutionary Committee, to give the Soviet a fighting force. It was no secret that plans for a Bolshevik coup were underway. On 22 October, Kerensky tried to prevent the coup by ordering the arrest of the Military Revolutionary Committee. The next day, Bolshevik newspapers were closed down and the telephone lines to the Bolshevik headquarters at the Smolny Institute were cut.

Kerensky's action provoked the very coup that he had been seeking to avoid. On 24 October, under the direction of the Military Revolutionary Committee, Bolshevik Red Guards (mainly young Bolshevik factory workers) and other troops loyal to the Soviet took action. They seized key communication points in the city (including bridges, railways stations, the central post office and the telephone exchange) and met very little resistance.

The so-called revolution of 25 October was in reality quite a tame affair. Military units surrounded the Winter Palace, where the remaining members of the Provisional Government were meeting. Between 9 and 10 pm, sailors aboard the battleship *Aurora*, moored on the River Neva, fired a series of blank shots. These did little damage but were sufficient to persuade most of the teenage cadets and women soldiers defending the palace to surrender. Shots were also fired from the artillery in the Peter and Paul Fortress on the opposite side of the River Neva (although only one actually hit the Palace).

Figure 6.7: A propaganda painting showing the Bolsheviks storming the Winter Palace.

On hearing the shots, soldiers entered through a back door and eventually found their way to the room where the remaining members of the government were waiting. The government representatives were duly arrested. (Kerensky had already managed to escape in a car belonging to the US Embassy. After a failed attempt to rally loyal forces, he lived out the rest of his life in exile in Paris and New York.) The incident was soon over and there were only two recorded deaths.

ACTIVITY

As a class, establish 10 to 12 reasons as to why the Provisional Government and Dual Power were overthrown in October 1917 and print each on a card. Divide into small groups, each with a complete set of cards. Each group should order the cards according to their importance. Having compared results, repeat the exercise, ordering the cards thematically.

Problems of interpretation

In one sense, it is easy to understand why there was a second revolution in 1917 because the February revolution had clearly left many issues unresolved. However, the enormous growth of Bolshevik power and influence between February and October also had a big impact on the nature and timing of the October revolution.

Traditional Soviet historians, at least until the end of the Stalinist era (1953), interpreted the October revolution as 'logically predetermined'. For many years, it was regarded in Russia as the 'victory of the workers' (represented by the Soviet) over 'the bourgeoisie' (represented by the Provisional Government). All these events were thought to have been guided, of course, by the wise hand of Lenin.

The Western approach during the early Cold War, at least until the 1960s, was to brand the Bolsheviks as a ruthless minority party. According to Western historians, the Bolsheviks' determination enabled them to impose their will on the majority in October, when the Provisional Government was in a weakened state. Indeed, these historians saw the behaviour of the leaders of the October revolution as foreshadowing Stalin's totalitarian approach (complete state control, under one all-powerful leader).

Theory of Knowledge

History and bias

How easy is it for historians to avoid national bias when writing history? What other forms of bias can affect the way historians write?

Since the 1960s, there have been considerable reappraisals on both sides. This became particularly marked in the East with the introduction of *glasnost* ('openness') in the 1980s and the break-up of the USSR in 1991. These events not only allowed greater freedom of interpretation, but also permitted access to archives that had previously been kept hidden. Some post-Stalinist historians, such as Eduard Burdzhalov and Pavel Volobuev, bravely challenged the official Communist Party line. Likewise, some Western historians (critical of American policies in the years following the Vietnam War) also challenged earlier Western accounts.

6

Yet it is only in the last 20 years that historians have come to accept that the October revolution was the result of a variety of factors (economic and social as well as political and linked to its leadership). It is now widely believed that Bolshevism succeeded less because of the party's centralisation, unity and discipline (all of which have been questioned) than because of its flexibility in the face of circumstances. Nevertheless, the question of how much weight should be assigned to each of these factors is still unresolved.

Whatever the underlying causes, it is now widely agreed that the actual events of 25–26 October were instigated by a small band of determined revolutionaries at a time when the Provisional Government had neither the support nor the coercive powers needed to retain control. Despite the later Bolshevik myths, partly spread by Sergei Eisenstein's film *October* (in which more damage was done to the Winter Palace than in the real October 1917), the 'storming' was not a spectacular people-led uprising. In fact, at the time, the majority of those living in Petrograd – let alone the rest of Russia – were hardly aware of what was going on. It should also be remembered that the 'revolution' was supposedly carried out in the name of the Petrograd Soviet, through its Military Committee. It was on the Petrograd Soviet's authority that the Provisional Government was ultimately disbanded and power transferred to the Second All-Russian Congress of Soviets. However, in practice, the victory was dominated by the Bolsheviks and they rapidly made it their own.

The historical debate about the October 1917 coup is discussed further in the Exam practice section at the end of Chapter 7. Some of the questions include the nature of the roles of Lenin and Trotsky, and whether it was indeed a Bolshevik coup or simply a tide of revolution on which the Bolsheviks were prepared to ride.

6.4 What roles did Lenin and Trotsky play in the events of 1917?

In many respects, the October revolution was the work of two very single-minded 'professional' revolutionaries: Lenin, who provided the leadership and fire; and Trotsky, who contributed the military brain. Neither had been in a position to play any part in the February revolution, since they were both in exile. Nevertheless, once the autocracy crumbled, both were determined to return to Russia and influence its future.

Neither Lenin nor Trotsky was very familiar with the lives of the ordinary people of Russia. They were both educated men from relatively wealthy backgrounds, who had spent most of their adult lives abroad. Lenin had lived outside Russia since 1900 (except for a very brief return during the 1905 revolution) and had spent the latter years in Switzerland. Meanwhile, Trotsky had spent most of the previous ten years in exile, living in various cities including Vienna, Zurich, Paris and – from January 1917 – New York. The two men shared a deep hatred of the old regime and a commitment to Marxism and political activism.

From Switzerland, Lenin tried to gain re-entry to Russia in 1917 through negotiations with the Germans, who believed his return would cause chaos and so undermine the Russian war effort. Nevertheless, the Germans were prepared to offer him safe passage by train through Frankfurt, Berlin and Stockholm (in neutral Sweden), although only in a 'sealed' train, confining Lenin and his band of followers to a locked compartment.

Lenin's arrival at Petrograd on 3 April marked the beginning of a series of events that would propel Russia towards the October revolution. Lenin was uncertain of what sort of reception awaited him, and half-expected to be arrested on leaving the train. However, his fears turned out to be unfounded. His reputation had gone before him, and he was greeted by a cheering band of soldiers and workers who were convinced that Lenin could somehow ensure that their needs were met.

SOURCE 6.7

On arriving in Petrograd in 1917, Lenin addressed the hundreds of workers and soldiers who thronged the station:

> Dear comrades, soldiers, sailors and workers. I am happy to greet in you the victorious Russian revolution; to greet you as the advance guard of the international proletarian army. The hour is not far when the people will turn their weapons against their capitalist exploiters. The Russian revolution achieved by you has opened a new epoch. ... The worldwide socialist revolution is dawning; European capitalism is on the brink of collapse. Soldiers, comrades! We must fight for a socialist revolution in Russia! We must fight until [we achieve] the total victory of the proletariat! Long live the worldwide socialist revolution!

Partly quoted in Sixsmith, M. 2011. **Russia.** *London, UK. BBC Books. p. 194: extended with information from the website http://en.international-ism.org which quotes* **History of the Russian Revolution (Vol. 1, Ch. 15),** *page 280–281*

QUESTION

With reference to origin and purpose, what are the value and limitations of Source 6.7 for historians studying Lenin's leadership in 1917?

Lenin's absolute confidence that a proletarian revolution would soon be achieved within Russia ensured that he stood out from other socialist leaders, who had argued that Russia had to go through a bourgeois/liberal phase before it would be possible to establish a working man's government. Lenin had reached the conclusion (as had Trotsky before him) that it was both possible and desirable to create a working–class government in Russia, despite the country's backwardness. He believed that the creation of such a government would help trigger revolutions in the more developed capitalist countries, which would in turn give support to the Russian workers. This theory of 'permanent revolution' made a proletarian revolution an immediate possibility. It also made it vital to have a policy of 'no compromise' with the bourgeoisie. The first two Bolsheviks to return from exile (in Siberia), Stalin and Kamenev, supported the Provisional Government. However, Lenin demonstrated his authority and leadership by declaring himself firmly against any such agreement.

Lenin also believed that the Provisional Government's liberal democracy was not in the proletariat's interests. He described it as a mere façade for the dictatorship (rule) of the bourgeoisie. Furthermore, because the trade unions wanted to work with the capitalists to improve their members' conditions, he condemned these unions too. According to Lenin, true revolutionary action on the proletariat's behalf required a vanguard party (a pioneering group) to educate the workers and peasants politically. This education would help them rise above the low political expectations of 'trade-union consciousness'. Lenin's theorising helped him to justify the Bolsheviks' quest for power. He claimed that the Bolsheviks were that vanguard party, who would develop 'true revolutionary class consciousness' and fulfil the 'dictatorship of the proletariat'. In other words, they would rule by, and in the interests of, the ordinary working people.

Lenin's first act in the Petrograd Soviet was to produce a manifesto, which became known as the April Theses. In this manifesto, he urged the soviets to overthrow the Provisional Government and create a dictatorship of the proletariat. He concluded with the powerful slogan 'All power to the soviets!' even though the Bolshevik Party was, as yet, only a minor influence within the soviets.

The April Theses also made promises that other leaders had hesitated to offer, such as an end to the war, land for the peasants and an improvement in the food supplies in the towns. This was just what the workers, peasants and soldiers wanted to hear, and 'peace, bread and land' became their rallying cry. Lenin rapidly understood and responded to the public mood. By June 1917, he was able to stand up in the Petrograd Soviet and declare, 'To those who say there is no political party ready to take full responsibility for power in Russia, I say, Yes there is! … We Bolsheviks will not shirk the task. We are ready here and now to assume the fullness of power.'

Trotsky left New York in March, but his ship was detained by British naval officials in Canada and he only arrived back in Russia on 4 May. Although Trotsky shared Lenin's ideas on permanent revolution, he did not commit himself to the Bolshevik Party immediately. Nevertheless, he quickly established his influence, joining the Executive Committee of the All-Russian Congress of Soviets, which had been formed in June.

Trotsky was arrested after the unsuccessful July Days rising in Petrograd. While he was in prison, he became a committed Bolshevik. After his release, following Kornilov's unsuccessful uprising, Trotsky was elected chairman of the Petrograd Soviet on 26 September. (The Bolsheviks had recently come to dominate the Petrograd Soviet by altering the membership regulations.) Trotsky was an expert strategist and he immediately set about turning the Soviet into an arm of the Bolshevik Party.

On 5 October, the commander of the Petrograd Military District, following Kerensky's instructions, ordered most of the capital's revolutionary-leaning garrison units to prepare for immediate transfer to the front. This action sparked a general mutiny, with most of the troops declaring their loyalty to the Petrograd Soviet.

On 9 October, the Soviet adopted a militant resolution, written by Trotsky. This called for the creation of a 'military revolutionary centre' to 'facilitate the defence of Petrograd from the attacks being openly prepared by military and civil Kornilovites'. This new body was known as the Military Revolutionary Committee.

Lenin, still in exile in Finland, believed the time was right for an immediate coup. However, his letters to the Bolshevik Central Committee in Petrograd did not find immediate favour. Even Trotsky initially urged that they should wait for the second Congress of Soviets before launching the revolution. Such was Lenin's frustration that he returned secretly and in disguise to a meeting of the Central Committee in Petrograd, on 10 October. At the meeting, he bullied the committee into supporting his plans. Trotsky was persuaded and took Lenin's side against Zinoviev and Kamenev. The vote was eventually agreed: ten in favour of an immediate coup, and two (Zinoviev and Kamenev) against such action.

It was largely left to Trotsky to organise the revolution. Speakers were sent round factories to ensure the vital support that was needed for success. Trotsky took personal charge of the new Military Revolutionary Committee of the Soviet, which (from 18 October onwards) began to gather troops at the Bolshevik headquarters in the Smolny Institute. Since the Mensheviks and Social Revolutionaries refused to join this group, it became a Bolshevik fighting force, which was made up of militias from the Bolshevik Red Guards, former soldiers and policemen.

Figure 6.8: Red Guards marching through Moscow in 1917.

The Garrison Crisis escalated and the Military Revolutionary Committee appointed commissars who were sent to all the city's troop units to win their loyalty. In total, 15 of the 18 garrisons declared allegiance to the Soviet rather than the Provisional Government. According to Czech historian Michael Reiman, this was the beginning of the October revolution. He wrote:

'Already on October 21st and 22nd the Military Revolutionary Committee, in effect, took upon itself authority over the [Petrograd] garrison. Its actions, from both a practical and a judicial standpoint, would be considered by any nation a clear case of mutiny and insurrection.'

Trotsky too argued, in *Lessons of October*, that the Petrograd Soviet entered a state of armed revolution before 25 October. He wrote:

'From the moment when we, as the Petrograd Soviet, invalidated Kerensky's order transferring two-thirds of the garrison to the front, we had actually entered a state of armed insurrection… the outcome of the insurrection of October 25 was at least three-quarters settled, if not more, the moment that we opposed

the transfer of the Petrograd garrison and created the Military Revolutionary Committee.'

Problems of interpretation

This interpretation of the events of October 1917 suggests that Trotsky's role was vital to the success of the revolution. It also suggests that he played a bigger part than Lenin, who eventually emerged from hiding to take charge on the night of 25 October only after the Military Revolutionary Committee had directed its units to seize the key points of the capital. But Eisenstein's film *October*, which originally gave both Lenin and Trotsky starring roles, was re-cut in the Stalinist era to portray Trotsky as a coward who hesitated at the start of revolution while the Bolshevik troops marched forward. Consequently, Trotsky was never given any credit by Soviet historians for his actions in October 1917. Indeed, some books on the period still emphasise the importance of Lenin's role, at Trotsky's expense.

The parts played by Lenin and Trotsky, both individually and collectively, are still interpreted in different ways. For example, Richard Pipes suggests that Lenin's drive, as the leader of a coup, was the main factor behind the October revolution. However, he also acknowledges the crucial role played by Trotsky in the actual organisation of the revolution. His view is that Lenin and Trotsky led an 'aggressive minority' and exploited the confusion that existed in Russia by October 1917 in order to seize power.

Stephen Smith challenges this interpretation and stresses the importance of the lower ranks of the Bolshevik Party. He also puts forward the view that the revolution was essentially a 'popular uprising', which both Lenin and Trotsky harnessed but did not propel.

Sheila Fitzpatrick also takes this line and questions Lenin's control over the party. She emphasises the importance of the radicalism of workers, peasants and soldiers. While she acknowledges Lenin's ability to mobilise the masses and his mastery of propaganda, and praises Trotsky's organisational skills, she suggests the revolution was driven 'from below'.

Alexander Rabinowitch supports this view and stresses the extent to which the leadership responded to grass-roots radicalism in the cities. In short, while no one denies the significance of the parts played by both Lenin and Trotsky, the most recent historical appraisals suggest their roles were more organisational than inspirational.

KEY CONCEPTS ACTIVITY

Significance and perspectives: Work with a partner to create a diagram that provides the key facts to support detailed appraisal of the roles of Lenin and Trotsky in the events of 1917. Take one individual each, and complete the diagram as far as possible. You can return to this diagram and add further detail after you have studied Bolshevik Russia.

Paper 3 exam practice

Question

Discuss the reasons why, despite the abdication of the tsar in March 1917, there was a second revolution in Russia in October 1917.
[15 marks]

Skill

Avoiding a narrative-based answer

Examiner's tips

Even once you have read the question carefully (and so avoided the temptation of including irrelevant material), produced your plan and written your introductory paragraph, it is still possible to go wrong.

By 'writing a narrative answer', history examiners mean supplying material that is potentially relevant to the question (and may well be very precise and accurate) **but** which is not clearly used in a way that answers the question. Instead of supporting comments that respond to the question, it merely **describes** what happened.

Your essay should be an argument, not simply an 'answer' in which you 'tell a story' or describe issues and developments. You should **address the demands/key words of the question** – and your response needs to be consistently analytical. You need to link each paragraph to the question and to the previous paragraph, in order to produce a clear 'joined-up' answer.

There is an increased danger of lapsing into a narrative essay when answering the final question – especially if you are running short of time. Despite all your good intentions at the start of the exam, you may be so keen to get started on your final (and perhaps least well-known) question that you set out without sufficient planning, before forming a proper judgement and so with little idea of 'where' you are going. If you are not careful, this will lead you to produce an **account**, as opposed to an analysis – writing around the question, rather than answering it directly. So, even if you are short of time, try to think and plan first and then write several analytical paragraphs that convey a view and show your understanding of the supporting information.

A good way of avoiding a narrative approach is to keep referring back to the question and to use its key words in your answer. This will help you to produce an answer that is focused on the specific demands of the question – rather than just giving information about the broad topic or period.

For this question, you will need to cover the following aspects:

- what changed as a result of the tsar's abdication in February 1917 – which grievances were resolved, and which remained or emerged
- why there was a revolution in October 1917 – the importance of the remaining/new grievances after February 1917 versus the importance of other factors
- your judgement as to why there was a second revolution in October 1917 – whether the tsar's abdication resolved anything, and whether it made the second revolution more or less likely.

Common mistakes

Every year, even candidates who have clearly revised well (and therefore have a good knowledge of the topic and of any historical debate surrounding it) still end up producing mainly narrative-based or descriptive answers. Very often, this is the result of not having drawn up a proper plan.

The extracts from the student's answer below show an approach that essentially just describes the revolutions of 1917, without any analysis linking the answer to the question.

Remember to refer to the simplified Paper 3 mark scheme in Chapter 8.

Sample paragraphs of narrative-based approach

Nicholas II abdicated in February/March 1917 because of the riots that broke out in Petrograd. On Thursday 23 February, International Women's Day, a march of women through the city centre turned political. Women who had been queuing for bread and unemployed workers from the nearby Putilov Works joined in. Fifty factories stopped work in the course of that day and there was chaos in

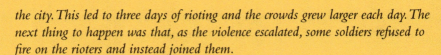

the city. This led to three days of rioting and the crowds grew larger each day. The next thing to happen was that, as the violence escalated, some soldiers refused to fire on the rioters and instead joined them.

By this point, almost the whole of the city's workforce has come out on strike and Petrograd is at a standstill. Although the duma president Rodzianko contacts Nicholas to tell him that all is not well and that he needs to return, when Nicholas gets the telegram, he ignores it. Then he has second thoughts and orders Major-General Khabalov, who is the commander in Petrograd, to open fire on the crowds. Following this, even more soldiers mutiny and this turns the protests into a revolution…

[The rest of the essay continues in the same way. There is plenty of accurate/relevant description of the February/March revolution and the events of March to August 1917, but time runs out and the later events are rushed and less detailed. There is only just time to mention that there was a revolution in October/November 1917, in the final paragraph. The whole point of the question – why there was a revolution in Russia in October/November 1917 – has been missed.]

> **EXAMINER'S COMMENT**
>
> This example, while accurate and detailed, shows what examiners mean by a narrative/descriptive answer. Note the 'time words' (such as 'By this point', 'Then' and 'Following this') and the way the writer slips into the present tense in order to 'tell the story'. This is something you should not copy!

Activity

In this chapter, the focus is on avoiding writing narrative-based answers. Using the information from this chapter, and any other sources of information available to you, try to answer **one** of the following Paper 3 practice questions in a way that avoids description. Do not use 'time words' and make sure your paragraphs begin with comments linking them to the question, so that they do not lead into narrative.

Paper 3 practice questions

1 To what extent was the First World War responsible for the final crisis of autocracy in February 1917?

2 Compare and contrast the causes, nature and consequences of the two Russian revolutions of 1917.

3 'The Russian revolutions of 1917 showed the depths of the Russian people's discontent.' To what extent do you agree with this statement?

4 To what extent did the Dual Power arrangement prevent the Provisional Government from consolidating and maintaining its power in Russia?

5 'The events of October/November 1917 were a protest against the inadequacies of the Provisional Government'. To what extent do you agree with this statement?

6 Examine the roles of Lenin and Trotsky in the 1917 Bolshevik Revolution in Russia.

7

Lenin's Russia, 1917–1924

TIMELINE

1917 **26 Oct:** Second All-Russian Congress of Soviets creates government, Soviet of People's Commissars, led by Lenin

Dec: Armistice (ceasefire) negotiated with Germans; Cheka formed

1918 **5 Jan:** Constituent Assembly meets and is dispersed

1 Feb: Gregorian calendar introduced

3 Mar: Treaty of Brest-Litovsk

4 Mar: A small party of British troops land at Murmansk

6–8 Mar: 7th Bolshevik Party Conference; 'Communist Party' name adopted

12 Mar: Capital transferred from Petrograd to Moscow

16–17 Jul: Murder of the tsar and his family

1 Aug: British attacked and occupied Arkhangelsk

1919 **8 Mar:** Party Secretariat and Politburo established; Comintern founded

Apr–Oct: Kolchak heads attack from western Siberia, Ukraine and Estonia

Nov: All White attacks defeated

Dec: Vesenkha (Supreme Council of National Economy) created

1920 **Apr:** Polish attack towards Kiev; Soviet counter-attack reaches Warsaw

Oct: Polish counter-attack

Nov: Polish armistice

1921 **Feb:** *Tambov* rising

Mar: Kronstadt uprising; 10th Communist Party Congress

1922 **Apr:** *Treaty of Rapallo*

Dec: USSR formed

1924 **Jan:** Lenin dies

KEY QUESTIONS

- How did the Bolsheviks consolidate power and win the Russian Civil War?
- Why was War Communism introduced in 1918 and replaced by the NEP in 1921?
- To what extent did the new Soviet state rely on terror and coercion?
- What was the relationship between Bolshevik Russia and the rest of the world?

The Bolshevik position in October 1917 was far from secure. In the following months, Vladimir Lenin showed both pragmatism and ruthlessness in cementing Bolshevik rule. He purged his opponents, set up the *Cheka* (a secret police force) and dismissed the elected Constituent Assembly at gunpoint when it failed to return a Bolshevik majority. He also, at some cost, made a much-needed peace treaty with the Germans, brought in measures to promote social equality, and provided the peasants with land.

The spring of 1918 saw the outbreak of a bloody civil war. This brought with it the policy of War Communism, which involved the requisitioning of the peasants' grain and the spread of the 'Red Terror' in a bid to destroy 'class enemies'. Although the Bolsheviks won the war, such policy extremes produced a crisis in 1921, when the Tambov peasant rebellion and the Kronstadt mutiny forced a change of strategy. The New Economic Policy (NEP) followed. This permitted private trade and partial capitalism, but there was an accompanying ban on factions within the Communist Party. Other parties (which had continued to exist during the civil war, even though their leaders were often imprisoned or executed) were also banned. Coming on top of the increased centralisation of the civil war years, this ban meant that Russia hardened into a tightly controlled and repressive state. While Russia grew more stable, more internationally accepted and economically stronger, it also therefore became more dependent on its leader, Lenin.

Overview

- Lenin's party was still in the minority in October 1917. He out-manoeuvred his rivals and forced the closure of the elected Constituent Assembly. This turned out to be the first step towards the creation of a one-party state.
- The Treaty of Brest-Litovsk was signed with Germany to end Russia's fighting in the First World War, even though its harsh terms caused discord.
- Between 1918 and 1921, the Bolsheviks fought a bitter civil war against their opponents, the Whites (who unleashed a 'White Terror'), in order to establish their hold over Russia. The tsar and his family were murdered in 1918 as a result of this war.
- To support their war effort, the Bolsheviks introduced a policy of War Communism, which put a great deal of pressure on peasants whose grain was requisitioned by the state.
- The combined effects of the Tambov peasant rising and the Kronstadt rebellion forced Lenin to change his economic policy in 1921 and introduce his New Economic Policy (NEP).
- Despite greater liberalisation of the economy, political repression (including terror and coercion) remained as central to communist rule as they had been during the civil war period.
- A temporary ban on other political parties – and on factions within the Communist Party – was also passed in 1921. This stifled debate within the Communist Party, reinforced moves towards greater centralisation, and increased the party leader's authority. Eventually, after Lenin's death in 1924, Stalin made these bans permanent.
- According to the terms of the treaty signed at Riga in March 1921 after the Russo-Polish War, Russia lost a considerable amount of territory to Poland.
- The relationship between the communist state and other countries was slightly eased by the ending of the civil war and the introduction of the NEP. Nevertheless, Russia remained vulnerable in a world that was hostile to communism.

Figure 7.1: A propaganda poster for Lenin, 'the people's hero'.

7.1 How did the Bolsheviks consolidate power and win the Russian Civil War?

Just over 500 of the 670 delegates present at the Second All-Russian Congress of Soviets, which met at the Smolny Institute on 25 October 1917, favoured a socialist government. However, not all the delegates approved of the Bolshevik revolution. The Menshevik leader Irakli Tsereteli predicted that Bolshevik power would last no longer than three weeks. There was even opposition to the revolution from Grigori Zinoviev and Lev Kamenev (within the Bolshevik Party). Meanwhile, Lenin and Trotsky clung to their belief that an international revolution would break out, and that this would save their own achievements.

The establishment of control

The Congress elected a new committee. The Executive Committee elected the previous June had been dominated by moderate socialists, but the new one had a majority of Bolsheviks and left-wing Social Revolutionaries. The Mensheviks and the right-wing faction of the Social Revolutionaries were unhappy at the way events were moving. They heckled Lenin and accused him of using violence to seize power illegally. In desperation, they walked out of the Congress, leaving a Bolshevik and left-wing Social Revolutionary coalition in control. Their action simply played into the Bolsheviks' hands, allowing them and their left-wing allies to dominate the Congress. Trotsky shouted at the retiring delegates the famous words, 'You're finished, you pitiful bunch of bankrupts. Get out of here to where you belong – in the dustbin of history.' Nevertheless, their seats were left empty – should they wish to return.

With the announcement of the collapse of the Provisional Government and the arrest of its ministers on the morning of 26 October, the Second Congress of Soviets declared itself the supreme authority in Russia. It appointed a new government – *Sovnarkom* (the Soviet of People's Commissars). Initially, this was entirely composed of Bolsheviks, and had Lenin as chairman and Trotsky as the commissar for foreign affairs. Therefore, in theory at least, the Bolsheviks assumed power as the majority party in the much-reduced Congress of Soviets. Taking power in the name of the soviets proved an advantage, since it helped win support from workers and peasants. However, the Bolsheviks were still in a very insecure position, with limited power outside Petrograd. They could not rely on the army or the police; the civil servants refused to serve under them; and the bankers refused to provide finance. It was only after ten days that the state bank was persuaded to hand over its reserves – and then only when it was threatened with armed force.

SOURCE 7.1

Lenin made a firm declaration in his decree announcing the assumption of power on 26 October 1917.

> The Soviet authority will at once propose a democratic peace to all nations and an immediate armistice on all fronts. It will safeguard the transfer without compensation of all land – landlord, imperial and monastic to the peasant committees; it will defend the soldiers' rights, introducing a complete democratisation of the army; it will establish workers' control over industry; it will ensure the Convocation of the Constituent Assembly on the date set; it will supply the cities with bread and the villages with articles of first necessity and it will secure to all nationalities inhabiting Russia the right of self determination. All local authority shall be transferred to the soviets of workers', soldiers' and peasants' deputies, which are charged with the task of enforcing revolutionary order. The fate of the revolution and democratic peace is in your hands!

Quoted in Christian, D. 1997. **Imperial and Soviet Russia.** *Basingstoke, UK. Palgrave Macmillan. pp. 208–09.*

QUESTION

What is the significance of Source 7.1 for a study of the Bolshevik consolidation of power in October 1917?

In order to fulfil his promises and show himself a man of his word, Lenin followed his decree on the assumption of power with a decree on peace and another on land. The decree on peace (following earlier promises) guaranteed an immediate end to the war, and a peace 'without annexation and indemnities'. The decree on land abolished private ownership of land and legitimised the seizures of land by peasants that were already well underway. It stated that there was to be no compensation for landowners because the land belonged to the 'entire people' and could not be 'owned' by anyone. Recognising peasant 'ownership' was a contradictory but pragmatic (practical) move. There was a chance that it would help reduce peasant support for the Social Revolutionaries and would also provide a breathing space for the Bolsheviks to consolidate their rule.

For the workers, the Bolsheviks promised an eight-hour working day and social insurance schemes to cover them for old age and unemployment. In fact, workers had already begun to take over factories that had been closed by their owners. Their actions were therefore legitimised by the workers' control decree issued in November. This decree went beyond what some Bolsheviks had wanted, as it gave workers a right to 'supervise management'. The soldiers also received what they wanted when the promise to remove class-ranks in the army was honoured in December. Officers were to be elected directly by the soldiers' soviets, and saluting and military decorations were outlawed.

The support of the soldiers was vital if the Bolsheviks were to establish full control over the towns and cities. Moscow was only taken after ten days of violence, and there was a dangerous moment when Alexander Kerensky sent 700 Cossacks under General Krasnov to retake Petrograd in November. However, by the end of the year the Bolsheviks had taken all the major towns and railways, even though large areas of the countryside were still beyond their authority.

Another decree, in November 1917, promised self-determination to the peoples of the former Russian Empire. This encouraged the separatist movements in Finland, the Baltic and the Caucasus. In December, Finland became an independent state and an elected *rada* (parliament) was set up in Ukraine. This is another example of the way the Bolsheviks tried to win support in the early months. The declaration of an armistice in November was also a popular move, particularly as it was accompanied by an official demobilisation of the troops (although many peasants had already deserted anyway).

In November 1917, the old legal system was abolished, in favour of a system of elected people's courts. The new government also outlawed sex discrimination and gave women the right to own property, in the hope of gaining female support. Decrees on the Church followed in December 1917, nationalising Church land and removing marriage and divorce from Church control. At the same time, the nationalisation of banks ended the flow of private capital.

Suppression of opposition

Anti-Bolshevik newspapers were closed down and a propaganda campaign was started against political and 'class' enemies, particularly the *burzhui* ('bourgeoisie'). The class system was abolished in November. Everyone became a *Grazhdani* ('Citizen') and party members were to be addressed as *Tovarisch* ('Comrade'). A general purge of the bureaucracy was carried out in the name of the workers' revolution, leaving only bureaucrats who were loyal to the Bolsheviks. The railway and communications workers, who went on strike in protest against the emergence of a one-party government, forced Lenin to appear to consider coalition with the other socialist parties. However, after the Social Revolutionary Party split into two parties – the Left and Right SRs – in December, the Bolshevik leaders overcame Lenin's reluctance and persuaded him to accept some Left SRs in *Sovnarkom*. When, later that month, the All-Russian Commission for the Suppression of Counter-Revolution, Sabotage and Speculation (soon known as the *Cheka*) was established, it imprisoned leading Kadets, Mensheviks and Right Social Revolutionaries – several of whom had begun to call for the overthrow of the new Soviet government.

ACTIVITY

Discuss with a partner what drove Lenin's actions in the early months of Bolshevik rule. You might like to consider the following: ideology, pragmatism, belief that the Bolshevik Party knew best, belief that Lenin knew best, reaction to opposition.

Opponents of the Bolsheviks pinned their hopes on the promise of a Constituent Assembly, and elections for this began in November. These elections produced a 41.7 million turnout. The Bolsheviks received only 9.8 million votes (24%), giving them 168 out of 703 seats. The Left Social Revolutionaries added a further 39 seats, but the Right Social Revolutionaries gained a big majority – 17.1 million votes (41%) and 380 seats.

Many votes had been cast without a full understanding of the political situation in Petrograd – in particular, of the decree on land reform – but Lenin was appalled and declared that 'we must not be deceived by the election figures. Elections prove nothing.' He argued that such a Constituent Assembly, comprising many political parties, was merely a remnant of bourgeois parliamentary democracy. To accept its rulings would be to take a step backwards in Russia's historical development. Instead, he argued that the more direct democracy of the soviets should prevail.

The Constituent Assembly met in the Tauride Palace for one day only – on 5 January 1918 – when it elected the Social Revolutionary Victor Chernov as its president, and refused to approve Lenin's decrees, which had been approved by the All-Russian Congress of Soviets. The Bolsheviks walked out and the other parties were evicted by pro-Bolshevik guards armed with rifles. When they tried to return, they found the palace locked and surrounded by soldiers. A crowd that demonstrated against this action was fired upon and 12 people died. Significantly, their bodies were buried on the anniversary of Bloody Sunday.

Figure 7.2: Members of the Constituent Assembly in January 1918.

Lenin wrote: 'Everything had turned out for the best. The dissolution of the Constituent Assembly means the complete and open repudiation of democracy in favour of dictatorship. This will be a valuable lesson.' In accordance with his theories on the 'dictatorship of the proletariat' (the rightful power of the workers – the majority of the population), Lenin believed he had acted in the workers' interests.

As Maxim Gorky commented, Lenin had 'a ruthless contempt, worthy of an aristocrat, for the lives of ordinary individuals'. Even Rosa Luxemburg, a fellow revolutionary, expressed alarm. She feared that Lenin's policy had brought about, 'not the dictatorship of the working classes over the middle classes', which she approved of, but 'the dictatorship of the Communist Party over the working classes'.

The end of the war

The result of the elections to the Constituent Assembly had shown all too clearly that Lenin's bid to consolidate his rule by building up popular support had not fully succeeded. This made it even more vital for him to fulfil his pledge to end the war.

The Bolsheviks had announced an armistice in November 1917, and in December peace negotiations began in Brest-Litovsk. The Germans were scornful of the Russian delegation, led by Trotsky, which was asking for peace without annexations or indemnities. There was fierce debate and argument among the Bolsheviks about the German demands. In early February, the Russian delegates walked out, with Trotsky saying there would be 'neither peace nor war'. This meant nothing to the Germans, who simply marched further into Ukraine.

Lenin forced further negotiations, and even talked of stepping down if others would not follow his demand for a treaty. He was opposed by the Revolutionary War Group (including Nikolai Bukharin), which even considered arresting Lenin. Trotsky refused to attend the final conference, but the Treaty of Brest-Litovsk was still signed on 3 March. Most of the territory on Russia's western border was surrendered, including Finland, Estonia, Latvia and Lithuania (which became independent republics) and Poland (which became an independent state). Bessarabia was ceded to Romania, a German ally, while semi-independent governments were set up in Georgia, Belarus and Ukraine.

Russia lost a sixth of its population (62 million people) and 2 million square kilometres (770 000 square miles) of land, including the fields that had provided almost one-third of Russia's agricultural produce. In addition, Russia had to give up 26% of its railway lines and 74% of its iron ore and coal supplies.

Lenin had instructed his negotiators to prolong the discussions in the hope that proletarian revolutions would break out in Europe, but no other revolutions had taken place. When the Treaty of Brest-Litovsk was signed, the harsh peace therefore united many Russians across the class divide, in opposition to Bolshevik domination. The treaty also caused further splits within the Bolshevik Party. For example, Bukharin claimed that Lenin had betrayed their cause by helping to prop up imperialist Germany, rather than continuing the fight for international revolution. The Left Social Revolutionaries left *Sovnarkom* in protest. There was now open, outright opposition to single-party Bolshevik rule.

DISCUSSION POINT

Why was Lenin able to hold on to power and consolidate Bolshevik rule in the months between October 1917 and April 1918?

How the Bolsheviks won the Russian Civil War

The October revolution had divided the country, and the signing of the Treaty of Brest-Litovsk proved to be the final stage in Russia's drift into civil war. Former tsarist army officers, moderate liberals and Kadets, Left and Right Social Revolutionaries, dispossessed landowners, anarchists and some of the ethnic minorities (particularly those affected by the peace terms) were all opposed to the Bolshevik government. Also adding to the turmoil were the peasant masses, most of whom were still very unsure about their future under the Bolsheviks. They were keen to take advantage of whatever situation they found themselves in, to assert their ownership of the land they farmed and protect their local areas.

ACTIVITY

As you work through this section, make a timeline of the key events of the civil war. Where relevant, add a comment on the significance of events

By spring 1918, an anti-Bolshevik volunteer army had been created in the south of the country. This was led by General Mikhail Alekseev and General **Lavr Kornilov** (Kornilov had escaped from his term in jail). **Anton Denikin** was initially made commander of the 1st Division. He would take command of the southern anti-Bolshevik army the following year, on the death of both generals.

> ### Lavr Kornilov (1870–1918):
>
> He was a military commander who had served during the Russo-Japanese War and the First World War. He became Commander-in-Chief of the Petrograd Garrison and Supreme Commander of the Russian Army in 1917. Following his attempt to take control of Petrograd in the 'the Kornilov coup,' he was arrested. He escaped from jail and formed the anti-Bolshevik Volunteer Army becoming one of the main commanders of the White Army during the Civil War. He was killed in action in April 1918.

> ### Anton Denikin (1872–1947):
>
> He had, like Kornilov served in the Imperial Russian Army, and became chief of staff to the Provisional Government's Commander-in-Chief, in March 1917. However, he conspired with Kornilov and was dismissed from his post. When Kornilov was killed in April 1918, Denikin became commander of the White forces in southern Russia. In 1919, he launched a major offensive toward Moscow but he was defeated, forced to retreat and in April 1920 resigned his command to General Pyotr Wrangel and settled in France, where he wrote his memoirs. He emigrated to the USA in 1945.

As well as tsarists and army officers, this southern force comprised mainly liberals and Kadets, although peasants made up most of the fighting forces. Several prominent civilian politicians (such as Peter Struve, Pavel Milyukov and Mikhail Rodzianko) also served at their headquarters. The southern volunteer army purchased arms and munitions from the Germans, and worked in a rough alliance with some of the Cossacks from the area. They also had the support of the new Ukrainian parliament, which resented the loss of land to Germany.

Anticipating the growing threat from the south, the Bolsheviks moved their capital from Petrograd to Moscow in March 1918. They also renamed themselves the Communist Party. However, despite some minor clashes that took place before March 1918, the civil war actually began elsewhere.

In March 1918, the Bolsheviks gave permission for the Czechoslovak Army of Liberation (the Czech Legion) to travel eastwards, through Siberia, to continue the fight against their enemies on the Western

Front. (The Czech Legion had been formed from Czech nationalists in Russia during the war against Germany and Austria-Hungary. By 1918, it numbered 45 000 soldiers.) A slow convoy of 60 trains set off along the Trans-Siberian Railway, transporting this force. When it reached Chelyabinsk Station in the Urals in May, there was a skirmish and some Bolshevik officials tried to arrest some Czech soldiers. This led to more fighting, in which the Czech Legion seized the railway line from Penza to Irkutsk. This gave the Czechs control over much of western Siberia and parts of Eastern European Russia. The emboldened Czech Legion abandoned their original plans, joined forces with anti-Bolsheviks, and began to advance westwards towards Moscow.

This sparked nearly three years of civil war (see Figure 7.3), during which most of the fighting was in the east and south, between the Bolshevik Reds and the anti-Bolshevik Whites. However, another, rather smaller White force was formed under the Russian general, Nikolai Yudenich, in the north in 1919. There were also peasant armies, loosely known as the Greens, whose loyalties frequently changed. Foreign powers intervened too, in the first half of 1918, on the side of the Whites. They were concerned about the loss of their wartime ally, as well as their own interests in Russia, particularly as the Bolsheviks were refusing to pay tsarist debts and were nationalising foreign-owned industries.

In March, the first British troops landed at Murmansk in March 1918 – a larger contingent then captured and occupied Arkhangelsk in August 1918. The troops successfully prevented supplies getting through to the communist government. Meanwhile, Japanese forces landed at Vladivostok in the Far East in April. In the second half of 1918, Italian, French and American troops joined the Japanese in the Far East, while British and French troops entered the Caucasus and Black Sea area. There were also German armies on the western borders of Russia and in Ukraine. In all, 250 000 troops, from more than 14 different states, took part in the fighting.

Figure 7.3: The Russian Civil War 1918–21.

ACTIVITY

Make a diagram to show the different sides in the civil war and their aims. Identify the main issues that might affect each side.

By early 1919, all the White forces acknowledged Admiral Alexander Kolchak as their overall commander. This allowed him to plan a triple offensive in March. Kolchak himself advanced towards Moscow from western Siberia with Czech support, while Denikin led an offensive from the south, and General Yudenich marched on Petrograd from Estonia. It was a tense time for the Leninist government, particularly when Yudenich reached Gatchina on the outskirts of Petrograd.

However, the Bolshevik military effort was increased and the attacks were subdued, so that the Reds gradually got the upper hand during 1920. The Whites also lost crucial foreign support – in April, Denikin resigned in favour of General Wrangel, and fled to the West. Wrangel was then defeated in November, when the remaining White forces in the south were evacuated by British and French ships.

Nonetheless, the war continued – against the Polish armies that had invaded western Ukraine in April and reached Kiev by May. General Mikhail Tukhachevsky mounted a successful communist counter-offensive in May. Under direct orders from Lenin, he led a full-scale invasion of Poland, driving the Poles back to Warsaw by July.

However, Lenin's hope – that a communist revolution would break out in Poland and spread westwards into Europe – proved unfounded. The Poles rose against communism again. Led by Marshal Joseph Piłsudski, they defeated the Red Army outside Warsaw in August, driving the Russians almost back to Minsk. It was only in October 1920 that an armistice was agreed. A peace treaty was finally signed at Riga in March 1921. To gain peace, Lenin had to grant self-rule to Poland, Galicia and parts of Belorussia, as well as confirming the independence of Estonia, Latvia and Lithuania. His controversial 'drive into Poland', which had split Bolshevik ranks and been opposed by Trotsky, therefore proved to be a disastrous failure.

By the end of 1920, most of the former Russian Empire was in communist hands. (In 1921, Georgia would be added. Joseph Stalin, himself a Georgian, went beyond Lenin's orders and brutally overthrew the Menshevik democratic socialist government in that province.) Only Poland, Finland and the Baltic states lay outside communist control. At the cost of perhaps as many as 10 million lives, lost to hunger and epidemic disease as well as military action, the Bolsheviks had triumphed over their enemies.

Reasons for the Bolshevik victory

To a large extent, the Bolshevik triumph was due to their enemies' disunity and the Bolsheviks' geographical advantages. The Whites had no single political programme and no unified government. Ex-radicals, such as Milyukov and Chernov, found it impossible to work with rightist aristocratic generals, such as Kolchak. When Kolchak was made supreme commander in 1919, he had hundreds of Social Revolutionaries arrested and executed. Meanwhile, a series of SR revolts helped undermine his position. White generals, such as Denikin, also refused to tolerate separatism and yet relied on the support of fighting forces from the ethnic minorities. Furthermore, the tsar's death deprived the White armies of a figurehead who might have rallied them and given them more impetus. Nine days before the arrival of the Czech forces in July 1918, panicking local Bolsheviks in Yekaterinburg had the tsar and his family shot.

So-called White allies such as the Cossacks, who wanted their own independence, or the Greens who fought variously for and against both Whites and Reds, proved to be unreliable. Foreign nations, whose interest faded with the end of the First World War and who, in any case, provided only half-hearted support because of their own commitments, proved equally untrustworthy. The intervention of foreigners actually provided some excellent propaganda material, allowing the Bolsheviks to portray themselves as 'the defenders of the Motherland'.

Although they had forces in Estonia, Arkhangelsk, the Caucasus and western Siberia in 1919, the distance between the White bases was enormous. Conveying messages, coordinating attacks and trying to move men and munitions between bases was almost impossible. In contrast, the Reds held the central area of Russia, including Petrograd and Moscow, which lay at the heart of the railway network. The Reds also controlled Russia's major armament factories at Tula and Petrograd, as well as the old tsarist arsenals. They were better able to mobilise human resources too, because they were controlling an area of dense population (as opposed to the Whites' more sparsely populated regions).

Theory of Knowledge

History, selection and bias

When historians write about wars, they already know the outcome and will often try to explain why events and developments lead to that outcome. Is history simply the product of the historians' selection of material and interpretation of the past?

The Whites could easily have taken advantage of the Bolsheviks' failure to win over the rural community. Instead, they treated the peasants with contempt, helping landowners to recover estates and giving land as a reward to followers. Peasants came to realise that only a Bolshevik victory would enable them to retain the lands they had taken.

The Cossack 'allies' of the southern army even drove thousands of non-Cossack peasants from their homes and villages. In addition, the many peasants who were conscripted into the White armies were subject to the most brutal discipline. As Orlando Figes has shown in his study, *Peasant Russia*, the Reds generally found it far easier than the Whites to recruit the peasants. The Reds also suffered fewer peasant desertions and uprisings. The communists set up elected councils (*Volispolkom* or VIK) to provide peasant representation of villages in dealings with the central government. These councils at least helped to maintain the illusion that the Bolsheviks wanted to respond to peasants' needs.

The Whites became infamous for the 'Terror' they brought. Resistance to troops could mean that whole villages and farms were burned down, bridges and water stations were destroyed, and hostages taken and shot. In the White Terror in the Yekaterinburg region, more than 25 000 people were shot or tortured to death by Kolchak's forces. Denikin's generals acted ruthlessly against the Jews. It has been estimated that between 100 000 and 150 000 Jews in Ukraine and southern Russia were killed in pogroms, while others were left homeless or died of disease. In the city of Yaroslavl, where a revolt broke out on 6–7 July 1918, the Whites captured about 200 people and crammed them on top of each other in a barge on the River Volga. There, they spent 13 days without food, exposed to the surrounding gunfire. The Cossack warlords were particularly cruel in their treatment of the peasants. Girls were raped and shot. Other victims could have their eyes gouged out, their tongues cut off, and even be buried alive.

ACTIVITY

Create a spider diagram to show why the Reds won the Russian Civil War. Plan your diagram carefully to group the different types of factors together.

Trotsky was appointed commissar for war on 8 April 1918. This signalled that the Reds were developing the Red Guards units into an efficient Red fighting force. In May 1918, compulsory military service was introduced. By August 1918, the size of the Red armies had increased from around 100 000 to over 500 000 men. By January 1920, 5 million men had been enlisted. Over 48 000 experienced former tsarist officers were recruited (including General Alexei Brusilov), sometimes by holding their relatives hostage.

To ensure the loyalty of both officers and men, political commissars were attached to every unit to provide 'political education' and spy for the government. The early experiments with soldiers' soviets and elected officers disappeared; ranks and harsh military discipline (including the death penalty) were re-introduced. Working parties of *burzhui* were created to do dangerous jobs at the front. Leather-clad special units were also set up to march behind the conventional soldiers, to prevent desertions. If any unit retreated without orders, its commissar and commander were immediately shot.

Figure 7.4: A Bolshevik propaganda vehicle loaded down with newspapers and a phonograph (early record player), manned by the Red Army in 1918.

Despite the severe discipline in their armies, the Reds generally managed to inspire greater loyalty among their troops than the Whites. They used propaganda very effectively to reinforce belief and maintain morale. Propaganda trains, trams, carts and riverboats carried books, newspapers, films and teachers to spread the Bolshevik message to more remote areas and to the army units on the front line.

ACTIVITY

Try to find some examples of Russian Civil War propaganda posters. Choose one to show the rest of your group, and explain its significance.

Trotsky's contribution to the civil war

Trotsky has often been credited by Western historians for the success of the Red armies. Although he declared 'War is the instrument of policy', he was not an expert military strategist; nor did he claim to be. However, he did travel the length and breadth of Russia – covering 104 000 km (65 000 miles) by train – to keep in contact with the fighting. The train was Trotsky's headquarters, communications centre and troop transporter. It also carried his own armoured car, which he used to get to the front lines.

Trotsky pursued military victory with energy and commitment. When Yudenich's army threatened Petrograd, Lenin wanted to abandon the city. However, Trotsky refused to give in. He travelled to the front line, where he helped save the city from the Whites. Trotsky apparently inspired troops to fight even when there seemed no hope, but some of his successes must be put down to the fact that he showed no mercy.

Although Western historians have usually praised Trotsky's achievements, the Soviets tried to write him out of history after Stalin assumed leadership. Any assessment therefore needs to be treated with caution. As Evan Mawdsley has written:

'The historian looking at Trotsky's Civil War career must beware of two myths. The first is the Soviet view dominant ever since his disgrace in the late 1920s that he played no beneficial role in the Civil War. The second might be called the "Trotskyist myth" that exaggerates his importance.'

Robert Service has written of 'Trotsky's brilliance' and Martin Sixsmith has said that 'the Red Army was led by a military genius'. However, Trotsky often took an independent line and clashed with subordinates (particularly Stalin), and not all Bolshevik followers loved him.

SOURCE 7.2

Victor Serge was a Russian revolutionary. During the Russian Revolution, he lived variously in Petrograd, Moscow and Berlin. He was a close associate of Trotsky.

> Trotsky was all tension and energy; he was, besides, an orator [public speaker] of unique quality… He outshone Lenin through his great oratorical talent, through his organising ability, first with the army, then on the railways, and by his brilliant gifts as a theoretician. His attitude was less homely than Lenin's, with something authoritarian about it. That, maybe, is how my friends and I saw him… we had much admiration for him, but no real love. His sternness, his insistence on punctuality in work and battle, the inflexible correctness of his demeanor struck me as proceeding from a character that was basically dictatorial.

Serge, V. 1984. (trans. P. Sedgwick). **Memoirs of a Revolutionary, 1901–1941.** *New York, USA. Writers and Readers Publishing Cooperative Society Ltd.*

QUESTION

What does Source 7.2 suggest about Trotsky? Is this a reliable source? Explain your answer

However, Lenin's role in the Red victory, which was exaggerated by later Soviet writers, must also not be over-stated. Lenin took little part in decision making, never visited the front line, and rarely even spoke to anyone in high command. He told a group of young communists, which happened to include Stalin (who recorded his words), that they should study military affairs but that for him it was 'too late'. Lenin's political judgement can also be questioned – particularly the economic policies he used to win the war, although he was flexible enough to change these when proven wrong. Although Lenin was an important leader in the October revolution and deserves credit for his part in negotiating the Brest-Litovsk Treaty, his personal contribution to the civil war victory must be judged quite minimal.

7.2 Why was War Communism introduced in 1918 and replaced by the NEP in 1921?

When the Bolsheviks seized power in October 1917, there was general agreement in the party that all members of society should have a share in resources. However, there were widely differing opinions on how this would be achieved. The initial decrees gave the peasants and urban workers control over their own labour through a system of land and factory committees, but went no further. Lenin himself seemed to favour a long transition period to socialism, during which markets would remain a major feature of economic life. He talked about a transitional era of 'state capitalism'.

Giving peasants and workers control had proved disastrous in economic terms. Workers had voted themselves pay rises, had failed to organise factories effectively, and had sometimes even stolen factory materials. The coming of the civil war made these problems worse. Supplies of raw materials disappeared and output shrank, causing acute inflation. This left the peasants reluctant to sell their produce, since there was little to be obtained from the cities in exchange. Soon money became worthless to them.

The hoarding of grain by the peasants, together with the loss of Ukraine, helped bring about an extreme food shortage that led to food riots in some urban areas. By February 1918, the citizens of Petrograd were living on rations of just 50 grams of bread a day and huge numbers of people were leaving for the countryside.

War Communism

ACTIVITY

As you read the rest of this section, make a diagram to illustrate the changes brought by War Communism and their significance.

Figure 7.5: This 1918 War Communism poster portrays the Russian worker as a heroic figure with its slogan 'On Your Horse, Proletarian!'

Consequently, the pressures of civil war forced a change, bringing the policy of War Communism. This turned the state into a centralised command economy. Industry was brought under state control, with the nationalisation of the railways and merchant fleet in the spring of 1918, and of the factories in June. In December, Vesenkha (the Supreme Council of the National Economy) was set up, and this council gradually assumed control over industrial enterprises. Professional state-employed managers, with a duty to increase production and maximise efficiency, replaced the factory committees. Often, these 'specialists' were actually the same bourgeois factory owners who had recently been displaced.

Labour discipline was tightened. Fines were re-introduced for workers who arrived late or failed to turn up to work. Furthermore, internal passports were issued, to try to stop workers leaving the cities. By 1921, workers could be imprisoned or shot if targets were not met. Unions became a means of keeping the workers under control and payment took the form of ration tokens. Only the labour force and the Red Army soldiers were given adequate food under the new rationing system. Essential civil servants and professionals, such as doctors, were given a lower level of rations. The former *burzhui* ('non-persons' or 'bourgeois parasites') were left on the edge of starvation.

Private trade and manufacture were forbidden, and money became less important as it was replaced with ration tokens. Rationing helped create a system of semi-controlled barter, which was suggestive of socialism. However, in the circumstances of civil war this meant a huge black market trade. According to Martin Sixsmith, 'A siege mentality informed the government's every act. Workers were no longer seen as agents of the revolution but as raw material, an expendable force to be exploited in the great experiment of building socialism.'

War Communism also brought more forcible requisitioning of grain from the peasants. The Food-Supplies Dictatorship, set up in May 1918, sent detachments of soldiers, Red Guards and workers from the large towns to force peasants to hand over their grain. Officially the grain was bought, but in fact it was often brutally confiscated and the requisitioning detachments were allowed to keep a share of whatever they collected, as a reward. This often caused the peasants great hardship by leaving them with insufficient grain for the months ahead. They also lost other important items, such as horses, carts and firewood, to the squads.

The peasants were divided into three categories. The poor and slightly less poor were regarded as allies of the proletariat, but the 'grasping fists' (the *kulaks* who had made personal wealth from their farming) were seen as 'enemies of the people'. The *Volispolkom* (VIK) encouraged the seizure of *kulak* stocks. The more efficient farmers therefore disappeared and grain supplies fell to dangerous levels. One-third of the land was abandoned to grass, while cattle and horses were slaughtered in their thousands.

There has been some debate as to whether War Communism was simply a pragmatic reaction to the civil war or a strategy that had been deliberately planned. There is evidence that Lenin saw War Communism as the natural extension of the class warfare that he had deliberately stirred up in the early days of the Bolshevik regime. He referred to it as the 'internal war to destroy "bourgeois attitudes"'.

Trotsky, on the other hand, had initially opposed War Communism and put forward his own mixed socialist/capitalist scheme in 1920, but this had been rejected by the party. Consequently, he had taken the view that greater discipline was the only way of countering Russia's imperial legacy and the economic devastation of the civil war. According to David Christian, 'The party emerged from the years of civil war, militarised, brutalised and aware that direct methods of mobilisation might be a workable alternative to the methods of capitalism.'

Whatever the reason, initial promises of freedom, justice and self-determination were swept aside by 1921. The early socialist experiments came to an end and a new autocratic political culture was established.

Theory of Knowledge

Evidence and interpretation

Historians have given the name War Communism to the economic system practised during the civil war. Do such labels help or obstruct our study of history?

Economic problems and political unrest

By 1921, the civil war was over and yet, for the peasants and workers, economic conditions were getting worse rather than better. Total industrial output had fallen to around 20% of its pre-war levels. With a collapse in the rail and river transport systems, factories were struggling to get necessary supplies. Worse still, food prices escalated as a severe famine hit Russia in 1921. The harvest of 1921 yielded only 48% of what had been produced in 1913.

A major drought in the south of the country had contributed to the famine but it was at least partly the result of communist policies. Price controls and requisitioning had encouraged the peasants to plant less, which meant there were no reserves to fall back on. Lenin must have known the dangers of his policies but, according to Richard Pipes, he repeatedly said that he would sooner the whole nation die of hunger than allow free trade in grain. Deaths from malnutrition and disease were certainly high, and possibly as many as 25 million died. According to Mawdsley, more than one million people died of typhus and typhoid in 1920, compared with 63 000 in 1917. A Northern European influenza epidemic also carried away thousands, and there were three million deaths as a result of higher child mortality. Numbers might have been higher still had it not been for foreign relief efforts. There were even reported incidents of cannibalism.

The famine was accompanied by a new outbreak of peasant violence. The worst occurred in Tambov province, 480 km (300 miles) south-east of Moscow, in August 1920. The requisitioning squads arrived here at a time when the peasants had almost no reserves. For nearly a year, until June 1921, the peasants fought for their freedom and their right to the land. They were led by Alexander Antonov, who gathered a 70 000-man peasant army. Over the next two years, the revolt spread across large areas of south-eastern Russia.

Figure 7.6: A Russian couple with their starving children during the famine of 1921–22

The government called up 100 000 Red Army troops to deal with the troubles, and even used poison gas to massacre the rebels as they hid in the forests.

237

SOURCE 7.3

Lenin blamed the kulaks for the unrest and demanded that they be punished.

> The insurrection of the *kulaks* must be suppressed without mercy. We need to set an example. You need to hang (I repeat, hang, without fail, in full public view) at least a hundred *kulaks*, the rich, the bloodsuckers. Then publish their names and take away all of their grain. Also execute the hostages. Do it in such a way that people for hundreds of miles around will tremble and cry out, 'let us choke and strangle those bloodsucking *kulaks*!'

Quoted in Sixsmith, M. 2011. **Russia.** *London, UK. BBC Books. p. 238.*

QUESTION

Compare and contrast Lenin's views in Sources 7.1 and 7.3.

There were also strikes and riots in the towns, as the food crisis deepened. Workers protested against the strict discipline in factories and the lack of union representation. Support for the other socialist parties revived, and there were calls for 'soviets without communism'. In January 1921, the bread ration was reduced by one-third in several cities, including Moscow and Petrograd. Martial law was declared and the *Cheka* was used to crush demonstrations, since regular soldiers refused to take action against the protesters.

This was the final straw for the 30 000 sailors stationed in the Kronstadt naval base. In March 1921, they sent a manifesto to Lenin. They demanded concessions that included free elections, free speech, freedom of the press and the ending of one-party Communist rule.

Although few of the original Kronstadt sailors of October 1917 remained (many had been killed in the civil war and others had moved on to become administrators), they were remembered as the 'shock troops' of the Bolshevik Revolution. Lenin was alarmed and ordered an immediate assault on the base. Red Army men marched 8 km (5 miles) across the ice, supported by artillery from the shore. The *Cheka* were positioned to their rear, in case any man should think of deserting. After nearly 24 hours of bitter and bloody fighting, which left more than 10 000 bodies strewn across the ice, the Kronstadt rebellion was crushed and the ringleaders were rounded up and shot. In total, 15 000 rebels were sent to the prison camp at Solovetsky on the White Sea. Lenin denounced the sailors as 'White Traitors', but the incident had shaken him, particularly as it came just when the Tambov peasant rising was reaching its peak.

These troubles also caused divisions within the Bolshevik Party itself. The Workers' Opposition Group, set up under Alexander Shiyapknikov and Alexandra Kollontai, argued for greater worker control and the removal of managers and military discipline in factories. This group strongly opposed those in the party, including Trotsky, who wanted to continue and intensify War Communism and use the Red Army to build socialism by force.

KEY CONCEPTS ACTIVITY

Causation: Make a chart summarising the reasons why Lenin was forced into a change of policy in 1921. Begin with the general reasons and work towards the more specific ones.

Lenin later claimed that the Kronstadt revolt was the 'flash that lit up reality'. But it was probably the combination of the many troubles of 1921 which persuaded him that a change of direction was necessary. Amid fierce debate at the 10th Party Congress, Lenin announced a New Economic Policy. Although he was supported by Nikolai Bukharin, Grigori Zinoviev and most of the leadership, many Bolsheviks saw this as a betrayal of their ideological principles.

The New Economic Policy

The New Economic Policy (NEP) of August 1921 reinstated a money economy, and was intended to encourage greater interaction between the town and countryside. Most importantly, it ended the requisitioning of grain in rural areas. Although peasants still had to give a certain proportion of their produce to the state as a form of tax, they were permitted to sell any surplus. The state retained control over the heavy, military and strategic industries – such as coal, iron and steel and oil – as well as the transport and banking systems. However, private ownership of smaller businesses (usually through cooperatives and trusts) and private trade were permitted once again. Rationing ended and industries had to pay their workers' wages from their own profits, thereby ensuring that they were run efficiently.

The NEP soon showed results. Although the larger industries took longer to revive and the production levels of 1913 were not reached until 1926, cereal production rose by 23%. Factory production increased (from a very low starting point) by a staggering 200% between 1920 and 1923. The peasants were encouraged to produce more, in order to sell grain for money, and they then bought the products of small-scale industry. Living standards rose, peasant revolts declined, and the industrial disputes ended. The change of policy also meant that foreign nations, such as Britain and Germany, were willing to make much-needed trade agreements with Russia.

Traders (known as Nepmen) travelled the country, buying grain and selling industrial goods. They could make big profits and enjoyed frequenting the gambling halls, night clubs, brothels and expensive restaurants that accompanied the return of private wealth. Lenin was not at ease with the changes, and the hardliners grumbled. But the breathing space allowed by the NEP ensured that the Bolsheviks continued to hold on to power.

There was one more adjustment to the policy in 1923, when the Scissors Crisis – as Trotsky called it – became acute (see graph below). As the peasants responded to the NEP more quickly than the industrial cooperatives, the towns became flooded with food, but had insufficient goods to offer in exchange. This encouraged peasants to hold back surpluses, as food prices started to fall and the cost of industrial goods was high. Consequently, from 1923, industrial prices were capped by the state and the peasants' food quotas were replaced by money taxes, so the peasants were forced to sell their produce.

SOURCE 7.4

Figures for 1913		% of 1913 figures							
	1913	1920	1921	1922	1923	1924	1925	1926
Industrial production 10 251 m. (1926) roubles	100	14	20	26	39	45	75	108
Coal 29 m. tonnes	100	30	31	33	47	56	62	95
Electricity 1945 m. kilowatt hours	100	–	27	40	59	80	150	180
Pig iron 4 216 000 tonnes	100	–	3	4	7	18	36	58
Steel 4 231 000 tonnes	100	–	4	9	17	27	50	74
Rail freight carried 132 m. tonnes	100	–	30	30	44	51	63	–
Cotton fabrics 2582 m. metres	100	–	4	14	27	37	65	89
Sown area 105 m. hectares	100	–	86	74	87	93	99	105
Grain harvest 80.1 m. tonnes	100	58	47	63	71	64	91	96

Table showing the Soviet economy under the New Economic Policy 1920–1926.

Notes: m. = million; – = figures not available; 1913 = 100 (baseline year)

The 1913 grain harvest was unusually high, so the figures in the final row exaggerate the decline in agricultural production in the early 1920s.

Adapted from Nove, A. 1992. **An Economic History of the USSR.** *3rd edn. Harmondsworth, UK. Penguin. p. 89.*

SOURCE 7.4 (CONT.)

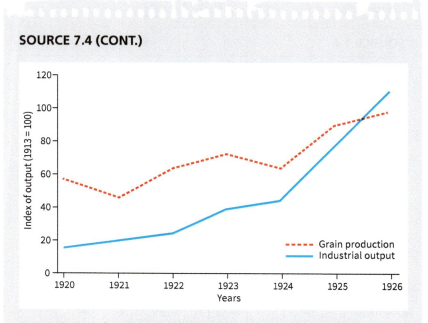

Economic growth under NEP 1920–26, based on the figures in Source 7.4; the Scissors Crisis got its name because the graph resembles scissors.

QUESTION

Using Source 7.4 and the information in this section, how successful was the New Economic Policy?

DISCUSSION POINT

What role do statistics play in history? Do statistics provide better evidence than written records?

7.3 To what extent did the new Soviet state rely on terror and coercion?

Terror and coercion were built into the Bolshevik state from its earliest days. The *Cheka* was established in December 1917 to root out political enemies. Over the following months and years, its activities expanded. In March 1918, the government requisitioned the Lubianka building, the former headquarters of the All-Russian Insurance Company, as the *Cheka*'s new base in Moscow. A prison was established inside and a contemporary joke referred to it as the tallest building in Moscow, since Siberia could be seen from its basement. 'Iron' Felix Dzerzhinsky was placed at the head of the operation.

Dzerzhinsky was well known for his ruthlessness and single-minded determination. He told *Sovnarkom*, 'Do not think I seek forms of revolutionary justice; we are not in need of justice. It is war now – face to face, a fight to the finish. Life or death!' By September 1918, most provinces had their own *Cheka* branch, with officials reporting directly to Lenin and the Politburo.

Initially, most of the *Cheka*'s work was directed at political opposition. In the summer of 1918, it pursued the Social Revolutionaries (SRs) so relentlessly that they reacted by capturing Dzerzhinsky, assassinating the German ambassador and murdering two Bolshevik Party leaders. Despite the capture and execution of 350 SR rebels, the Social Revolutionary Fanny Kaplan nearly succeeded in assassinating Lenin on 30 August 1918 by firing three bullets into his arm, neck and jaw. Although Lenin survived (albeit with injuries that would contribute to his early death five years later), the incident had severe consequences.

Red Terror was extended throughout the country as civil war tensions intensified because of the White Terror and foreign intervention. All remaining SRs and Mensheviks were branded traitors, and 500 were shot in Petrograd alone. A determined onslaught was launched against 'class enemies' everywhere, in an attempt to enforce loyalty to the Bolshevik Revolution and communism. Yakov Sverdlov, chairman of the Bolshevik Central Committee, spoke of 'merciless mass terror against all opponents of the revolution!'. On 5 September 1918, *Sovnarkom* authorised the *Cheka* to find, question, arrest and destroy the families of any suspected traitors. 'Class enemies' were identified by their aristocratic or middle-class backgrounds, or from information gathered by spies or collected from informers. 'Confessions' were obtained under torture and the convicted faced immediate execution.

DISCUSSION POINT

If Fanny Kaplan had not attempted to assassinate Lenin, would this have affected the course of Russian history? Is all history based on chance events of this type?

Once terror became a legitimate policy of the state, it was hard to control. Local *Cheka* agents acted as their own masters, keen to show their enthusiasm. An estimated half a million people were shot in the following three years. Victims ranged from the tsar and his family, shot on 17 July 1918 (though not only for ideological reasons), to townsfolk suspected of associating with another 'class enemy' or perhaps with the misfortune to have neighbours who bore a grudge. Priests, Jews, Catholics and, to a lesser extent, Muslims also suffered. Around 8000 priests were executed in 1921 for failing to hand over Church relics, supposedly for the relief of famine victims.

In addition, the Red Terror meant that 'class enemies' were discriminated against in the wartime rationing system, so they were left to beg or barter their remaining possessions for food. They were also ordered by the city soviets to undertake duties such as street cleaning, snow clearing and sweeping tramlines.

In the countryside, the *Cheka* enforced grain requisitions and its agents showed no mercy. They executed black marketeers, hoarders and speculators as well as arresting *kulaks*, who were sent to labour camps or shot. Families, friends and even entire villages might suffer punishments because of their association with 'class enemies'. Many villages were destroyed in the Tambov region, for example, after 1921. The number of people in the prison camps, according to Pipes, reached about 50 000 in 1920 and 70 000 by 1923. Prisoners were treated as slave labour and given physically demanding tasks, such as mining or digging Arctic canals, while receiving pitifully small food rations.

Figure 7.7: Russian labour camp inmates working in freezing temperatures; many did not survive the harsh conditions.

KEY CONCEPTS ACTIVITY

Perspectives: Carry out some further research into the effects of the Red Terror and the Leninist prison camps. You might like to begin with Orlando Figes' book A People's Tragedy, which contains many first-hand accounts.

Robert Service has suggested that the Red Terror was more the product of local-level decisions than a policy of the Bolshevik state itself, but this does not mean that the state was unsupportive of coercion. Lenin believed in class warfare and he signed the execution lists. He also supported the show trials to which 34 of the rebel leaders of 1921 were subjected. At these trials, they were made to denounce others and admit their crimes in public.

From 1922, the *Cheka* was renamed the GPU (Main Political Administration) and new coercive legislation and action were introduced. The early censorship of the press turned into a full-scale

245

pre-publication scrutiny of all writings from 1921. Meanwhile, the Union of the Militant Godless was established in 1921, as part of a systematic campaign to weaken the power of the Church within the state, and to strip the Church of its wealth.

Theory of Knowledge

Historians and moral judgements

Historians have often expressed horror at events such as the Red Terror. Should historians make moral judgements about the past?

Although Lenin spoke of 'democratic centralism', coercion seems to have been more important to him than democracy. In theory, workers and peasants influenced state decisions by electing members of their local soviets. These soviet members, in turn, chose those who would sit on higher-level soviets and so on, while the central authorities passed decisions down to the masses. But the system actually became a means for passing orders downwards, particularly with the increased centralisation of the civil war years.

Commands were passed down from the Communist Party's seven- to nine-man Politburo (selected from the Central Committee), as *Sovnarkom* gradually met less frequently. Local soviets, led by party nominees rather than elected representatives after 1919, did as they were commanded. In 1921, the 10th Party Congress passed a ban on other political parties, and a ban on factions within the Communist Party. This meant that any decision taken by the Central Committee had to be accepted by the whole party, on pain of expulsion. The bans were originally intended as temporary measures but later became permanent under Stalin. From 1923, the nomenklatura system made appointment to an estimated 5500 key party and government posts dependent on the agreement of the Central Committee. This new loyal party élite could expect rewards in return for ensuring that central instructions were always obeyed without question.

The Communist government also abandoned its earlier support for 'national self-determination' for the ethnic minorities after 1921. Although displays of national culture and native languages were permitted, independence movements were denounced as 'counter-revolutionary'. In 1922, demands from Georgia for greater independence were brutally crushed on the orders of Stalin, a Georgian himself and the people's commissar for nationalities (although his actions were condemned by Lenin). The Union of Soviet Socialist Republics (USSR) was formally established in December 1922. This replaced the Russian Soviet Federal Republic (RSFR) created in January 1918, but in practice the difference was minimal. The states that made up the union were kept under very strict control and, when necessary, coerced from the centre.

KEY CONCEPTS ACTIVITY

Change and continuity: In pairs, choose one of the ethnic minority groups mentioned in this book. Using the information here and the results of your own research, assess the treatment of this group in tsarist and Bolshevik times. Then prepare a presentation to give to the rest of your class about your ethnic group.

7.4 What was the relationship between Bolshevik Russia and the rest of the world?

Lenin kept tight control of foreign policy. Although Trotsky was initially made commissar for foreign affairs, Trotsky's refusal to attend the signing of the Brest-Litovsk Treaty led to his replacement in April 1918 by Georgi Chicherin. Chicherin held this post until July 1930 and, for most of that time, he was forced by circumstances to seek 'peaceful co-existence' with the Western capitalist powers.

Initially, Lenin hoped that the revolution in Russia would lead to a proletarian revolution in the rest of Europe. Indeed, the Bolsheviks never expected to stay in power for long after October 1917. Rather, they saw themselves sparking off revolutions elsewhere, and setting an example of how to drive a proletarian revolution forward. (Revolutions did break out in Germany and Hungary after the First World War, but they were soon crushed.) In an attempt to spread revolution around the world, Lenin held a congress, which set up the Communist

International (Comintern) in Moscow in March 1919, and another in 1920. Despite the civil war and famine within Russia itself, the Comintern pursued its role actively – particularly in Germany.

However, the activities of the Comintern only made the Western powers more determined to resist the march of communism. The Bolshevik Party's attempts to order foreign communist parties to follow the Leninist model (and have their programmes for revolution vetted and agreed by the Comintern) weakened the support of foreign workers for the cause. In 1924, the so-called 'Zinoviev letter' was published in Britain. This document appeared to suggest that the Comintern was encouraging the British Labour Party to work for revolution. Its publication was enough to ensure a resounding British Conservative victory in that year's election, even though it was shown to be a forgery.

The Soviet-dominated Comintern had little success. In particular, its attempts to stir up proletarian revolution in Germany and Hungary failed miserably. Similarly, it never succeeded in provoking a proletarian uprising in Poland. Lenin's hopes of taking Warsaw, and spreading revolution into Germany, came to nothing.

The pressures of the civil war (and the activities of some foreign nations in support of the Whites), as well as the failures of the Comintern, forced Lenin to accept that peaceful co-existence was a more realistic policy. His main concern was to ensure that the capitalist countries remained divided so they could not unite against Russia. However, he was also keen to establish trading links. Of course, he had to overcome the suspicions of the Western powers, who had been angered by the Soviet government's cancellation of former tsarist debts – and its publication of secret treaties which revealed their war aims as regards territorial ambitions. Fortunately for Lenin, the liberalisation represented by the NEP persuaded the British government to make a trading treaty with Russia in 1921, although this was only an economic agreement.

In April 1922, Chicherin boosted the security of the Communist state by reaching an understanding with Germany (the other post-war outcast state of Europe) in the Treaty of Rapallo. Germany and Russia agreed to recognise one another, cancel all claims for debts, develop their trade relations and cooperate secretly in military matters. The treaty provided economic benefits and would prove significant in the years after Lenin's death, as the tension over the failed communist risings of 1921–23 receded.

The Soviet Union gradually obtained diplomatic recognition from other major powers, beginning with the Labour government in Britain in February 1924. Furthermore, private Western and American firms began to extend technological assistance and to develop commercial links with Russia in the 1920s.

Figure 7.8: Russian delegates went to Genoa, Italy, to negotiate the Treaty of Rapallo.

KEY CONCEPTS QUESTION

Change and significance: Analyse the key developments that changed Russia's/the USSR's relationship with the rest of the world in the 1853–1924 period.

Lenin's declaration that 'the underlying chief task and basic condition of our victory is the propagation of revolution at least to several of the more advanced countries' was never to be fulfilled. The Soviet leadership was forced to restrict its revolutionary activity to the promotion of opposition among colonial peoples against 'imperialist exploitation'. This was seen, for example, in the aid sent to help the struggles of the non-Marxist Guomindang (Nationalist Party) in China.

In this respect, as in so many other aspects of government, Lenin died before he had a chance to address the consequences of the revolution he had led. Lenin had helped to shape the Russia of 1924 but, as Robert Service said, 'his times also moulded him'.

DISCUSSION POINT

In the study of Bolshevik Russia, a lot of emphasis has been placed on the importance of Lenin's leadership. Is the course of history determined by the actions of 'great men'?

Epilogue

Lenin suffered three strokes after May 1922. The first two impaired his speech and partially paralysed the right side of his body. The third, in March 1923, left him both mute and bed-ridden. It was after his first stroke that Lenin chose to dictate his Testament in December 1922, signalling his intentions for the future of Russia. He did not make specific provision for future leadership, but provided appraisals and criticisms of Zinoviev, Kamenev, Bukharin and Trotsky. His strongest condemnation was of Stalin, whose behaviour in Georgia had caused Lenin alarm. Stalin had become the party's first general-secretary in 1922, but Lenin wrote that the 'unlimited authority' he exercised was unacceptable and suggested (in a Postscript written in 1923) that 'comrades think about a way of removing Stalin from that post'. He also commented on Stalin's 'personal rudeness, unnecessary roughness and lack of finesse', flaws 'intolerable in a Secretary-General'.

In fact, Lenin was so concerned about Stalin that he joined forces with Trotsky to restore some democracy in the Communist Party, and prevent Stalin pushing through his plans for a more centralised constitution. However, their attempts to block Stalin's progress came to nothing, as Lenin's health was rapidly declining and Trotsky was too isolated within the party.

Lenin's Testament was never read to the Party Congress as he had intended. After his death, the Central Committee members decided among themselves to suppress it. The way was therefore left open for Stalin, the 'rough' general-secretary, to emerge as the sole leader of Soviet Russia by 1929, and for a new stage in Russia's history to begin.

Paper 3 exam practice

Question 1

'The Russian Civil War destroyed the idealism of the October 1917 revolution and led to the emergence of an autocratic and repressive Communist state.' To what extent do you agree with this statement? **[15 marks]**

Skill

Using your own knowledge analytically and combining it with awareness of historical debate

Examiner's tips

Historical knowledge and analysis should be the core of your answer. However, references to issues that have provoked historical debate, and some awareness of what historians have thought about a topic, are desirable extras when relevant. By integrating relevant knowledge about historical debates and interpretations, and showing that you understand issues that have provoked differences between historians, you may be able to write an answer that qualifies for the higher mark bands.

Having followed the advice given previously, you should already be aware of the need to read the question carefully, draw up a plan, make a judgement, work out a line of argument and write a focused introductory paragraph. You should also know how to avoid both irrelevance and simple narrative. Your task now is to follow your plan by writing a series of linked paragraphs that contain relevant analysis, precise supporting own knowledge and, where appropriate, brief references to historical debates and interpretations.

For this question, you will need to:

- outline the Bolshevik 'idealism' that existed in October 1917, and contrast this with the type of state that existed in Russia in 1921
- question the extent of the idealism of October 1917, and consider whether there was continuity of ideology through to 1921

- question whether the type of state that existed in Russia in 1921 was the product of the civil war or of other factors, such as a logical outcome of Bolshevik ideology
- provide a judgement, making it clear whether you agree or disagree with the statement.

Since this topic has been the subject of historical debate, you should also be able to refer to different historians' views.

Common mistakes

Some students, who have been made aware of historical debate and know that extra marks can be gained by showing this, tend to write in a descriptive way: 'Historian X says... and historian Y says...' However, they make no attempt to comment on these views and explain which is more convincing. The views of others are only useful when they are fully **evaluated** (for example, has one historian had access to more/better information than another, perhaps because they were writing at a different time?). Views should be **integrated** into an answer with some personal comment. Another weak use of historical debate is to write comments such as 'Historian X is biased because she is American.' Such comments will not receive credit.

Remember to refer to the simplified Paper 3 mark scheme in Chapter 8.

Sample paragraphs containing analysis and historical debate

[Following an introduction setting out a view...]

It is sometimes suggested that the civil war destroyed the idealism of the October revolution and diverted it away from its Marxist roots in freedom, equality and justice. Martin Sixsmith, for example, has written, 'As his hold on power became more fragile, Lenin abandoned his promises... the rhetoric of liberation gave way to what became known as War Communism, harsh, enslaving and repressive.'

These are obviously strong words and would reinforce the view that the Bolshevik regime was changed for the worse by the experience of civil war. However, Evan Mawdsley in 'The Russian Civil War' took a different line. His study offers a more convincing case for continuity than those of historians such as Alec Nove, who claimed that Lenin 'went off the rails'.

7 Imperial Russia and the Soviet Union (1855–1924)

There would certainly appear to be a contrast between what was done in the immediate euphoria of victory, in 1917, with the decrees on land and workers' control, the changes to the judicial system and the removal of ranks and the more stringent discipline of the military, and the tough repressive measures brought by the civil war, which apparently reversed earlier decrees. However, this contrast fails to recognise the fragility of the Bolsheviks' position in October 1917. They had little choice but to put political and economic systems in place that would enable them to keep power. When they could get away with more authoritarian action, for example using Sovnarkom to undermine the soviets' power, or dismissing the Constituent Assembly in January 1918, they did so. Lenin never intended that the peasants should have private ownership of land, for example, and his earlier writings say as much. However, he allowed this in 1917 because he could not stop what was already happening and still retain power.

Much of what happened during the civil war can be seen as the product of the same Bolshevik 'idealism' that accompanied their seizure of power. Class conflict was inherent in Bolshevism from the beginning. In October 1917, striking civil servants were arrested and the civil service was purged. The burzhui were victimised and condemned to beg and do hard labour. These traits were also common to the period of the civil war when 'non-persons' were drafted into Labour Brigades, and merciless discipline was used to enforce loyalty. According to Mawdsley, 'any form of socialism claiming absolute control over society is bound to lead to totalitarian excesses'. Sheila Fitzpatrick has also lent weight to the view that the coercion of the peasants in the civil war was necessary for the development of communism and led directly to the collectivisation of the 1930s. Although a link to later developments does not necessarily prove that there was continuity between October 1917 and 1921, such totalitarian tendencies were clearly present in the early months as Lenin purged the opposition and established the Cheka to ensure conformity in his new Communist state...

[There follow further examples of actions in the early months that foreshadowed what had happened by 1921, and discussion of the continuity of ideology between 1917 (and before) and 1921.]

Activity

In this section, the focus is on writing an answer that is analytical, well-supported by precise own knowledge, and which refers to relevant historical interpretations/debates. Making use of information from this chapter, and any other sources of information available to you, try to answer **one** of the Paper 3 practice questions using these skills.

Question 2

Evaluate Lenin's successes and failures as ruler of Russia from October 1917 to his death in 1924. **[15 marks]**

Skill

Writing a conclusion to your essay

Examiner's tips

Provided you have carried out all the steps recommended so far, it should be relatively easy to write a concluding paragraph.

For this question, you might include some of the following ideas:

- Lenin's effective establishment of Bolshevik rule, and the development of a one-party state
- Lenin's contribution to the Treaty of Brest-Litovsk and support for Trotsky in the creation of a Red Army, which won the civil war
- Lenin's 'image', which provided a focus for internal stability through the difficult years of civil war
- Lenin's pragmatism, which led him to replace War Communism with the NEP and disperse potential opposition forces
- Lenin's failure to promote world revolution

- Lenin's reliance on repression and the *Cheka* to keep himself and his party in power
- Lenin's changes of policy, suggesting he was forced to act against his original intentions.

With a question like this, which asks you to consider successes and failures, you may wish to address successes and balance these against failures, as suggested here. Alternatively, you might prefer to think of themes – perhaps the early months/the civil war/foreign relations/ economic policy/political control – and look at the successes and failures in each area.

Although the question merely asks you to 'analyse', never forget that your essay must be an argument. This means that you are required to come to some kind of **judgement** about whether Lenin was primarily a success or failure – or perhaps a success in certain areas and a failure in others.

Common mistakes

Sometimes, conclusions can become very long and rambling, going over what has already been said and making the examiner read the same things twice or even more!

Another common fault is to introduce new material into the conclusion. This is sometimes tempting, when some 'extra' piece of information that has not been thought of before pops into a candidate's mind. However, the conclusion is not the place for new material; the conclusion exists for the summing up of the argument.

The best type of conclusion will convince the examiner that the candidate has followed through the view set out in the introduction, has proved their judgement using supporting material, and has a full and thorough understanding of the issues raised. A poor conclusion will serve none of these purposes. It may suggest that the candidate's view has changed, or that the writer does not have a view. It may reinforce suspicions that the candidate's understanding is woolly and the material imperfectly known, and it will leave the examiner feeling disappointed and unconvinced.

Remember to refer to the simplified Paper 3 mark scheme in Chapter 8.

Sample student conclusion

It is clear that Lenin's successes far outweighed his failures during his time in power. He successfully avoided a coalition government to assert his own and his party's leadership, and he issued decrees that kept the peasants and workers loyal in the early months. Furthermore, he persuaded the Bolsheviks to sign the treaty of Brest-Litovsk, led the Bolshevik state through a successful civil war, and fearlessly promoted War Communism to meet the needs of the army and ensure internal loyalty. He should be applauded for his courage to use terror to defeat counter-revolution and his pragmatism in allowing economic concessions when they were needed in 1921. He never faltered in his fight for the strong central control that Russia needed, and while Lenin may have been criticised for his ruthlessness, there is no doubting his total commitment and dedication. He may have misjudged the readiness of Western Europe for revolution, and have been forced to change policies according to circumstance, but none of this detracts from the overall success of his time as leader of Russia.

EXAMINER'S COMMENT

This is a good conclusion. It makes the judgement clear and pulls together the main threads of the argument, without repeating endless detail. It ends strongly, with reference to the weakness of the opposing argument, and leaves the reader convinced that the candidate understands the issues. Provided that the preceding material is equally fluent, convincing and detailed, this conclusion suggests a high-scoring answer.

Activity

In this section, the focus is on writing a strong conclusion. Using the information from this chapter and any other sources of information available to you, write concluding paragraphs for **at least two** of the following Paper 3 practice questions. Remember: to do this, you will need to make full plans for the questions you choose.

Paper 3 practice questions

1   Examine the causes and consequences to 1921 of the Russian Revolution of October 1917.

2   'The Bolshevik state under Lenin between 1918 and 1921 failed to live up to the expectations of those who had supported it in 1917.' To what extent do you agree with this statement?

3   Evaluate the reasons for, and results of, the establishment of a Marxist/Communist state in Russia between October 1917 and the beginning of 1921.

4   To what extent did the Reds win the Russian Civil War because of their unity and organization?

5   'Between October 1917 and 1924, Lenin was more interested in power than ideology.' To what extent do you agree with this statement?

6   Discuss the view that the Bolshevik state under Lenin between 1918 and 1924 is best described as a dictatorship.

Exam practice

8

Introduction

You have now completed your study of the main events and developments that took place in imperial Russia and the Soviet state between 1855 and 1924. You have also had a chance to examine the various historical debates and differing historical interpretations that surround some of these developments.

In Chapters 1–7, you have encountered examples of Paper 3-type essay questions, with examiner's tips. You have also had some basic practice in answering such questions. In this chapter, these tips and skills will be developed in more depth. Longer examples of possible student answers are provided, accompanied by examiner's comments. These should increase your understanding of what examiners will be looking for when they mark your essays. Following each question and answer, you will find tasks to give you further practice in the skills needed to gain high marks in this exam.

IB History Paper 3 exam questions and skills

Those of you following HL Option 4 – *History of Europe* – will have studied in depth three of the eighteen sections available for this HL Option. *Imperial Russia, Revolution and the Establishment of the Soviet Union (1855–1924)* is one of those sections. For Paper 3, two questions are set from each of the 18 sections, giving 36 questions in total; and you have to answer **three** of these.

Each question has a specific mark scheme. However the 'generic' mark scheme in the *IB History Guide* gives you a good general idea of what examiners are looking for, in order to be able to put answers into the higher bands. In particular, you will need to acquire precise historical knowledge so that you can address issues such as cause and effect, and change and continuity. This knowledge will be required in order to explain historical developments. You will also need to understand relevant historical debates and interpretations, and be able to refer to these and critically evaluate them.

Essay planning

Make sure you read each question **carefully**, noting all the important dates, key words and 'command' words – you might find it useful to highlight these words on your question paper. You should think about the key words and dates as you produce a rough plan (for example, a spider diagram) before you begin each of the three essays you attempt. Making a plan before you begin will not only help you to structure your essay well, it will also ensure that you have enough own knowledge to answer the question adequately and confirm that you have made a sensible choice. It is far better to think and plan **before** you begin to write than to realise you don't know enough about the topic, or to change your mind about the argument you are trying to present, halfway through an answer!

Relevance to the question

Remember that you need to keep your answers relevant and focused on the words of the question. Don't go outside the dates mentioned in the question (unless the question invites you to do so), and don't write an answer to a similar but differently worded question that you might have revised or written before. It is not enough to describe the events or developments – nor to focus on one key word, date or individual, and write down everything you know about it. Instead, you need to select your evidence carefully in order to support the comments you make in relation to the question as a whole. If the question asks for 'causes/reasons' and 'results', 'continuity and change', 'successes and failures', 'strengths and weaknesses' or 'nature and development', make sure you deal with all the parts of the question, otherwise you will severely limit your mark.

Examiner's tips

For Paper 3 answers, examiners are looking for well-structured arguments which:

- are consistently relevant/linked to the question
- offer clear/precise analysis
- are supported by accurate, precise and relevant own knowledge

- offer a balanced judgement
- refer to different historical debates/interpretations or, where relevant, refer to the ideas of historians and offer some critical evaluation of these.

Simplified mark scheme

Band		Marks
1	Consistently clear understanding of and focus on the question, with all main aspects addressed. Answer is fully analytical, balanced and well-structured/organised. Own knowledge is detailed, accurate and relevant, with events placed in their historical context. There is developed critical analysis, and sound understanding of historical concepts. Examples used are relevant, and used effectively to support analysis/evaluation. The answer also integrates evaluation of different historical debates/perspectives. All/almost all of the main points are substantiated, and the answer reaches a clear/reasoned/consistent judgement/conclusion.	13–15
2	Clear understanding of the question, and most of its main aspects are addressed. Answer is mostly well-structured and developed, though, with some repetition/lack of clarity in places. Supporting own knowledge mostly relevant/accurate, and events are placed in their historical context. The answer is mainly analytical, with relevant examples used to support critical analysis/evaluation. There is some understanding/evaluation of historical concepts and debates/perspectives. Most of the main points are substantiated, and the answer offers a consistent conclusion.	10–12
3	Demands of the question are understood – but some aspects not fully developed/addressed. Mostly relevant/accurate supporting own knowledge, and events generally placed in their historical context. Some attempts at analysis/evaluation but these are limited/not sustained/inconsistent.	7–9

Band		Marks
4	**Some understanding** of the question. **Some relevant own knowledge,** with some factors identified – but with **limited explanation. Some attempts at analysis,** but answer **lacks clarity/ coherence, and is mainly description/narrative.**	4–6
5	**Limited understanding of/focus on** the question. **Short/generalised** answer, with very **little accurate/ relevant own knowledge.** Some **unsupported assertions,** with **no real analysis.**	0–3

Student answers

The extracts from student answers that follow will have brief examiner's comments, and a longer overall comment at the end. Those parts of student answers that are particularly strong and well-focused (such as demonstrations of precise and relevant own knowledge, or examination of historical interpretations) will be highlighted in red. Errors/ confusion/irrelevance/loss of focus will be highlighted in blue. In this way, students should find it easier to follow why marks were awarded or withheld.

Question 1

To what extent were the reforms of Alexander II's reign driven only by a desire to preserve the autocracy? **[15 marks]**

Skills

- Factual knowledge and understanding
- Structured, analytical and balanced argument
- Awareness/understanding/evaluation of historical interpretations
- Clear and balanced judgement

Examiner's tip

Look carefully at the wording of this question, which asks you to evaluate the motivation for the reforms carried out during Alexander II's reign. Obviously you will need to consider whether a desire to maintain autocracy was important, but don't forget the key word 'only'. You might wish to take issue with this, and you should certainly consider whether other factors played a part. Plan your answer carefully before you begin to write so that you know what you will argue and how you will structure your argument.

Figure 8.1: Russian peasants visiting a lawyer, attempting to settle their land rights following the emancipation of the serfs in 1861.

Student answer

It is wrong to say that the reforms of Alexander II's reign were 'only' driven by a desire to preserve the autocracy. There were many other factors involved. While maintaining the autocracy was doubtless of great importance to the tsar, the fact that he was prepared to liberate the serfs, set up local government institutions (the zemstvas *and* dumas*), support a favourable climate for economic growth, and was even ready to consider Loris-Melikov's proposals for some minor constitutional reform, show that modernising and strengthening his country was important to him. It was at least equally important to him to create stability by responding to criticisms.*

EXAMINER'S COMMENT

This is a well-directed introduction. It begins with a clear judgement or thesis, and supports this with reference to some specific reforms of Alexander II's reign. It suggests that the candidate knows where the argument will lead and that the issues have already been thought through.

Alexander II was certainly concerned about the preservation of the God-given autocracy that he had inherited from his father, Nicholas I, in 1855. He took his power to issue ukases *seriously, and was fully committed to his secular and religious responsibilities within the Orthodox Church. Ruling in cooperation with the landed nobility was accepted without question, but there were a number of other factors in 1855 that were pushing Alexander II to consider reform. Russia had only just emerged from a disastrous war in the Crimea that had exposed the weakness of its transport systems, its inability to provide up-to-date weaponry, and the risks of relying on serf conscripts for the army. The war years had seen many peasant disturbances. More enlightened thinkers within Russia, particularly those from the 'Westerner' tradition, believed time was ripe for change. Alexander was intelligent enough to see that serfdom (which had outlived such practices elsewhere in Europe) was holding Russia back, and it was his desire to modernise and strengthen his country that drove him to embark on his reforms.*

EXAMINER'S COMMENT

This paragraph is very well focused on the question and presents an argument that shows understanding of the issues. That argument is supported by some specific information, conveying a range of reasons concisely and without falling into over-description.

Alexander chose to emancipate the serfs in 1861 because the practice of serfdom was inefficient. Although there were plenty of other reasons put forward at the time, not least that it was immoral and unfair, Alexander was driven above all by the need to catch up with his Western competitors. Serf labour was incapable of meeting the needs of Russia's growing population, and the 'mir' or peasant commune (which insisted that the serfs worked together in traditional ways) was seen as an obstruction to efficient modern farming practices. Furthermore, serfdom failed to provide the nobles, on whom Alexander depended, with a decent income. Food shortages also provoked peasant unrest, undermining social stability. The military failures of the Crimean War were probably the final trigger. So, although Alexander showed his concern for autocracy in managing the emancipation 'from above', he carried through the reform in order to ensure Russia's survival as a 'Great Power' and for reasons of greater economic efficiency and social stability.

The emancipation of the serfs had wide implications for society and necessitated a series of further reforms, which were also intended to modernise and strengthen Russia. These included the creation of the district and provincial zemstva in 1864 and the reform of municipal government, establishing the duma in 1870, as well as the introduction of judicial reforms, bringing, for example, trial by jury in 1864 and changes in military service in 1874. If Alexander II's sole concern had been to preserve his autocracy, he would hardly have gone down such a path, for example allowing representation of 'ordinary people', including peasants, for the first time in the zemstva. The promotion of primary education, welfare and other public services were all progressive causes championed by the zemstva and favoured by the tsar.

Although the electoral system was admittedly based on property ownership, and lack of control over the police limited the new councils' power, the changes nevertheless showed a genuine concern to modernise and strengthen the country and not simply to preserve autocracy. The tsar's autocracy could have been maintained without any such changes.

[There then follow several paragraphs that continue the same argument, and comment on the motivation behind other reforms (judicial, military, cultural, economic). These show strong, precise knowledge and also refer to the limitations of the reforms and how the government remained an autocracy. However, they all emphasise the view that this was not the reason for change.]

It is sometimes suggested that the modifications made to Alexander II's reforms after 1866, particularly the restrictions re-imposed on education when Dmitri Tolstoy became education minister, suggest that Alexander II was not truly interested in reform and only in preserving his autocracy. This is untrue, although he may have been alarmed at the growth of populism and violent opposition, which affected him personally and naturally encouraged him to take action to stop the spread of opposition. However, the military reforms (which placed efficiency first) took place in the 1870s, as did some much-needed economic changes. Just before his life was ended by a bomb in 1881, Alexander had even agreed to proposals by the minister of the interior, Loris-Melikov, which would have given local representatives an advisory role in government.

Alexander experienced difficulty in carrying through far-reaching reforms while still preserving an autocracy, but simply because he accepted the preservation of autocracy does not mean he only reformed for that reason. To say this would be to do Alexander II a great injustice. His concern to modernise and strengthen his country, and to create a stable, prosperous nation that could compete with the West on equal terms, were of great importance to him.

EXAMINER'S COMMENT

The second-last paragraph is analytical, introducing an alternative argument while upholding the earlier judgement. It is, however, rather less developed than the earlier sections, suggesting that perhaps too much time has been devoted to the individual reforms, leaving insufficient time for an analysis of the 'period of reaction'. The conclusion is direct, but brief. It upholds the judgement given in the introduction but is a little disappointing in that it lacks some depth and 'punch' to round off the high level of argument that has been presented throughout the answer. Again, it suggests that time may have been running out.

Overall examiner's comments

This is a very good, analytical response. It has a clear judgement, which is sustained throughout the answer. It also employs a highly analytical approach. There is precise and specific supporting information and a high level of understanding has been shown. It is certainly deserving of Band 1, although it would only be awarded a mark at the bottom of that Band – 13 out of 15 – for two reasons. First, the end is rushed and there is insufficient analysis of the so-called 'reactionary period', and second, it needed greater depth in its exploration of historical concepts.

Activity

Look again at the student answer. Now try to write your own answer, writing the middle section in full and developing the final section and conclusion further. You should also try to incorporate some historiography so that the answer can get to the top band and obtain the full 15 marks.

Question 2

Examine the similarities and differences between the two Russian revolutions of 1917. **[15 marks]**

Skills

- Factual knowledge and understanding
- Structured, analytical and balanced argument
- Awareness/understanding/evaluation of historical interpretations
- Clear and balanced judgement

Examiner's tip

Look carefully at the wording of this question, which asks you to look at similarities and differences. This means you need to compare the two revolutions of 1917 in a variety of aspects, most specifically their causes, events and consequences. As with all questions, you also need to adopt a view. This means that before you begin you will need to decide if there were more differences than similarities, more similarities than differences, or whether the truth lies somewhere between the two. In making your plan, which should be separated into similarities and differences, you will be able to decide whether you can produce more evidence on one side than the other. It does not really matter what you argue, as long as you have an argument and can support your comments with relevant and precise own knowledge in order to write convincingly. Both aspects of the question will need to be addressed thoroughly in order to achieve high marks. It is important that you do not merely describe the revolutions but provide detailed and relevant analysis of them in your answer.

Figure 8.2: Striking workers from the Putilov metal works in Petrograd on the first day of the February 1917 revolution.

Student answer

Russian history recorded two important revolutions in the year 1917, which were to shape the future of the state. These revolutions included the February 1917 revolution against Tsar Nicholas II and the October revolution against the Provisional Government. These two revolutions were different in terms of who organised them, who they were against, and what their results were.

EXAMINER'S COMMENT

This is a basic introduction. It shows some knowledge of the two revolutions of 1917 and so identifies the topic that the question is asking about. It also appears to give a view in stating that there were differences between the two revolutions. However, since it does not explicitly mention similarities, it is hard to know whether this is a deliberate attempt to present a thesis or a sign that the question has not been read properly.

The February 1917 revolution against the tsar is often considered as a general outburst of feeling from the people of Russia. The tsar's regime was becoming increasingly unpopular. In order to analyse the February 1917 revolution, it is important to take into consideration the fact that in 1905 there was an attempt at revolution, which the tsar avoided by compromising at the very last moment. The general position of Russia at that time was quite bad. There was widespread poverty all around the country. In such a position, the Russo-Japanese war did no good to the tsar. People were increasingly upset with his regime and Russian failures in the war. However, on the advice of senior army officers and ministers, the tsar announced the formation of a Duma *to introduce some sort of democracy to calm the increasing rage of the people. Unfortunately, the tsar soon forgot his promises and dissolved the first* Duma *only ten weeks after it was formed. Even though the* Duma *consisted of the middle class and landlords, it still put forward demands such as genuine democracy, the* Duma's *right to appoint the tsar's ministers, and the redistribution of land. These demands were far too big for the tsar, who kept changing the mode of election of the* Duma *until he had a conservative, less demanding* Duma.

EXAMINER'S COMMENT

Although there is some accurate own knowledge, this is mostly background material, and so is not explicitly linked to the demands of the question. While some brief reference to the historical context preceding the February revolution is a sound idea, and important in any explanation of the causes of that revolution, it is not wise to give too much descriptive information on this. What is needed is precise own knowledge of what contributed to the outbreak of revolution in February, so that this can be compared with the situation in October. The amount of detail provided about the 1905 revolution and its aftermath suggests that this answer might easily slip into irrelevant narrative.

This is a general factor in understanding why there was an outburst in February 1917 that saw the end of the tsar. People were angry about the tsar's broken promises, there was a shortage of bread, and soldiers were dying on the front. Though the initial February riots were bread riots, the people were soon joined by hundreds of factory workers who were on strike. The tsar asked the troops to disperse the crowds. However, soon the soldiers refused to fire on unarmed crowds. Reports of mutiny and mobs seizing buildings were widespread.

The tsar's ministers and army officers advised him to set up a constitutional monarchy but he refused to do so and sent more troops. The position was worsened by the fact that the tsar appointed himself as the army chief in the war. The increasing deaths of soldiers enraged many. Some soldiers were reported to leave the war, deserting back home. The army, key individuals and ministers now knew that the tsar had to go. People who had defended the tsar in 1905 now wanted to get rid of him, as they feared a full-scale revolution would completely change the structure of Russia. Hence they had to save their own skin. Therefore, on an imperial train, the tsar was asked by army officers to abdicate. Nicholas abdicated in favour of his brother, Archduke Michael, who refused the throne and hence imperial Russia came to an end. The result, apart from the tsar's dismissal, was the setting up of the Provisional Government.

EXAMINER'S COMMENT

These paragraphs show awareness of the causes of the February revolution, although there is limited evaluation of these, and they tend to be described in a semi-narrative way. Note the tell-tale use of 'now', which always suggests an essay is turning into a story. Furthermore, there has been no attempt, as yet, to look comparatively at similarities or differences between the developments in February and those in October. Therefore, although the information is linked to what is asked for, the focus is not fully on the question.

While the February revolution was a result of general discontent, the October revolution was mainly a Bolshevik revolution. Though the Bolsheviks claimed that they had agitators working in industries to help cause the February revolution, it would be more correct to say that the February revolution was organised by no one in particular. Contrary to this, the October revolution was designed by the Bolshevik leadership, namely Lenin and Trotsky. Lenin returned to Russia after his exile, from Switzerland. It was he who came up with what became known as the magnificent April Theses, chanting 'bread, land, peace and all power to the soviets'.

Lenin convinced the Bolsheviks that they should not wait for a complete bourgeois revolution (i.e. when Russia became fully industrialised) before a workers' revolution, but should take power from the Provisional Government. Lenin and Trotsky capitalised on the mistakes of the Provisional Government. The Provisional Government took the unpopular decision to continue the war with Germany. They postponed the elections, stating that elections could not take place with so many troops away. Furthermore, the conditions at home for the general population were not improving at all. Hence, Lenin and Trotsky used the mistakes of the Provisional Government for their own gain. They criticised it so that when the Bolsheviks take over, there is minimal resistance.

[There then follows a paragraph describing the October revolution.]

*Therefore it can be stated that the two revolutions were of different natures and
had different results or consequences. The February revolution was not planned.
It was a bloody revolution and resulted in the abdication of the tsar. The October
revolution was a well-planned revolution. It was bloodless, thanks to the
leadership of the Bolsheviks. However, it resulted in the civil war and eventually
Russia became a single party state under the Bolsheviks. The February revolution
can be said to be a mass mobilisation of general people, while the October
revolution was mainly a Bolshevik revolution. Hence, there are more differences
than similarities.*

Overall examiner's comments

Much of this answer is descriptive, although a basic understanding is
shown, together with some attempt to compare in passing, as well as
some valid comparisons in the final paragraph. However, not all the
implications of the question are considered, particularly with reference
to similarity. Too often, the emphasis is on the context rather than
genuine comparison. This answer will consequently be placed in Band 3
with 8 marks It needs a more analytical approach and a greater focus on
'similarity and difference' in order to rise higher.

Activity

Look again at the simplified mark scheme, and the student answer. Now try to draw up a plan focused on the demands of the question. Then try to write several paragraphs that will be good enough to get into the top band, and so obtain the full 15 marks. As well as making sure you address **both** aspects of the question, try to integrate some references **and** evaluation of relevant historians/historical interpretations into your answer.

Figure 8.3: A propaganda painting showing the Bolsheviks storming the Winter Palace in October 1917.

Question 3

Evaluate the reasons for, and the nature of, opposition to tsardom in Russia between 1881 and 1914. **[15 marks]**

Imperial Russia and the Soviet Union (1855–1924)

Skills

- Factual knowledge and understanding
- Structured, analytical and balanced argument
- Awareness/understanding/evaluation of historical interpretations
- Clear and balanced judgement

Examiner's tip

Look carefully at the wording of this question, which requires two areas to be addressed – the various reasons for opposition, and the 'nature' of the opposition during the reigns of Alexander III and Nicholas II to 1914. Both parts of the question (reasons **and** nature) will have to be addressed if high marks are to be achieved. You will need to formulate arguments about why opposition developed and why it took the form it did, and there will need to be precise knowledge given in support of those arguments. There is also some relevant historiography that could be made part of the answer.

Figure 8.4: The police raid the premises of a *Nihilist* group engaged in printing a dissident journal in St Petersburg in the 1880s.

Student answer

There was a lot of opposition to the tsarist autocracy between 1881 and 1914. The main reason for the opposition was repressive and conservative tsarist rule. The nature of opposition varied from the opposition of the ethnic minority groups to political opposition from liberals, Social Revolutionaries and Social Democrats (Communists). There was also opposition from workers, who resented their poor living and working conditions, and peasants who wanted more land and rights.

Opposition grew because of Russia's economic growth at the end of the 19th century. This produced a new middle class and many workers, both of which were hostile to the regime. The middle class wanted political reform and the workers wanted better conditions. The educational reforms introduced by Alexander II, and the expansion in the numbers of students in universities, also produced opposition from those known as 'the intelligentsia', who read about new radical ideas and wanted to put them into practice. The disasters of the Russo-Japanese war in 1904–05 encouraged the opposition even more, but different groups wanted very different things. The opposition continued to 1914 because, although Nicholas granted a Duma or National Assembly, he tried to curb the power of the four Dumas that were called and never really listened to opposition demands or made any radical changes.

EXAMINER'S COMMENT

This is a fair start. The first paragraph focuses on an overall reason and addresses 'nature' in terms of the composition of the opposition movements. The second paragraph gives an overview of the opposition, providing some accurate, specific detail. Ideally these two paragraphs should have been merged into a single introduction. A clearer judgement should also have been made as the basis for an argument in the body of the essay.

In 1881, the People's Will (which was a more extreme organisation that developed out of Land and Liberty, and which demanded a national constitution, universal suffrage, freedom of speech and press, local self-government and national self-determination) succeeded in assassinating Alexander II. This led Alexander III to crack down on opposition movements, and many leading figures from the People's Will were imprisoned. The violence and extremism simply increased the persecution of all who acted against the autocracy. Even moderate opposition groups (such as the Liberals who spoke out in the zemstva and Dumas) were suppressed, along with the more extreme socialists and Communists. Many were forced into exile, thanks to the activities of the Okhrana.

> ### EXAMINER'S COMMENT
> This paragraph has become more descriptive. While it describes
> what the People's Will wanted and did, it would have been better
> if 'reasons for' and 'nature of' had been addressed more directly.
> It provides some useful context but by this stage the answer really
> needs to move forward.

*The Liberals were the most moderate of the opposition groups. The aim of the
Liberals was to introduce parliamentary democracy. They opposed the tsar through
the* zemstva, *but Alexander III curbed their power and banned an attempt at an
'all-*zemstva *organisation' in 1896. In 1903, Pyotr Struve founded the Union
of Liberation and a series of 'reform banquets' was organised in 1904 but they
had little real influence. In 1905, the Liberals held a series of congresses and set
up the 'Union of Unions' under Milyukov, demanding full civil and political
rights, universal suffrage and nationwide elections to a National Assembly.*

The Liberals got some of what they wanted when Nicholas granted a Duma *in
1905, but in practice they were disappointed by its limited powers and remained
in opposition in 1914.*

*The second major opposition group was the Social Revolutionaries, who favoured
a new Russian society based on the traditional peasant* mir, *or commune. They
grew out of the populist tradition but were more violent. In 1886, for example,
a group of students who had made bombs to assassinate Alexander III were
arrested and hanged. These students included Lenin's brother, Alexander Ulyanov.
In 1901, some of these populist groups founded the Social Revolutionary Party,
which adopted the views of* Chernov. *The party was active in the troubles
of 1904–05, assassinating von* Plehve, *the minister of the interior, in 1904
and Nicholas II's uncle, Grand-Duke Sergei, in 1905. They also stirred up
discontent in the countryside, and were forceful in their opposition within the*
Dumas *after 1907. They succeeded in assassinating Stolypin in 1911.*

*The third group was the Communists, who believed that the proletariat would
eventually rise against the middle and upper classes and seize control of the
means of production. They emerged from the development of industry in Russia
in the 1880s and 1890s, when the Emancipation of Labour movement helped
circulate Marxist ideas as interpreted by Plekhanov. In 1898 the 1st Congress
of the Russian Social Democratic Workers' Party was held, but was broken
up by* Okhrana *agents. A 2nd Congress took place in 1903. However, the
Communists split among themselves on this occasion – between the Bolsheviks,
led by Lenin, who believed that a Communist revolution in Russia could only*

be achieved under the guidance of a small elite of professional revolutionaries, and the Mensheviks who wanted a Communist revolution that was not controlled by one person or a small group.

The SDs did not play a major role in events before 1914 because of this split, although Trotsky briefly led a St Petersburg Soviet in 1905. Nicholas II used the secret police to persecute them and their leaders were forced into exile or prison camps. They were not interested in moderate government through the Duma *and boycotted the first* Duma, *although they played a part in the second.*

EXAMINER'S COMMENT

The last few paragraphs are over-descriptive. While they contain a good deal of accurate and precise information, they present a list of opposition groups and their activities without analysing them. To answer this question properly, it is necessary to consider why the opposition groups developed as they did, not simply describe what happened.

[There follows a more detailed analysis of the events of 1904–05, with reference to the types and effectiveness of opposition activities. There is also a paragraph on 1906–14, assessing the extent to which opposition activities (as opposed to tsarist/ministerial action) prevented the *Dumas* from working effectively. There is some reference to historiography and interpretation. The answer ends…]

Robert Service has emphasised that political opposition was strong and growing in 1914. Other historians, such as Timasheff, have suggested that the opposition was being gradually won over or destroyed, and that all Russia needed was some more years of peace for the opposition to be appeased and a modern system of government to develop.

The opposition did not achieve much success before 1914. This is partly because of the tsarist power of repression, which meant groups had to be secretive, found it difficult to circulate printed material, and had leaders living abroad or in Siberia. Perhaps the most important reason why the opposition failed to destroy the tsarist autocracy was because it was too divided.

When Nicholas II granted a Duma in 1905, some more moderate opposition groups thought that they had what they wanted, while others wanted to continue to fight. So the opposition never seriously challenged the tsar, and Russia was still led by an all-powerful autocrat when it went to war in 1914.

> ## EXAMINER'S COMMENT
>
> The material on 1904–05 and the *Dumas* 1905–14 brings in some
> analysis and interpretation, although the words of the question are
> not explicitly used, and some of the text is more concerned with
> the 'success' of groups. This is again seen in the opening sentence
> of the conclusion, which suggests that the answer has strayed
> into 'why did the opposition movements achieve little before
> 1914?' The conclusion makes no explicit reference back to the
> introduction or key words of the question.

Overall examiner's comments

This answer contains a good deal of potentially relevant information
but there is very little attempt, after the opening, to address the question
directly. It fails to develop an argument, and by the end has wandered
off into a different question. Furthermore, some relevant issues raised
at the beginning of this answer – about the opposition of the ethnic
minorities, or of the workers and peasants – are ignored in the rest
of the answer. This suggests that inadequate planning was undertaken
before writing. However, there is some analysis, some good, precise
detail, and the answer certainly moves beyond description. While it
needed greater focus for higher marks, there is enough here for this
answer to be placed at the top of Band 3 with 9 marks.

Activity

Look again at the simplified mark scheme, and the student answer above.
Now write your own answer to the question, and try to make it good
enough to get into the top band and so obtain the full 15 marks. In
particular, make sure you are aware of the main historical debates about
this topic – and incorporate some critical evaluation of these debates in
your answer.

Further reading

For supplementary student reference

Bromley, Jonathan. 2002. *Russia 1848–1917*. Oxford, UK. Heinemann.

Corin, Chris and Fiehn, Terry. 2002. *Communist Russia Under Lenin and Stalin*. London, UK. Hodder Education.

Darby, Graham. 1998. *The Russian Revolution*. Harlow, UK. Longman.

Hite, John. 2004. *Tsarist Russia 1801–1917*. Ormskirk, UK. Causeway Press.

Laver, John. 2002. *The Modernisation of Russia 1856–1985*. Oxford, UK. Heinemann.

Lee, Stephen. 2006. *Russia and the USSR, 1855–1991*. London, UK. Routledge.

Lynch, Michael. 2005. *Reaction and Revolutions: Russia 1881–1924* (2nd edn) London, UK. Hodder Murray.

Phillips, Steve. 2000. *Lenin and the Russian Revolution*. Oxford, UK. Heinemann.

Service, Robert. 1991. *The Russian Revolution 1900–1927*. London, UK. Macmillan.

Waller, Sally. 2009. *Tsarist Russia 1855–1917*. Cheltenham, UK. Nelson Thornes.

Williams, Beryl. 2000. *Lenin (Profiles in Power)*. Harlow, UK. Longman.

Wood, Alan. 1986. *The Russian Revolution*. (2nd edn) Harlow, UK. Longman.

For further research

Acton, Edward. 1990. *Rethinking the Russian Revolution*. London, UK. Hodder Arnold.

Christian, David. 1986. *Imperial and Soviet Russia*. Basingstoke, UK. Palgrave Macmillan.

Crankshaw, Edward. 1976. *The Shadow of the Winter Palace: Russia's Drift to Revolution 1825–1917*. New York, USA. Viking Penguin.

Figes, Orlando. 1997. *A People's Tragedy: The Russian Revolution 1891–1924*. London, UK. Pimlico.

Freeze, Gregory. 2009. *Russia: A History*. (3rd edn) Oxford, UK. Oxford University Press.

Hosking, Geoffrey. 2002. *Russia and the Russians*. London, UK. Penguin.

Hutchinson, John. 1999. *Late Imperial Russia 1890–1917*. Harlow, UK. Longman.

McCauley, Martin. 2007. *The Soviet Union*. (2nd edn) Harlow, UK. Longman

Moon, David. 1999. *The Russian Peasantry, 1600–1930*. Harlow, UK. Longman.

Mosse, Werner. 1995. *Alexander II and the Modernization of Russia*. (2nd edn) London, UK. I. B. Tauris.

Rogger, Hans. 1983. *Russia in the Age of Modernisation and Revolution 1881–1917*. Harlow, UK. Longman.

Rothnie, Niall. 1989. *The Russian Revolution*. Basingstoke, UK. Palgrave Macmillan.

Serge, Victor. (trans. Peter Sedgwick). 1984. *Memoirs of a Revolutionary*. New York, USA. Writers and Readers Publishing Inc.

Service, Robert. 2002. *Lenin: A Biography*. London, UK. Pan Books.

Sixsmith, Martin. 2011. *Russia*. London, UK. BBC Books.

Waldron, Peter. 1997. *The End of Imperial Russia 1855–1917*. Basingstoke, UK. Palgrave Macmillan.

Further information

Sources and quotations in this book have been taken from the following publications.

Christian, David. 1986. *Imperial and Soviet Russia*. Basingstoke, UK. Palgrave Macmillan.

Corin, Chris and Fiehn, Terry. 2002. *Communist Russia Under Lenin and Stalin*. London, UK. Hodder Education.

Crankshaw, Edward. 1976. *The Shadow of the Winter Palace: Russia's Drift to Revolution 1825–1917*. New York, USA. Viking Penguin.

Figes, Orlando. 1997. *A People's Tragedy: The Russian Revolution 1891–1924*. London, UK. Pimlico.

Graham, Stephen. 1968. *Tsar of Freedom*. New York, USA. Archon.

Holland, Andrew. 2010. *Russia & its Rulers, 1855–1964*. London, UK. Hodder Education.

Mawdsley, Evan. 2001. *The Russian Civil War*. Edinburgh, Scotland. Birlinn.

Rogger, Hans. 1983. *Russia in the Age of Modernisation and Revolution 1881–1917*. Harlow, UK. Longman.

Saunders, David. 1992. *Russia in the Age of Reaction and Reform, 1801–81*. Harlow, UK. Longman.

Seton-Watson, Hugh. 1952. *The Decline of Imperial Russia, 1855–1914*. London, UK. Methuen.

Sixsmith, Martin. 2011. *Russia*. London, UK. BBC Books.

Waller, Sally. 2009. *Tsarist Russia 1855–1917*. Cheltenham, UK. Nelson Thornes.

Westwood, John. 2002. *Endurance and Endeavour: Russian History 1812–2001*. Oxford, UK. Oxford University Press.

Wood, Alan. 2007. *The Romanov Empire 1613–1917*. London, UK. Hodder Arnold.

Index

Acknowledgements

The authors and publishers acknowledge the following sources of copyright material and are grateful for the permissions granted. While every effort has been made, it has not always been possible to identify the sources of all the material used, or to trace all copyright holders. If any omissions are brought to our notice, we will be happy to include the appropriate acknowledgements on reprinting.

Front Cover Getty Images: Hulton Archive / Stringer; Figure 1.1 TopFoto: The Print Collector / HIP; Figure 1.2 Corbis: Hulton-Deutsch Collection; Figure 1.4 TopFoto: Roger-Viollet; Figure 2.1 TopFoto: World History Archive; Figure 2.2 Mary Evans: INTERFOTO / Sammlung Rauch; Figure 2.3 Getty Images: Imagno; Figure 2.4 Mary Evans: John Massey Stewart Russian Collection; Figure 2.5 Mary Evans: John Massey Stewart Russian Collection; Figure 3.1 Corbis: Hulton-Deutsch Collection; Figure 3.2 TopFoto: World History Archive; Figure 3.4 Mary Evans: John Massey Stewart Russian Collection; Figure 3.5 TopFoto: Roger-Viollet; Figure 3.6 TopFoto: RIA Novosti; Figure 3.8 TopFoto: The Granger Collection; Figure 4.1 Corbis: Reproduced by permission of The State Hermitage Museum, St. Petersburg, Russia; Figure 4.2 TopFoto: Fotomas; Figure 4.4 Corbis: Bettmann; Figure 4.5 Corbis: Austrian Archives; Figure 4.7 TopFoto; Figure 4.10 TopFoto; Figure 5.1 Getty Images: Universal History Archive; Figure 5.3 Getty Images: DEA / G. DAGLI ORTI / De Agostini; Figure 5.4 TopFoto: ullsteinbild; Figure 5.5 Corbis: Hulton-Deutsch Collection; Figure 5.6 Getty Images: Slava Katamidze Collection; Figure 5.7 TopFoto: Topham Picturepoint / The monk Grigoriji Rasputin between Tsar Nicholas II and Tsarina Alexandra Fedorovna, caricature, Russia, 20th Century; Figure 6.1 Corbis: Bettmann; Figure 6.3 Getty Images: Hulton Archive; Figure 6.4 Getty Images: Universal History Archive; Figure 6.5 Corbis; Figure 6.6 Mary Evans Picture Library: ALEXANDER MELEDI; Figure 6.7 Getty Images: Universal History Archive; Figure 6.8 Corbis; Figure 7.1 Getty Images: Universal History Archive; Figure 7.2 TopFoto: ullsteinbild; Figure 7.4 Mary Evans Picture Library: Alexander Meledin; Figure 7.5 TopFoto: Alexander Apsit / Fine Art Images / Heritage-Images; Figure 7.6 TopFoto: Roger-Viollet;

Figure 7.7 TopFoto: Topham Picturepoint; Figure 7.8 Getty Images: Topical Press Agency; Figure 8.1 Mary Evans Picture Library: John Massey Stewart Russian Collection; Figure 8.2 TopFoto: Fine Art Images / Heritage-Images; Figure 8.3 Getty Images: Universal History Archive.